# HOW TO TALK SO KIDS WILL LISTEN & Listen So KIDS WILL TALK

Adele Faber and Elaine Mazlish are internationally acclaimed, award-winning experts on adult-child communication. They lecture throughout the United States and the workshop programmes they have created are being used by thousands of groups around the world to improve communication between adults and children. Their books, printed in twenty languages, have sold over three million copies.

Adele and Elaine both live in Long Island, New York, and each has three adult children.

*Books by Adele Faber and Elaine Mazlish,*
*available from Piccadilly Press:*

How to Talk so Kids Will Listen,
and Listen so Kids Will Talk

How to Talk so Teens Will Listen,
and Listen so Teens Will Talk

Siblings Without Rivalry

How to Talk so Kids Can Learn

# HOW TO TALK SO KIDS WILL LISTEN & LISTEN SO KIDS WILL TALK

## AdeLe Faber & ELaine MazLish

With a New Afterword:
The Next Generation by Joanna Faber

Illustrations by Kimberly Ann Coe

PICCADILLY PRESS

First published in Great Britain in 2001 by
Piccadilly Press, a Templar/Bonnier publishing company
Deepdene Lodge, Deepdene Avenue, Dorking, Surrey RH5 4AT
www.piccadillypress.co.uk

This 30th anniversary edition published 2013

First edition published by Avon Books, Inc in 1982
Revised edition in 1999

A catalogue record for this book is available
from the British Library

ISBN: 978 1 84812 309 0  (paperback)

9 11 13 15 17 19 20 18 16 14 12 10 8

Print

# Contents

# Acknowledgments

To Leslie Faber and Robert Mazlish, our consultants-in-residence, who were always there for us—with a better phrase, a new thought, a word of encouragement.

To Carl, Joanna, and Abram Faber, to Kathy, Liz, and John Mazlish, who cheered us on—just by being who they are.

To Kimberly Coe, who took our stick figures and scribbled instructions and sent us back drawings of parents and children for whom we felt immediate affection.

To Robert Markel for his support and guidance at a critical time.

To Gerard Nierenberg, friend and advisor, who gave generously of his experience and expertise.

To the parents in our workshops for their thoughtful feedback and written contributions.

To Ann Marie Geiger and Patricia King for giving of themselves unstintingly when we needed them.

To Jim Wade, our editor, whose unflagging good spirits and concern for quality made him a joy to work with.

To Dr. Haim Ginott, who introduced us to new ways of communicating with children. When he died, the children of the world lost a great champion. He cared so much that there be "no more scratches on their souls."

# A Letter to Readers

Dear Reader,

The last thing we ever thought we'd be doing was writing a "how-to" book on communication skills for parents. The relationship between each parent and child is a very personal and private matter. The idea of giving anyone instructions on how to talk in such a close relationship just didn't feel right to us. In our first book, *Liberated Parents/Liberated Children*, we tried not to teach or preach. We had a story to tell. Our years of workshops with the late child psychologist Dr. Haim Ginott had affected our lives deeply. We were sure that if we told the story of how our new skills had changed the way we treated both our children and ourselves, that our readers would catch the spirit behind the skills and be inspired to improvise on their own.

To some extent it did work that way. Many parents wrote to tell us proudly of what they had been able to accomplish in their homes just from reading about our experiences. But there were other letters, and a common appeal ran through them all. They wanted a second book—a book with "lessons" . . . "practice exercises" . . . "rules of thumb" . . . "tear-out reminder pages" . . . some kind of materials that would help them to learn the skills "step-by-step."

For a while we considered the idea seriously, but our initial resistance returned and we pushed the thought to the back of our minds. Besides, we were too busy concentrating on the speeches and workshops we were preparing for our lecture tours.

During the next few years we traveled around the country, conducting workshops for parents, teachers, school principals, hospital staffs, teenagers, and child-care workers. Wherever we went, people shared with us their personal experiences with these new methods of communication—their doubts, their frustrations, and their enthusiasm. We were grateful to them for their openness and we learned from them all. Our files were bulging with exciting new material.

Meanwhile, the mail continued to come in, not only from the United States but from France, Canada, Israel, New Zealand, the Philippines, India. Mrs. Anagha Ganpule from New Delhi wrote:

"There are so many problems about which I would like to take your advice. . . . Please let me know what I could do to study the subject in depth. I am at a dead end. The old ways do not suit me, and I do not have the new skills. Please help me get over this."

That was the letter that did it.

We started to think again about the possibility of writing a book that showed "how." The more we talked about it, the more comfortable we became with the idea. Why not a "how-to" book with exercises so that parents could teach themselves the skills they wanted to know?

Why not a book that would give parents a chance to practice what they've learned at their own pace—either by themselves or with a friend?

Why not a book with hundreds of examples of helpful dialogues so that parents could adapt this new language to their own personal style?

The book could have cartoons that would show the skills in action, so that a harried parent could glance at a picture and give himself or herself a quick refresher course.

We'd personalize the book. We'd talk about our own experiences, answer the most commonly asked questions, and include the stories and new insights that parents in our groups have shared with us over the past six years. But, most important, we'd always keep sight of our larger goal—the constant search for methods that affirm the dignity and humanity of both parents and children.

## A Letter to Readers

Suddenly our original uneasiness about writing a "how-to" book vanished. Every other art or science has its skill books. Why not one for parents who want to learn how to talk so their kids will listen, and listen so their kids will talk?

Once we decided, we started writing rapidly. We hope to get a complimentary copy off to Mrs. Ganpule in New Delhi before her children are grown.

Adele Faber
Elaine Mazlish

# How to Read
# and Use This Book

It seems presumptuous for us to be telling anyone else how to read a book (particularly when both of us have been known to start books in the middle or even read them backward). But since this is our book we'd like to tell you how we think it should be tackled. After you've gotten the feel of it by flipping through and glancing at the cartoons, start with Chapter I. Actually *do* the exercises as you go along. Resist the temptation to skip over them and get to the "good parts." If you have a compatible friend with whom to work on the exercises, so much the better. We hope you'll talk and argue and discuss your answers at length.

We also hope you'll write your answers down so that this book becomes a personal record for you. Write neatly or illegibly, change your mind and cross out or erase, but do write.

Read the book slowly. It took us more than ten years to learn the ideas in it. We don't suggest that you take that long to read it; but if the methods suggested here make sense to you, you might want to make some changes, and it's easier to change a little at a time than all at once. After you've read a chapter, lay the book aside and give yourself a week to do the assignment before going on. (You may be thinking, "With everything else I have to do, the last thing I need is an assignment!" Nevertheless, experience tells us that the discipline of having to put skills into action and record the results helps put the skills where they belong—inside you.)

Finally, you may wonder why some portions of this book, which is written by two people, are told from the point of view of one person. It was our way of solving the bothersome problem of constantly having to identify who was speaking about whose experience. It seemed to us that "I" would be easier for our readers than a constant repetition of "I, Adele Faber . . ." or "I, Elaine Mazlish. . . ." As for our conviction of the value of the ideas in this book, we speak in unison. We have both seen these methods of communication at work with our own families and with thousands of others. It is a great pleasure for us to share them with you now.

All we are given is possibilities—
to make ourselves one thing or another.

**José Ortega y Gasset**

# 1 | Helping Children Deal with Their Feelings

I was a wonderful parent before I had children. I was an expert on why everyone else was having problems with theirs. Then I had three of my own.

Living with real children can be humbling. Every morning I would tell myself, "Today is going to be different," and every morning was a variation of the one before: "You gave her more than me!" . . . "That's the pink cup. I want the blue cup." . . . "This oatmeal looks like throw-up." . . . "He punched me." . . . "I never touched him!" . . . "I won't go to my room. You're not the boss over me!"

They finally wore me down. And though it was the last thing I ever dreamed I'd be doing, I joined a parent group. The group met at a local child-guidance center and was led by a young psychologist, Dr. Haim Ginott.

The meeting was intriguing. The subject was "children's feelings," and the two hours sped by. I came home with a head spinning with new thoughts and a notebook full of undigested ideas:

*Direct connection between how kids feel and how they behave.*

1

*When kids feel right, they'll behave right.*

*How do we help them to feel right?*

*By accepting their feelings!*

*Problem—Parents don't usually accept their children's feel-
ings. For example:*
  *"You don't really feel that way."*
  *"You're just saying that because you're tired."*
  *"There's no reason to be so upset."*

*Steady denial of feelings can confuse and enrage kids. Also
teaches them not to know what their feelings are—not to
trust them.*

After the session I remember thinking, "Maybe other parents do that. I don't." Then I started listening to myself. Here
are some sample conversations from my home—just from a
single day.

| | |
|---|---|
| CHILD: | Mommy, I'm tired. |
| ME: | You couldn't be tired. You just napped. |
| CHILD: | (*louder*) But I'm tired. |
| ME: | You're not tired. You're just a little sleepy. Let's get dressed. |
| CHILD: | (*wailing*) No, I'm tired! |

| | |
|---|---|
| CHILD: | Mommy, it's hot in here. |
| ME: | It's cold. Keep your sweater on. |
| CHILD: | No, I'm hot. |
| ME: | I said, "Keep your sweater on!" |
| CHILD: | No, I'm hot. |

| | |
|---|---|
| CHILD: | That TV show was boring. |
| ME: | No, it wasn't. It was very interesting. |
| CHILD: | It was stupid. |
| ME: | It was educational. |
| CHILD: | It stunk. |
| ME: | Don't talk that way! |

Can you see what was happening? Not only were all our conversations turning into arguments, I was also telling my children over and over again not to trust their own perceptions but to rely on mine instead.

Once I was aware of what I was doing, I was determined to change. But I wasn't sure how to go about it. What finally helped me most was actually putting myself in my children's shoes. I asked myself, "Suppose I were a child who was tired, or hot or bored? And suppose I wanted that all-important grown-up in my life to know what I was feeling . . . ?"

Over the next weeks I tried to tune in to what I thought my children might be experiencing, and when I did, my words seemed to follow naturally. I wasn't just using a technique. I really meant it when I said, "So you're still feeling tired—even though you just napped." Or "I'm cold, but for you it's hot in here." Or "I can see you didn't care much for that show." After all, we were two separate people, capable of having two different sets of feelings. Neither of us was right or wrong. We each felt what we felt.

For a while, my new skill was a big help. There was a noticeable reduction in the number of arguments between the children and me. Then one day my daughter announced, "I hate Grandma," and it was *my mother* she was talking about. I never hesitated for a second. "That is a terrible thing to say," I snapped. "You know you don't mean it. I don't ever want to hear that coming out of your mouth again."

That little exchange taught me something else about myself. I could be very accepting about most of the feelings the children had, but let one of them tell me something that made me angry or anxious and I'd instantly revert to my old way.

I've since learned that my reaction was not that unusual. On the following page you'll find examples of other statements children make that often lead to an automatic denial from their parents. Please read each statement and jot down what you think a parent might say if he were denying his child's feelings.

3

I. CHILD: I don't like the new baby.
   PARENT: (*denying the feeling*)

_____

_____

_____

II. CHILD: I had a dumb birthday party. (After you went "all
    out" to make it a wonderful day.)
    PARENT: (*denying the feeling*)

_____

_____

_____

III. CHILD: I'm not wearing this stupid retainer anymore. It
     hurts. I don't care what the orthodontist says!
     PARENT: (*denying the feeling*)

_____

_____

_____

IV. CHILD: I hate that new coach! Just because I was one
    minute late he kicked me off the team.
    PARENT: (*denying the feeling*)

_____

_____

_____

Did you find yourself writing things like:

"That's not so. I know in your heart you really love the
baby."

"What are you talking about? You had a wonderful party—
ice cream, birthday cake, balloons. Well, that's the last party
you'll ever have!"

4

"Your retainer can't hurt that much. After all the money we've invested in your mouth, you'll wear that thing whether you like it or not!"

"You have no right to be mad at the coach. It's your fault. You should have been on time."

Somehow this kind of talk comes easily to many of us. But how do children feel when they hear it? In order to get a sense of what it's like to have one's feelings dismissed, try the following exercise:

Imagine that you're at work. Your employer asks you to do an extra job for him. He wants it ready by the end of the day. You mean to take care of it immediately, but because of a series of emergencies that come up you completely forget. Things are so hectic, you barely have time for your own lunch.

As you and a few coworkers are getting ready to go home, your boss comes over to you and asks for the finished piece of work. Quickly you try to explain how unusually busy you were today.

He interrupts you. In a loud, angry voice he shouts, "I'm not interested in your excuses! What the hell do you think I'm paying you for—to sit around all day on your butt?" As you open your mouth to speak, he says, "Save it," and walks off to the elevator.

Your coworkers pretend not to have heard. You finish gathering your things and leave the office. On the way home you meet a friend. You're still so upset that you find yourself telling him or her what had just taken place.

Your friend tries to "help" you in eight different ways. As you read each response, tune in to your immediate "gut" reaction and then write it down. (There are no right or wrong reactions. Whatever you feel is right for you.)

I. *Denial of Feelings:* "There's no reason to be so upset. It's foolish to feel that way. You're probably just tired and blowing the whole thing out of proportion. It can't be

as bad as you make it out to be. Come on, smile . . . You look so nice when you smile."
Your reaction:

_____

_____

_____

II. *The Philosophical Response:* "Look, life is like that. Things don't always turn out the way we want. You have to learn to take things in stride. In this world, nothing is perfect."
Your reaction:

_____

_____

_____

III. *Advice:* "You know what I think you should do? Tomorrow morning go straight to your boss's office and say, 'Look, I was wrong.' Then sit right down and finish that piece of work you neglected today. Don't get trapped by those little emergencies that come up. And if you're smart and you want to keep that job of yours, you'll make sure nothing like that ever happens again."
Your reaction:

_____

_____

_____

IV. *Questions:* "What exactly were those emergencies you had that would cause you to forget a special request from your boss?"

"Didn't you realize he'd be angry if you didn't get to it immediately?"

"Has this ever happened before?"

"Why didn't you follow him when he left the room and try to explain again?"

Your reaction:

_____

_____

_____

V.  *Defense of the Other Person:* "I can understand your boss's reaction. He's probably under terrible pressure. You're lucky he doesn't lose his temper more often."

Your reaction:

_____

_____

_____

VI.  *Pity:* "Oh, you poor thing. That is terrible! I feel so sorry for you, I could just cry."

Your reaction:

_____

_____

_____

VII.  *Amateur Psychoanalysis:* "Has it ever occurred to you that the real reason you're so upset by this is because your employer represents a father figure in your life? As a child you probably worried about displeasing your father, and when your boss scolded you it brought back your early fears of rejection. Isn't that true?"

Your reaction:

_____

_____

_____

VIII. *An Empathic Response* (an attempt to tune into the feelings of another): "Boy, that sounds like a rough experience. To be subjected to an attack like that in front of other people, especially after having been under so much pressure, must have been pretty hard to take!"
Your reaction:

_____

_____

_____

You've just been exploring your own reactions to some fairly typical ways that people talk. Now I'd like to share with you some of my personal reactions. When I'm upset or hurting, the last thing I want to hear is advice, philosophy, psychology, or the other fellow's point of view. That kind of talk makes me only feel worse than before. Pity leaves me feeling pitiful; questions put me on the defensive; and most infuriating of all is to hear that I have no reason to feel what I'm feeling. My overriding reaction to most of these responses is "Oh, forget it. . . . What's the point of going on?"

But let someone really listen, let someone acknowledge my inner pain and give me a chance to talk more about what's troubling me, and I begin to feel less upset, less confused, more able to cope with my feelings and my problem.

I might even say to myself, "My boss is usually fair. . . . I suppose I should have taken care of that report immediately. . . . But I still can't overlook what he did. . . . Well, I'll go in early tomorrow and write that report first thing in the morning. . . . But when I bring it to his office I'll let him know how upsetting it was for me to be spoken to in that way. . . . And I'll also let him know that, from now on, if he has any criticism I would appreciate being told privately."

The process is no different for our children. They too can help themselves if they have a listening ear and an empathic response. But the language of empathy does not come naturally to us. It's not part of our "mother tongue." Most of us grew up having our feelings denied. To become fluent in this new language of acceptance, we have to learn and practice its methods. Here are some ways to help children deal with their feelings.

## TO HELP WITH FEELINGS

1. Listen with full attention.

2. Acknowledge their feelings with a word—"Oh" . . . "Mmm" . . . "I see."

3. Give their feelings a name.

4. Give them their wishes in fantasy.

On the next few pages you'll see the contrast between these methods and the ways that people usually respond to a child who is in distress.

It can be discouraging to try to get through to someone
who gives only lip service to listening.

# I. LISTEN WITH FULL ATTENTION.

It's much easier to tell your troubles to a parent who is really listening.
Sometimes a sympathetic silence is all a child needs.

It's hard for a child to think clearly or constructively
when someone is questioning, blaming, or advising her.

There's a lot of help to be had from a simple "Oh . . . mmm . . ." or
"I see." Words like these, coupled with a caring attitude, are invitations
to a child to explore her own thoughts and feelings, and possibly
come up with her own solutions.

It's strange. When we urge a child to push a bad feeling away—
however kindly—the child seems to get only more upset.

## III. GIVE THE FEELING A NAME.

Parents don't usually give this kind of response, because they fear that by giving a name to the feeling they'll make it worse. Just the opposite is true. The child who hears the words for what she is experiencing is deeply comforted. Someone has acknowledged her inner experience.

When children want something they can't have,
adults usually respond with logical explanations of
why they can't have it. Often, the harder we explain,
the harder they protest.

# IV. GIVE A CHILD HIS WISHES IN FANTASY.

Sometimes just having someone understand
how much you want something makes reality easier to bear.

So there you have it—four possible ways to give first aid to a child in distress: by listening with full attention, by acknowledging his feelings with a word, by giving a name to his feelings, and by granting him his wishes in fantasy.

But more important than any words we use is our attitude. If our attitude is not one of compassion, then whatever we say will be experienced by the child as phony or manipulative. It is when our words are infused with our real feelings of empathy that they speak directly to a child's heart.

Of the four skills you've just seen illustrated, perhaps the most difficult is to have to listen to a child's emotional outpourings and then "give a name to the feeling." It takes practice and concentration to be able to look into and beyond what a child says in order to identify what he or she might be feeling. Yet it's important that we give our children a vocabulary for their inner reality. Once they have the words for what they're experiencing, they can begin to help themselves.

This next exercise has a list of six statements that a child might make to her parents. Please read each statement and figure out:

1. A word or two that describe what the child might be feeling.
2. A statement you might make to the child to show you understand the feeling.

## Helping Children Deal with Their Feelings

### ACKNOWLEDGING FEELINGS

| The child says. | A word that describes what he or she might be feeling. | Use the word in a statement that shows you understand the feeling. (Don't question or give advice.) |
|---|---|---|
| EXAMPLE: "The bus driver yelled at me and everybody laughed." | Embarrassment | That must have been embarrassing (or) Sounds as if that was embarrassing |
| 1. "I'd like to punch that Michael in the nose!" | | |
| 2. "Just because of a little rain my teacher said we couldn't go on our field trip. She's dumb." | | |
| 3. "Mary invited me to her party, but I don't know. . . ." | | |
| 4. "I don't know why teachers have to load you down with so much homework over the weekend!" | | |

5. "We had
basketball prac-
tice today and
I couldn't sink
that ball once."

_____    _____
                    _____
                    _____
                    _____
                    _____

6. "Janey is
moving away
and she's my
best friend."

_____    _____
                    _____
                    _____
                    _____

Did you notice how much thought and effort it takes to let a child know you have a sense of what it is he or she might be feeling? For most of us it doesn't come naturally to say things like:

"Boy, you sound angry!" or
"That must have been a disappointment for you," or
"Hmm. You seem to be having some doubts about going to that party," or
"Sounds as if you really resent all that homework," or
"Oh, that must have been so frustrating!" or
"To have a dear friend move away can be pretty upsetting."

And yet it's statements like these that give children comfort and free them to begin to deal with their problems. (By the way, don't worry about using words that are too big. The easiest way to learn a new word is to hear it used in context.)

You may be thinking, "Well, in this exercise I was able to give an initial response that showed I understood—more or less. But where would the conversation go from there? How would I continue? Is it okay to give advice next?"

Hold off on giving advice. I know how tempting it is to try to solve a child's problem with an immediate solution:

"Ma, I'm tired."
"Then lie down and rest."

"I'm hungry."
"Then eat something."

"I'm not hungry."
"Then don't eat."

Resist the temptation to "make better" instantly. Instead of giving advice, continue to accept and reflect on your child's feelings.

Here's an example of what I mean. A father in our group reported that his young son came storming into the house with the first statement you worked on in your workbooks: "I'd like to punch that Michael in the nose!"

The father said, "Normally the conversation would have gone like this:"

SON: I'd like to punch that Michael in the nose!
FATHER: Why? What happened?
SON: He threw my notebook in the dirt!
FATHER: Well, did you do something to him first?
SON: No!
FATHER: Are you sure?
SON: I swear, I never touched him.
FATHER: Well, Michael is your friend. If you take my advice, you'll forget about the whole thing. You're not so perfect, you know. Sometimes you start up and then blame someone else—the way you do with your brother.
SON: No, I don't. He starts up with me first . . . Oh, I can't talk to you.

But the father had just attended a workshop on helping his children deal with their feelings, and this is what actually took place:

| | |
|---|---|
| SON: | I'd like to punch that Michael in the nose! |
| FATHER: | Boy, you're angry! |
| SON: | I'd like to push his fat face in! |
| FATHER: | You're *that* mad at him! |
| SON: | You know what that bully did? He grabbed my notebook at the bus stop and threw it in the dirt. And for no reason! |
| FATHER: | Hmmm! |
| SON: | I bet he thought I was the one who broke his dumb clay bird in the art room. |
| FATHER: | You think so. |
| SON: | Yeah, he kept looking at me all the time he was crying. |
| FATHER: | Oh. |
| SON: | But I didn't break it. I didn't! |
| FATHER: | You *know* you didn't. |
| SON: | Well, I didn't do it on purpose! I couldn't help it if that stupid Debby pushed me into the table. |
| FATHER: | So Debby pushed you. |
| SON: | Yeah. A lot of things got knocked down, but the only thing that broke was the bird. I didn't mean to break it. His bird was good. |
| FATHER: | You really didn't mean to break it. |
| SON: | No, but he wouldn't believe me. |
| FATHER: | You don't think he'd believe you if you told him the truth. |
| SON: | I dunno . . . I'm gonna tell him anyway—whether he believes me or not. And I think he should tell me he's sorry for throwing my notebook in the dirt! |

The father was astonished. He hadn't asked questions and yet the child had told him the whole story. He hadn't given one word of advice, and yet the child had worked out his own solution. It seemed unbelievable to him that he could have been so helpful to his son just by listening and acknowledging his feelings.

It's one thing to do a written exercise and read a model dialogue. It's another to put listening skills into action in a real situation with our own children. Parents in our groups report that it's helpful to role-play with one another and get a little practice before dealing with actual situations in their own homes.

On the following page you'll find a role-playing exercise to try with a friend or spouse. Decide which of you will play the child and which will play the parent. Then read only your part.

## Child's Situation
### (Role-Playing)

I. The doctor said that you have an allergy and need to have shots every week so that you won't sneeze so much. Sometimes the shots are painful and sometimes you hardly feel them at all. The shot you had today was the kind that really hurt. After you leave the doctor's office, you want your parents to know how it felt.

Your parent will respond to you in two different ways. The first time, your feelings will be denied, but keep trying to get your parent to understand anyway. When the conversation comes to a natural conclusion, ask yourself what your feelings were and share your answer with the person who is role-playing with you.

Start the scene by rubbing your arm and saying,
*"The doctor nearly killed me with that shot!"*

II. The situation is the same, only this time your parent will respond differently. Again, when the conversation comes to a natural conclusion ask yourself what your feelings were this time and share your answer.

Begin the scene in the same way, by saying,
*"The doctor nearly killed me with that shot!"*

**When you've played the scene twice, you might want**

**to reverse roles so that you can experience the parent's point of view.**

### Parent's Situation
*(Role-Playing)*

I. You have to take your child for allergy shots every week. Although you know your youngster dreads going, you also know that most of the time the shots just hurt for a second. Today, after leaving the doctor's office your child complains bitterly.

You'll be playing the scene twice. The first time, try to get your child to stop complaining by denying his or her feelings. Use the following statements (if you like, you can make up some of your own):

*"Come on, it can't hurt that much."*

*"You're making a big fuss over nothing."*

*"Your brother never complains when he has a shot."*

*"You're acting like a baby."*

*"Well, you'd better get used to those shots. After all, you're going to have to get them every week."*

When the conversation comes to a natural conclusion, ask yourself what your feelings were and share your answer with the person who is role-playing with you.

Your child will start the scene.

II. The scene is the same, only this time you will really listen.

Your responses will show that you can both hear and accept whatever feelings your child might express. For example:

*"Sounds as if it really hurt."*

*"Mmmm, that bad!"*

*"Wouldn't it be great if someone would discover a pain-free way to treat allergies?"*

*"It's not easy to get these shots week after week. I bet you'll be glad when they're over."*

When the conversation comes to a natural conclusion, ask yourself what your feelings were this time and share your answer.

Your child will start the scene again.

**When you've played the scene twice, you might want to reverse roles so that you can experience the child's point of view.**

When you played the child whose feelings were brushed aside and denied, did you find yourself becoming more and more angry? Did you start out being upset about your shot and end up being mad at your parent?

When you played the parent who tried to stop the complaining, did you find yourself getting more and more irritated with your "unreasonable" child?

That's usually the way it goes when feelings are denied. Parents and children become increasingly hostile toward each other.

Parent, when you were accepting of your child's feelings, did you sense the fight going out of your interchange? Did you experience your power to be genuinely helpful?

Child, when your feelings were accepted, did you feel more respected? More loving toward your parent? Was the pain easier to bear when someone knew how much it hurt? Could you face it again next week?

When we acknowledge a child's feelings, we do him a great service. We put him in touch with his inner reality. And once he's clear about that reality, he gathers the strength to begin to cope.

## ASSIGNMENT

At least once this week have a conversation with a child in which you accept his or her feelings. Jot down what was said while it's still fresh in your mind.

*A Quick Reminder . . .*

---

**Helping Children Deal with Their Feelings**

Children Need to Have Their Feelings
Accepted and Respected.

1. YOU CAN LISTEN QUIETLY AND ATTENTIVELY.

2. YOU CAN ACKNOWLEDGE THEIR FEELINGS WITH A WORD.

   "Oh . . . Mmm . . . I see . . ."

3. YOU CAN GIVE THE FEELING A NAME.

   "That sounds frustrating!"

4. YOU CAN GIVE THE CHILD HIS WISHES IN FANTASY.

   "I wish I could make the banana ripe for you
   right now!"

   • • •

   All feelings can be accepted.
   Certain actions must be limited.

   "I can see how angry you are at your brother.
   Tell him what you want with words, not fists."

---

Note: You may find it useful to make a copy of this and other
"reminder" pages and put them up in strategic locations
around the house.

## Part II: COMMENTS, QUESTIONS, AND PARENTS' STORIES

### *Questions Parents Have Asked*

## 1. Is it important that I always empathize with my child?

No. Many of our conversations with our children consist of casual exchanges. If a child were to say, "Mom, I decided to go to David's house after school today," it would seem unnecessary for the parent to reply, "So you made a decision to visit a friend this afternoon." A simple "Thanks for letting me know" would be sufficient acknowledgment. The time for empathy is when a child wants you to know how he feels. Reflecting his positive feelings presents few problems. It's not hard to respond to a youngster's exuberant "I got ninety-seven on my math test today!" with an equally enthusiastic "Ninety-seven! You must be so pleased!"

It's his *negative* emotions that require our skill. That's where we have to overcome the old temptation to ignore, deny, moralize, etc. One father said that what helped him become more sensitive to his son's emotional needs was when he began to equate the boy's bruised, unhappy feelings with physical bruises. Somehow the image of a cut or a laceration helped him realize that his son required as prompt and serious attention for his hurt feelings as he would for a hurt knee.

## 2. What's wrong with asking a child directly, "Why do you feel that way?"

Some children can tell you why they're frightened, angry, or unhappy. For many, however, the question "Why?" only adds to their problem. In addition to their original distress, they must now analyze the cause and come up with a reasonable explanation. Very often children don't know why they feel as they do. At other times they're reluctant to tell because they fear that in the adult's eyes their reason won't seem good enough. ("For *that* you're crying?")

It's much more helpful for an unhappy youngster to hear, "I see something is making you sad," rather than to be interrogated with "What happened?" or "Why do you feel that way?" It's easier to talk to a grown-up who accepts what you're feeling rather than one who presses you for explanations.

## 3. Are you saying we should let our children know we agree with their feelings?

Children don't need to have their feelings agreed with; they need to have them acknowledged. The statement "You're absolutely right" might be satisfying to hear for the moment, but it can also prevent a child from thinking things through for himself.

*Example:*

CHILD: The teacher says she's calling off our class play. She's mean!

PARENT: After all those rehearsals? I agree with you. She must be mean to do a thing like that!

End of discussion.

Notice how much easier it is for a child to think constructively when his feelings are accepted:

CHILD: My teacher says she's calling off the class play. She's mean.

PARENT: That must be a big disappointment for you. You were looking forward to it.

CHILD: Yeah. Just because some kids fool around at rehearsal. It's *their* fault.

PARENT: *(listens silently)*

CHILD: She's mad because nobody knows their parts, too.

PARENT: I see.

CHILD: She said if we "shaped up" she might give us one more chance. . . . I better go over my lines again. Would you cue me tonight?

Conclusion: What people of all ages can use in a moment of distress is not agreement or disagreement; they need someone to recognize what it is they're experiencing.

### 4. If it's so important to show my child I understand, what's wrong with simply saying, "I understand how you feel"?

The problem with saying "I understand how you feel" is that some children just don't believe you. They'll answer, "No, you don't." But if you take the trouble to be specific ("The first day of school can be scary—so many new things to get used to"), then the child knows you really do understand.

### 5. Suppose I try to identify a feeling and it turns out that I'm wrong. What then?

No harm done. Your child will quickly set you right.
*Example:*

CHILD: Dad, our test was postponed till next week.

FATHER: That must have been a relief for you.

CHILD: No, I was mad! Now I'll have to study the same stuff again next week.

FATHER: I see. You were hoping to get it over with.
CHILD: Yeah!

It would be presumptuous for any one person to assume he could always know what another person is feeling. All we can do is attempt to understand our children's feelings. We won't always succeed, but our efforts are usually appreciated.

**6. I know feelings should be accepted, but I find it hard to know how to react when I hear "You're mean" or "I hate you" from my own child.**

If "I hate you" upsets you, you might want to let your child know, "I didn't like what I just heard. If you're angry about something, tell it to me in another way. Then maybe I can be helpful."

**7. Is there any way to help a child who's upset other than by letting him know you understand his feelings? My son has very little tolerance for any kind of frustration. Occasionally it does seem to help when I acknowledge his feelings and say something like "That must be so frustrating!" But usually when he's in such an emotional state he doesn't even hear me.**

Parents in our groups have found that when their children are extremely upset, sometimes a physical activity can help relieve some of the painful feelings. We've heard many stories about angry children who have felt calmer after punching pillows, hammering old grocery cartons, pounding and kneading clay, roaring like a lion, throwing darts. But the one activity that seems most comfortable for parents to watch, and most satisfying for children to do, is to draw their feelings. The two examples that follow happened within a week of each other:

I had just come back from a workshop session and found my three-year-old son lying on the floor having a tantrum. My husband was just standing there looking disgusted. He said, "Okay, child specialist, let's see if you can handle this one." I felt I had to rise to the occasion. I looked down at Joshua, who was still kicking and screaming, and grabbed a pencil and the pad near the phone. Then I knelt down, handed the pencil and pad to Joshua, and said, "Here, show me how angry you are. Draw me a picture of the way you feel."

Joshua jumped up immediately and began to draw angry circles. Then he showed it to me and said, "This is how angry I am!"

I said, "You really *are* angry!" and tore another piece of paper from the pad. "Show me more," I said.

He scribbled furiously on the page, and again I said, "Boy, *that* angry!" We went through the whole thing one more time. When I handed him a fourth piece of paper, he was definitely calmer. He looked at it a long time. Then he said, "Now I show my happy feelings," and he drew a circle with two eyes and a smiling mouth. It was unbelievable. In two minutes he had gone from being hysterical to smiling—just because I let him show me how he felt. Afterward my husband said, "Keep going to that group."

At the next session of our group, another mother told us about her experience using the same skill.

When I heard about Joshua last week, my first thought was "How I wish I could use that approach with Todd." Todd is also three, but he has cerebral palsy. Everything that comes naturally to other kids was monumental for him—standing without falling, keeping his head erect. He's made remarkable progress, but he's still so easily frustrated. Anytime he tries to do something and can't, he screams for hours on end. There is no way in the world I can get through to him. The worst part is that he kicks me and tries to bite me. I guess he thinks that somehow his difficulties are all my fault, and that I should be able to do something about it. He's angry at me most of the time.

On the way home from last week's workshop I thought, "What if I catch Todd *before* he goes into his full tantrum?" That afternoon he was playing with his new puzzle. It was a very simple one, with just a few big pieces. Anyway, he couldn't get the last piece to fit, and after a few tries he began to get that look on his face. I thought, "Oh no, here we go again!" I ran over to him and shouted, "Hold it! . . . Hold everything! . . . Don't move! . . . I've gotta get something!" He looked startled. I frantically searched in his bookshelves and found a big purple crayon and a sheet of drawing paper. I sat down on the floor with him and said, "Todd, is this how angry you feel?" And then I drew sharp zigzag lines up and down, up and down.

"Yeah," he said, and yanked the crayon out of my hand and made wild slashing lines. Then he stabbed the paper over and over again until it was full of holes. I held the paper up to the light and said, "You are so mad . . . You are absolutely furious!" He grabbed the paper away from me and, crying all the while, tore it again and again until it was nothing more than a pile of shreds. When he was all finished, he looked up at me and said, "I love you, Mommy." It was the first time he'd ever said that.

I've tried it again since and it doesn't work all the time. I guess I have to find some other physical outlet for him, like a punching bag or something. But I'm beginning to realize that what's most important is that, while he's punching or pounding or drawing, I be there—watching him, letting him know that even his angriest feelings are understood and accepted.

**8. If I accept all of my child's feelings, won't that give him the idea that anything he does is all right with me? I don't want to be a permissive parent.**

We too worried about being permissive. But gradually we began to realize that this approach was permissive only in the sense that all feelings were permitted. For example, "I can see that you're having fun making designs in the butter with your fork."

But that doesn't mean that you have to permit a child to behave in a way that's unacceptable to you. As you remove the butter, you can also let the young "artist" know that "Butter is not for playing with. If you want to make designs, you can use your clay."

We found that when we accepted our children's feelings they were more able to accept the limits we set for them.

**9. What is the objection to giving children advice when they have a problem?**

When we give children advice or instant solutions, we deprive them of the experience that comes from wrestling with their own problems.

Is there ever a time for advice? Certainly.

For a more detailed discussion of when and how to give advice, see "More About Advice" on pages 164 to 166.

**10. Is there anything you can do if you realize afterward that you've given your child an unhelpful response? Yesterday my daughter came home from school very upset. She wanted to tell me about how some kids picked on her in the playground. I was tired and preoccupied, and so I brushed her off and told her to stop crying, that it wasn't the end of the world. She looked very unhappy and went up to her room. I know I made her feel worse, but what can I do now?**

Every time a parent says to himself, "I wish I hadn't said that. Why didn't I think to say . . . ," he automatically gets another chance. Life with children is open-ended. There's always another opportunity—later in the hour, day, or week—to say, "I've been thinking about what you told me before, about those kids teasing you at the playground. And I realize now how upsetting that must have been for you."

Compassion is always appreciated, whether it comes sooner or later.

### Cautions

**I. Children usually object when their exact words are repeated back to them.**

*Example:*

CHILD:   I don't like David anymore.

PARENT:   You don't like David anymore.

CHILD:   *(with annoyance)* That's what I just said.

This child might have preferred a less parrotlike response, such as:

"Something about David bothers you."

OR

"Sounds as if you're really annoyed with him."

**II. There are youngsters who prefer no talk at all when they're upset. For them, Mom or Dad's presence is comfort enough.**

One mother told us about walking into the living room and seeing her ten-year-old daughter slumped on the sofa with tear-stained eyes. The mother sat down beside her daughter, put her arms around her, murmured, "Something happened," and sat silently with her for five minutes. Finally, her daughter sighed and said, "Thanks, Mom. I'm better now." The mother never did find out what happened. All she knew was that her comforting presence must have been helpful, because an hour later she heard her daughter humming to herself in her room.

### III. Some children become irritated when they express an intense emotion and their parent's response is "correct" but cool.

A teenager in one of our workshops told us that she came home one afternoon in a rage because her best friend had betrayed a very personal secret. She told her mother what had happened, and very matter-of-factly her mother commented, "You're angry." The girl said she couldn't help snapping back with a sarcastic, "No kidding."

We asked her what she would have liked her mother to say. She thought awhile and answered, "It wasn't the words; it was how she said it. It was as if she was talking about the feelings of someone she didn't even care about. I guess I wanted her to show me that she was right in there with me. If she had just said something like 'Boy, Cindy, you must be *furious* at her!' then I would have felt she understood."

### IV. It's also not helpful when parents respond with more intensity than the child feels.

*Example:*

TEENAGER: *(grumbling)* Steve kept me waiting on the street corner for half an hour, and then he made up some story that I know isn't true.

MOTHER: That is inexcusable! How could he do such a thing to you? He's inconsiderate and irresponsible. You must feel like never seeing him again.

It probably never occurred to the teenager to react so violently to his friend or to consider so drastic a retaliation. All he probably needed from his mother was an understanding grunt and a shake of the head to convey sympathy for his irritation at his friend's behavior. He didn't need the additional burden of having to cope with her strong emotions.

## V. Children don't appreciate having the names they call themselves repeated by their parents.

When a child tells you he's dumb or ugly or fat, it's not helpful to reply with "Oh, so you think you're dumb," or "You really feel you're ugly." Let's not cooperate with him when he calls himself names. We can accept his pain without repeating the name.

*Example:*

CHILD: The teacher said we're only supposed to spend fifteen minutes a night on our math. It took me a whole hour to finish. I must be dumb.

PARENT: It can be discouraging when work takes longer than you expect.

*Example:*

CHILD: I look terrible when I smile. All you can see are my braces. I'm ugly.

PARENT: You really don't like the way you look in those things. And it probably doesn't help to know that to me you're a pleasing sight—with or without your braces.

We hope our "cautions" haven't scared you off. It's probably obvious to you by now that dealing with feelings is an art, not a science. Yet we have faith (based upon years of observation) that parents, after some trial and error, can master the art. You'll sense after a while what is helpful to your individual child and what isn't. With practice you'll soon discover what irritates and what comforts, what creates distance and what invites intimacy, what wounds and what heals. There is no substitute for your own sensitivity.

## *Parents' Stories*

We teach the same basic principles to every group. Yet we never cease to be surprised at the originality of parents or the variety of situations in which these principles are applied. Each of the following stories is presented basically as parents have written them. In most cases the children's names have been changed. You'll notice that not every single thing the parents say is a "model" response. But their basic willingness to listen and their attitude of acceptance are what make the difference.

The parents who told these first two stories to the group found it difficult to believe that when they refrained from giving advice the child really did start to work toward his own solution. This mother introduced her story with, "Listen to how little I said!"

Nicky, age eight, comes home from school and says, "I'd like to punch Jeffrey."

ME: You're *really* mad at Jeffrey!

NICKY: Yeah! Whenever we play soccer and I get the ball he says, "Give it to me, Nicky, I'm better than you are." Wouldn't that make *anybody* mad?

ME: Yes.

NICKY: But Jeffrey's not really like that. In first grade he was always nice. But I think when Chris came in the second grade Jeffrey picked up the habit of boasting from him.

ME: I see.

NICKY: Let's call Jeffrey and invite him to the park.

My son is a first grader who is not aggressive and doesn't get into fights. Therefore I tend to be overprotective because he seems so vulnerable. On Monday he came home from school and told me that a boy in his class, who is much bigger than he is, sent a "deputy" over to tell him that he

37

was going to be "beat up" tomorrow. My first reaction was pure hysteria: keep him home from school, teach him overnight self-defense—anything to save him pain and fear.

Instead of showing him my alarm, I decided to listen attentively and just answered, "Umm." Then Douglas launched into a nonstop monologue. He said, "Yes, so I've figured out three strategies for defense. First, I'll try to talk him out of fighting. I'll explain that you shouldn't fight because it's uncivilized. Then if that doesn't work, I'll put on my glasses, but (he paused and thought here) if he's a bully that won't stop him, and he must be a bully because I never even spoke to him and now he wants to beat me up. Then, if nothing else works, I'll get Kenny to attack him. Kenny is so strong the bully will just look at him and be scared."

I was shocked and just said, "Oh," and he said, "Okay . . . it'll be okay . . . I have plans to use," and he walked out of the room relaxed. I was so impressed with my son. I had no idea he could be so brave or so creative about handling his own problems. And all this came about because I just listened and kept out of his way.

But I didn't let it go there. I said nothing to Douglas, but I called his teacher that afternoon and alerted her to what was going on. She said it was good I called, because in today's world no threat should be overlooked.

The next day it took all my self-control not to ask him what happened, but he said to me, "Mommy, guess what, the bully never came near me today."

Some parents reported their amazement at the calming effect their "accepting" statements had. The old "Calm down!" or "Cut it out!" seemed only to agitate the children further. But a few words of acknowledgment often soothed the most savage feelings and changed the mood dramatically. This first example is from a father.

My daughter, Holly, came in from the kitchen.

"Mrs. G. really yelled at me in gym today."

"Oh."

"She screamed at me."

"She was really mad."

"She yelled, 'You don't hit the ball *that* way in volleyball. You do it *this* way!' How should I know? She never told us how to hit it."

"You were angry at her for yelling."

"She made me so mad."

"It can be frustrating to be yelled at for no good reason."

"She had no right!"

"You feel she shouldn't have yelled at you."

"No. I'm so mad at her, I could step on her . . . I'd like to stick pins in a doll of her and make her suffer."

"Hang her by the thumbs."

"Boil her in oil."

"Turn her over a spit."

At this point Holly smiled. I smiled. She began to laugh, and so did I. She then remarked that it was really silly the way Mrs. G. yelled. Then she said, "I sure know *now* how to hit the volleyball to satisfy her."

Usually I might have said, "You probably did something wrong to make her yell. Next time listen when the teacher corrects you and then you'll know what to do." She would probably have slammed the door and raged in her room about what an insensitive idiot she had for a father, along with a miserable teacher.

Setting: My kitchen.

I have just put the baby down for her nap. Evan comes home from nursery school all excited because he's going to Chad's house to play.

EVAN: Hi, Mom. Let's go to Chad's now!

MOM: Nina (*the baby*) is sleeping now, but we'll go later.

EVAN: (*getting upset*) I want to go now. You said we could.

MOM: How about if I walk you over with your bike?

EVAN: No! I want you to stay with me. (*starts to cry hysterically*) I want to go now! (*He takes the drawings he has just brought home from school, crumples them, and stuffs them in the garbage.*)

MOM: (*My lightbulb goes on.*) Boy, are you furious! You're so angry you threw your drawings away. You must really be upset. Here you were, so looking forward to playing with Chad, and Nina is sleeping. That's so disappointing.

EVAN: Yeah, I really wanted to go to Chad's. (*stops crying*) Can I watch TV, Mom?

MOM: Sure.

Situation: Father was going fishing and four-year-old Danielle wanted to go with him.

DADDY: All right, honey, you can come along, but remember we'll be standing outside for a long, long time and it's cold outside this morning.

DANIELLE: (*Confusion is spread across her face and she answered with great hesitation.*) I changed my mind . . . I want to stay home.

Two minutes after Daddy left the tears began.

DANIELLE: Daddy left me and he knew I wanted to go!

MOMMY: (*preoccupied at the time and not in the mood to cope*) Danielle, we both know that *you* decided to stay home. Your crying is distracting and I don't want to listen, so if you're going to cry go to your room.

She runs to her room wailing.

Minutes later Mommy decides to try the new method.

MOMMY: (*going to Danielle's room and sitting on her bed*) You really wanted to be with Daddy, didn't you? Danielle stopped crying and nodded her head.

MOMMY: You felt confused when Daddy mentioned how cold it would be. You couldn't make up your mind.

Relief showed in her eyes. Nodding again, she dried her eyes.

MOMMY: You felt you didn't have enough time to make up your mind.

DANIELLE: No, I didn't.

At this point I hugged her. She bounced off her bed and went off to play.

It also seemed to help the children to know that they could have two very different feelings at the same time.

After the baby was born, I always told Paul that he loved his new brother. Paul would shake his head, "Nooooo! Nooooo!"

This past month I've been saying, "It seems to me, Paul, you have two feelings about the baby. Sometimes you're glad you have a brother. He's fun to watch and play with. And sometimes you don't like having him around at all. You just wish he'd go away."

Paul likes that. At least once a week now, he'll say to me, "Tell me about my two feelings, Mommy."

Some parents particularly appreciated having the skills to be helpful when a child's mood was one of discouragement or despair. They were glad to know they didn't have to take on their children's unhappiness and make it their own. One mother said, "I've just begun to realize what unnecessary pressure I've been putting myself under to make sure my kids are happy all the time. I first became aware of how far gone I was when I found myself trying to Scotch-tape a broken pretzel together to stop my four-year-old from crying. I've also begun to realize what a burden I've been putting on the children. Think of it! Not only are they upset about the original problem, but then they get more upset because they see me suffering over their suffering. My mother used to do that to me, and I remember feeling so guilty—as if there was something wrong with me for not being happy all the time. I want my kids to know that they're entitled to be miserable without their mother falling apart."

My son, Ron, came in with muddied overalls and down-cast face.

FATHER: I see a lot of mud on your pants.

RON: Yeah, I suck at football.

FATHER: You had a hard game.

RON: Yeah, I can't play. I'm too weak. Even Jerry knocks me down.

FATHER: It's so frustrating to get knocked down.

RON: Yeah. I wish I was stronger.

FATHER: You wish you were built like Superman.

RON: Yeah, then I could knock *them* down.

FATHER: You could run right over those tacklers.

RON: I could find plenty of running room.

FATHER: You could run.

RON: I can pass, too. I'm good on the short pass, but I can't throw a bomb (long pass).

FATHER: You can run and pass.

RON: Yeah, I can play better.

FATHER: You feel you could play better.

RON: Next time I'm going to play better.

FATHER: You know you'll play better.

Ordinarily I would have greeted Ron with some re-marks such as: "You're a good player. You just had one bad game. Don't worry, you'll do better next time." He prob-ably would have sulked and gone to his room.

I've made a tremendous discovery in this group. The more you try to push a child's unhappy feelings away, the more he becomes stuck in them. The more comfortably you can accept the bad feelings, the easier it is for kids to let go of them. I guess you could say that if you want to have a happy family you'd better be prepared to permit the expression of a lot of unhappiness.

Hans has been going through a difficult period. He has a teacher who is very hard on him and whom he doesn't like. When he is most unhappy with himself and most down in the dumps (usually when he is taking the school pressures out on us at home), he calls himself "stupid," feels no one likes him because he is stupid, says he is the "stupid" of his class, and so on.

On one of these nights my husband sat down with him, with all the concern in the world:

FRANK: (*gently*) Hans, you're not stupid.

HANS: I am too stupid. I'm a stupid stupid.

FRANK: But, Hans, you're not stupid. Why, you're one of the smartest eight-year-olds I know.

HANS: I am not. I'm stupid.

FRANK: (*still gently*) You're not stupid.

HANS: I am too stupid.

On and on it went. I didn't want to butt in and I couldn't bear to listen, so I left the room. To his credit Frank never lost his temper, but Hans went to bed still saying he was stupid, still down in the dumps.

I went in to him. I had had a horrendous day with him. He had devoted most of the afternoon and evening to aggravating me, and I didn't think I had it in me to cope with much more. But there he was lying in bed, miserably saying he was stupid and everyone hated him, so I went in. I didn't even know what I had left in me to say. I just sat on the edge of the bed, exhausted. Then a phrase we used in class came to me and I said it almost mechanically: "Those are rough feelings to have."

Hans stopped saying he was stupid and was silent for a minute. Then he said, "Yeah." That somehow gave me the strength to go on. I just began talking randomly then

43

about some of the nice or special things he'd said or done over the years. He listened for a while and then began participating with some of his own memories. He said, "Remember when you couldn't find your car keys and you were looking all over the house and I said to look in the car and they were there." After about ten minutes of this, I was able to kiss a boy good night who had restored his faith in himself.

Some parents were very comfortable with the idea of granting their children in fantasy what they couldn't give them in reality. It was so much easier for these parents to say, "You wish you had . . ." than to have an all-out battle over who was right and why.

DAVID: (*ten*) I need a new telescope.

FATHER: A new telescope? Why? There's nothing wrong with the one you already have.

DAVID: (*heatedly*) It's a kid's telescope!

FATHER: It's perfectly adequate for a boy your age.

DAVID: No, it isn't. I need a 200-power telescope.

FATHER: (*I could see we were headed for a big fight. I decided to try to shift gears.*) So you'd really like a 200-power telescope.

DAVID: Yeah, 'cause then I could see into the craters.

FATHER: You want to get a really close look at them.

DAVID: That's right!

FATHER: You know what I wish? I wish I had enough money to buy you that telescope. No, with your interest in astronomy, I wish I had enough money to buy you a 400-power telescope.

DAVID: A 600-power telescope.

FATHER: An 800-power telescope.

DAVID: (*getting enthusiastic*) A 1,000-power telescope!

FATHER: A . . . A . . .

DAVID: (*excitedly*) I know . . . I know . . . If you could, you'd buy me the one at Mount Palomar!

As we both laughed, I realized what made the difference. One of the keys to giving in fantasy was to really let yourself go, to be "far out" fantastic. Even though David knew it wasn't going to happen, he seemed to appreciate it that I took his longing so seriously.

My husband and I took Jason and his older sister, Leslie, to the Museum of Natural History. We really enjoyed it, and the kids were just great. Only on the way out we had to pass a gift shop. Jason, our four-year-old, went wild over the souvenirs. Most of the stuff was overpriced, but we finally bought him a little set of rocks. Then he started whining for a model dinosaur. I tried to explain that we had already spent more than we should have. His father told him to quit his complaining and that he should be happy for what we *did* buy him. Jason began to cry. My husband told him to cut it out, and that he was acting like a baby. Jason threw himself on the floor and cried louder.

Everyone was looking at us. I was so embarrassed that I wanted the floor to open up. Then—I don't know how the idea came to me—I pulled a pencil and paper out of my bag and started writing. Jason asked what I was doing. I said, "I'm writing that Jason wishes he had a dinosaur." He stared at me and said, "And a prism, too." I wrote, "A prism, too."

Then he did something that bowled me over. He ran over to his sister, who was watching the whole scene, and said, "Leslie, tell Mommy what you want. She'll write it down for you, too." And would you believe it, that ended it. He went home very peacefully.

I've used the idea many times since. Whenever I'm in a toy store with Jason and he runs around pointing to everything he wants, I take out a pencil and a scrap of paper and write it all down on his "wish list." That seems to satisfy him. And it doesn't mean I have to buy any of the things for him—unless maybe it's a special occasion. I guess what Jason likes about his "wish list" is that it shows that I not only know what he wants but that I care enough to put it in writing.

This final story speaks for itself.

I've just been through one of the most harrowing experiences of my life. My six-year-old daughter, Suzanne, has had croup before, but never an attack like this. I was terrified. She couldn't breathe and started to turn color. I couldn't get an ambulance, so I had to drive her to the emergency room along with my son Brian and my mother, who was visiting for the day.

My mother was completely hysterical. She kept repeating, "Oh, my God! She can't breathe. We'll never make it! What have you done to this child?"

In a voice louder than my mother's I said, "Suzie, I know you're having trouble breathing. I know it's scary. We're on our way now to get help. You're going to be all right. If you like, you can hold on to my leg while I drive." She held on to my leg.

At the hospital, two doctors and a few nurses crowded around. My mother was still ranting and raving. Brian asked me if Suzie will really die like Grandma keeps saying. I didn't have time to answer, because the doctors were trying to keep me out of the room and I knew Suzie needed me to be there. I could see by her eyes that she was terrified.

They gave her a shot of Adrenalin. I said, "That hurts, doesn't it?" She nodded. Then they put a tube down her throat. I said, "I know the tube must hurt, but it will help you." She still wasn't breathing normally, and they put her into an oxygen tent. I said, "It must feel strange with all that plastic around you. But this is also to help you breathe and get well." Then I put my hand through the zippered part of the tent and held her hand and told her, "I will not leave you. I'll be here with you even when you're asleep. I'll be here as long as you need me."

Her breathing became a little easier, but her condition was still critical and I stayed with her for seventy-two hours with practically no sleep. Thank God she pulled through.

I know that without these workshops it would have been very different. I would have been in a complete panic. By talking to her the way I did, by letting her know I knew what she was going through, I relaxed her so she didn't fight all the medical treatment she was getting.

I really feel I helped to save Suzie's life.

# 2 | Engaging Cooperation

By this time, your children have probably presented you with numerous opportunities to put your listening skills into action. Kids usually let us know—loud and clear—when something is bothering them. I know that in my own house any day with the children was like a night at the theater. A lost toy, a "too short" haircut, a report due for school, new jeans that didn't fit right, a fight with brother or sister—any of these crises could generate enough tears and passion for a three-act drama. We never lacked for material.

The only difference is that in the theater the curtain falls and the audience can go home. Parents don't have that luxury. Somehow we have to deal with all the hurt, anger, and frustration and still retain our sanity.

We know now that the old methods don't work. All our explaining and reassuring bring no relief to the children, and wear us out. Yet the new methods can present problems, too. Even though we're aware of how much more comforting the empathic response can be, it's still not easy to give. For many of us the language is new and strange. Parents have told me:

"I felt so awkward at first—not like myself—as if I were playing a part."

48

"I felt phony, but I must have been doing something right, because my son, who never says more than 'Yup,' 'Nope,' and 'Do I have to?,' suddenly began to talk to me."

"I felt comfortable, but the children seemed uneasy. They looked at me suspiciously."

"I discovered that I never listened to my kids before. I'd wait for them to finish talking so I could say what I had to. Real listening is hard work. You have to concentrate if you're not just going to give a pat response."

One father reported, "I tried it and it didn't work. My daughter came home from Sunday school with a long face. Instead of my usual 'Why the sour puss?,' I said, 'Amy, you seem very upset about something.' She burst into tears, ran to her room, and slammed the door."

I explained to that father that even when it "doesn't work," it "works." Amy heard a different sound that day—one that told her that someone cared about her feelings. I urged him not to give up. In time, when Amy knows she can count on an accepting response from her father, she'll feel it's safe to talk about what's bothering her.

Perhaps the most memorable response I heard was from a teenager who knew that his mother was attending my workshops. The boy came home from school muttering angrily, "They had no right to keep me off the team today just because I didn't have my gym shorts. I had to sit and watch the whole game. It was so unfair!"

"That must have been very upsetting to you," she said to him with concern.

He snapped at her, "Oh, you, you always take their side!"

She grabbed his shoulder. "Jimmy, I don't think you heard me. I said, 'That must have been very upsetting for you.'"

He blinked and stared at her. Then he said, "*Dad* should go to that course, too!"

• • •

Until now we've been concentrating on how parents can help children deal with their negative feelings. Now we would like to focus on helping parents deal with some of their own negative feelings.

One of the built-in frustrations of parenthood is the daily struggle to get our children to behave in ways that are acceptable to us and to society. This can be maddening, uphill work. Part of the problem lies in the conflict of needs. The adult need is for some semblance of cleanliness, order, courtesy, and routine. The children couldn't care less. How many of them would, of their own volition, take a bath, say "please" or "thank you," or ever change their underwear? How many of them would even wear underwear? A lot of parental passion goes into helping children adjust to societal norms. And somehow the more intense we become, the more actively they resist.

I know there were times when my own children thought of me as the "enemy"—the one who was always making them do what they didn't want to do: "Wash your hands . . . Use your napkin . . . Keep your voices down . . . Hang up your coats . . . Did you do your homework? . . . Are you sure you brushed your teeth? . . . Come back and flush the toilet . . . Get into pajamas . . . Get into bed . . . Go to sleep."

I was also the one who stopped them from doing what they wanted to do: "Don't eat with your fingers . . . Don't kick the table . . . Don't throw dirt . . . Don't jump on the sofa . . . Don't pull the cat's tail . . . Don't put beans up your nose!"

The children's attitude became "I'll do what I want." My attitude became "You'll do as I say," and the fight was on. It got to the point where my insides would churn every time I had to ask a child to do the simplest thing.

Take a few minutes now to think about what it is that you insist your children do, or not do, during a typical day. Then list your personal daily dos and don'ts in the space below.

In a single day I see to it that my children (or child) do the
following:

IN THE MORNING            IN THE AFTERNOON            IN THE EVENING

_____            _____            _____

_____            _____            _____

_____            _____            _____

_____            _____            _____

_____            _____            _____

_____            _____            _____

_____            _____            _____

I also make sure that my children (or child) don't do the following:

IN THE MORNING            IN THE AFTERNOON            IN THE EVENING

_____            _____            _____

_____            _____            _____

_____            _____            _____

_____            _____            _____

_____            _____            _____

_____            _____            _____

_____            _____            _____

Whether your list is long or short, whether your expectations are realistic or unrealistic, each item on that list
represents your time and your energy and contains all the
ingredients necessary for a battle of wills.

Are there any solutions?

Let's first look at some of the methods most commonly
used by adults to get children to cooperate. As you read the
example that illustrates each method, go back in time and

pretend you're a child listening to your parent speak. Let the words sink in. What do they make you feel? When you have your answer, write it down. (Another way to do this exercise is to have a friend read each example aloud to you as you listen with closed eyes.)

### I. Blaming and Accusing

"Your dirty fingerprints are on the door again! Why do you always do that? . . . What's the matter with you anyway? Can't you ever do anything right? . . . How many times do I have to tell you to use the doorknob? The trouble with you is you never listen."

As a child I'd feel

_____

_____

### II. Name-Calling

"It's below freezing today and you're wearing a light jacket! How dumb can you get? Boy, that really is a stupid thing to do."

"Here, let me fix the bike for you. You know how unmechanical you are."

"Look at the way you eat! You're disgusting."

"You have to be a slob to keep such a filthy room. You live like an animal."

As a child I'd feel

_____

_____

### III. Threats

"Just you touch that lamp once more and you'll get a smack."

"If you don't spit that gum out this minute, I'm going to open your mouth and take it out."

"If you're not finished dressing by the time I count to three, I'm leaving without you!"

As a child I'd feel

_____

_____

## IV. Commands

"I want you to clean up your room right this minute."

"Help me carry in the packages. Hurry up!"

"You still didn't take out the garbage? Do it now! . . . What are you waiting for? Move!"

As a child I'd feel

_____

_____

## V. Lecturing and Moralizing

"Do you think that was a nice thing to do—to grab that book from me? I can see you don't realize how important good manners are. What you have to understand is that if we expect people to be polite to us, then we must be polite to them in return. You wouldn't want anyone to grab from you, would you? Then you shouldn't grab from anyone else. We do unto others as we would have others do unto us."

As a child I'd feel

_____

_____

## VI. Warnings

"Watch it, you'll burn yourself."

"Careful, you'll get hit by a car!"

"Don't climb there! Do you want to fall?"

"Put on your sweater or you'll catch a bad cold."
As a child I'd feel

_____

_____

### VII. Martyrdom Statements

"Will you two stop that screaming! What are you trying to do to me . . . make me sick . . . give me a heart attack?"

"Wait till you have children of your own. Then you'll know what aggravation is."

"Do you see these gray hairs? That's because of you. You're putting me in my grave."

As a child I'd feel

_____

_____

### VIII. Comparisons

"Why can't you be more like your brother? He always gets his work done ahead of time."

"Lisa has such beautiful table manners. You'd never catch her eating with her fingers."

"Why don't you dress the way Gary does? He always looks so neat—short hair, shirt tucked in. It's a pleasure to look at him."

As a child I'd feel

_____

_____

### IX. Sarcasm

"You knew you had a test tomorrow and left your book in school? Oh, smart! That was a brilliant thing to do."

"Is that what you're wearing—polka dots and plaid? Well, you ought to get a lot of compliments today."

"Is this the homework you're bringing to school tomorrow? Well, maybe your teacher can read Chinese; I can't."

As a child I'd feel

_____

_____

## X. Prophecy

"You lied to me about your report card, didn't you? Do you know what you're going to be when you grow up? A person nobody can trust."

"Just keep on being selfish. You'll see, no one is ever going to want to play with you. You'll have no friends."

"All you ever do is complain. You've never once tried to help yourself. I can see you ten years from now—stuck with the same problems and still complaining."

As a child I'd feel

_____

_____

Now that you know how the "child" in you would react to these approaches, you might be interested in finding out the reaction of others who have tried this exercise. Evidently, different children respond differently to the same words. Here are some sample reactions from one group.

*Blaming and Accusing.* "The door is more important than I am" . . . "I'll lie and tell her it wasn't me" . . . "I'm a yuk" . . . "I'm shrinking" . . . "I want to call her a name" . . . "You say I never listen, so I won't."

*Name-Calling.* "She's right. I am stupid and unmechanical" . . . "Why even try?" . . . "I'll fix her. Next time I won't even wear a jacket" . . . "I hate her" . . . "Ho hum, there she goes again!"

*Threats.* "I'll touch the lamp when she's not looking" . . . "I want to cry" . . . "I'm afraid" . . . "Leave me alone."

*Commands.* "Try and make me" . . . "I'm frightened" . . . "I don't want to move" . . . "I hate his guts" . . . "Whatever I do, I'll be in trouble" . . . "How do you get transferred out of this lousy outfit?"

*Lecturing and Moralizing.* "Yak yak yak . . . Who's even listening?" . . . "I'm dumb" . . . "I'm worthless" . . . "I want to get far away" . . . "Boring, boring, boring."

*Warnings.* "The world is scary, dangerous" . . . "How will I ever manage by myself? Whatever I do, I'll be in trouble."

*Martyrdom Statements.* "I feel guilty" . . . "I'm scared. It's my fault she's sick" . . . "Who even cares?"

*Comparisons.* "She loves everyone more than me" . . . "I hate Lisa" . . . "I feel like a failure" . . . "I hate Gary, too."

*Sarcasm.* "I don't like being made fun of. She's mean" . . . "I'm humiliated, confused" . . . "Why try?" . . . "I'll get back at her" . . . "No matter what I do, I can't win" . . . "I'm boiling with resentment."

*Prophecy.* "She's right. I never will amount to anything" . . . "I can too be trusted; I'll prove him wrong" . . . "It's no use" . . . "I give up" . . . "I'm doomed."

If we as adults experience these feelings just from reading some words on a page, what must real children feel?

Are there alternatives? Are there ways to engage our children's cooperation without doing violence to their self-esteem or leaving them with such a backwash of bad feelings? Are there methods that are easier for parents, that exact less of a toll from them?

We'd like to share with you five skills that have been helpful to us and to the parents in our workshops. Not every one of them will work with every child. Not every skill will suit your personality. And there isn't any one of them that is effective all the time. What these five skills do, however, is create a climate of respect in which the spirit of cooperation can begin to grow.

## *To Engage Cooperation*

1. Describe. Describe what you see or describe the problem.

2. Give information.

3. Say it with a word.

4. Talk about your feelings.

5. Write a note.

# I. DESCRIBE.

*Describe what you see, or describe the problem.*

*Instead of*

*Describe*

*Instead of*

It's hard to do what needs to be done when people are telling you what's wrong with you.

*Describe*

It's easier to concentrate on the problem when someone just describes it to you.

# DESCRIBE (continued)

When grown-ups describe the problem, it gives children a chance to tell themselves what to do.

# II. GIVE INFORMATION.

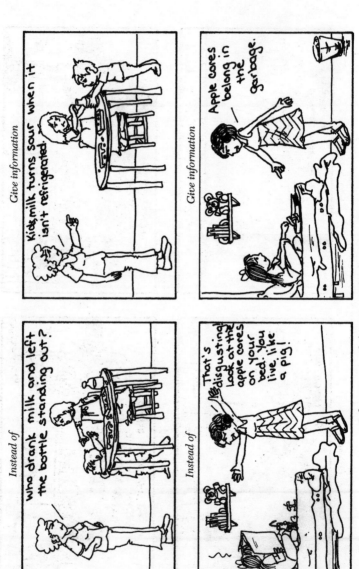

Instead of

*Who drank milk and left the bottle standing out?*

Give information

*Kids, milk turns sour when it isn't refrigerated.*

Instead of

*That's disgusting! Look at the apple cores on your bed. You live like a pig!*

Give information

*Apple cores belong in the garbage.*

Information is a lot easier to take than accusation.

# GIVE INFORMATION (continued)

*Instead of*

If I catch you writing on the walls once more you're going to get a spanking!

*Give information*

Walls are not for writing on. Paper is for writing on.

*Instead of*

It would never occur to you to give me a hand with the housework, would it?

*Give information*

It would really be helpful if the table were set for dinner now.

When children are given information, they can usually figure out for themselves what needs to be done.

# III. SAY IT WITH A WORD.

Look at the contrast between the effect of the
long paragraph and the effect of a single word.

*Instead of*

*Say it with a word*

In this case "less is more."

## SAY IT WITH A WORD (continued)

*Instead of*             *Say it with a word*

*Instead of*             *Say it with a word*

Children dislike hearing lectures, sermons, and long explanations. For them, the shorter the reminder, the better.

# IV. TALK ABOUT YOUR FEELINGS.

Make no comment about the child's character or personality.

*Instead of*

*Talk about your feelings*

Children are entitled to hear their parents' honest feelings.

By describing what we feel, we can be genuine without being hurtful.

# TALK ABOUT YOUR FEELINGS (continued)

Notice, when parents are being helpful they talk about their feelings only. They use the word "I" or "I feel . . .".

*Talk about your feelings*

*Instead of*

You're rude! You always interrupt.

I feel so frustrated when I start to say something and can't finish!

*Talk about your feelings*

*Instead of*

What do you mean, I have to take you? You sound like a spoiled brat!

I object to being told I have to do anything. What I'd like to hear is, "Dad, I'm ready to go. Can you take me now?"

It's easier to cooperate with someone who is expressing irritation or anger, as long as you're not being attacked.

## WRITE A NOTE.

Sometimes nothing we say is as effective as the written word.
The note below was written by a father who was tired of
cleaning his daughter's long hairs from the sink drain.

This was written by a working mother
who taped it to the family TV set.

## WRITE A NOTE (*continued*)

This note was hung on the back of a bedroom door. It was a two-sided sign that netted two tired parents an extra hour of sleep on Sunday morning. When they were ready to let the children in, they flipped the sign over.

# WRITE A NOTE (*continued*)

This father got tired of yelling and finally decided
to let a note do the talking for him.

Mother flew in a paper airplane with words on it to her son
and his friend—neither of whom could read. They ran in to
ask what the words said, and when they found out
they ran back to put away their toys.

There you have it—five skills that encourage cooperation and leave no residue of bad feelings.

If your kids happen to be in school now or in bed or are, by some miracle, playing quietly, then this is your chance to fit in a few minutes of practice. You can sharpen your skills on some hypothetical children before your own descend on you.

*Exercise I.* You walk into your bedroom and find that your freshly bathed child has just thrown a wet towel on your bed.

A. Write a typical statement that might be made to the child that would not be helpful.

———————————————————————

———————————————————————

B. In the same situation show how each of the skills listed below could be used to invite your child's cooperation.

1. Describe:

(Describe what you see, or describe the problem.)

———————————————————————

———————————————————————

2. Give information:

———————————————————————

———————————————————————

3. Say it with a word:

———————————————————————

———————————————————————

4. Talk about your feelings:

———————————————————————

———————————————————————

5. Write a note:

_____

_____

_____

_____

_____

You've just applied five different skills to the same situation. In these next situations, choose the one skill that you think would be most effective with your own child.

*Exercise II.* Situation A. You are about to wrap a package and can't find your scissors. Your child has a pair of scissors but is constantly borrowing yours and not returning them.
   Unhelpful statement:

_____

_____

Skilled response:

_____

_____

Skill used:

_____

_____

Situation B. Your youngster keeps leaving his sneakers in the kitchen doorway.

   Unhelpful statement:

_____

_____

Skilled response:

_____

_____

Skill used:

_____

_____

Situation C. Your child has just hung his wet raincoat in the closet.
Unhelpful statement:

_____

_____

Skilled response:

_____

_____

Skill used:

_____

_____

Situation D. You realize your child has not been brushing his teeth lately.
Unhelpful statement:

_____

_____

Skilled response:

_____

_____

Skill used:

_____

_____

I remember my own experience when I first experimented with these skills. I was so gung ho to get this new approach going in my family that I came home from a meeting, tripped over my daughter's skates in the hall, and sweetly told her, "Skates belong in the closet." I thought I was wonderful. When she looked up at me blankly, and then went back to reading her book, I hit her.

I've since learned two things:

1) *It's important to be authentic.* Sounding patient when I'm feeling angry can only work against me. Not only do I fail to communicate honestly; but because I've been "too nice," I wind up letting it out on my child later on. It would have been more helpful had I bellowed, "Skates belong in the closet!" For that, my daughter might have bestirred herself.

2) *Just because I don't "get through" the first time doesn't mean I should revert to the old ways.* I have more than one skill at my disposal. I can use them in combination and, if necessary, in increasing intensity. For example, in the case of the wet towel I might start by calmly pointing out to my daughter, "The towel there is getting my blanket wet."

I could combine that with "Wet towels belong in the bathroom."

If she's off in one of her daydreams and I really want to penetrate her thoughts, I can increase the volume: "*Jill, the towel!*"

Suppose she doesn't budge and my gorge begins to rise. I can get louder still: "JILL, I DON'T WANT TO HAVE TO SLEEP IN A COLD, WET BED ALL NIGHT!"

I might want to save my voice. I could conceivably drop a note onto her ever-present book: "Wet towels on my bed make me see red!"

I could even imagine myself getting mad enough to tell her, "I don't like being ignored. I'm putting away your wet towel, and now you have a resentful mother!"

There are many ways to match the message to the mood.

You might want to apply these skills now to the realities of your own home. If so, take a second look at your list of daily "dos and don'ts" on page 51. Is it possible that some of the "musts" on that list could be made easier for you and your child by using the skills you worked with just now? Perhaps the skills in Chapter 1, on how to accept a child's negative feelings, could also help to ease the situation.

Give it some thought and write down the skills you think you might like to try this week.

THE PROBLEM                                      THE SKILLS I MIGHT USE

_____

_____

_____

_____

_____

_____

Some of you may be thinking, "But suppose my child still doesn't respond, what then?" In the next chapter we'll explore some more advanced skills for engaging our children's cooperation. We'll be talking about problem-solving and other alternatives to punishment. Your assignment for the coming week will help you solidify what you've been working on today. In the meantime I hope that the ideas in this chapter will make the days ahead a little easier for you.

## ASSIGNMENT

**I. One unhelpful thing I did not say this week:**
   (Sometimes what we don't say can be as helpful as what we do say.)
   Situation:

_____

_____

I didn't say:

_____

_____

## II. Two new skills I put to use this week:
Situation 1.

_____

_____

Skill used:

_____

Child's reaction:

_____

My reaction:

_____

Situation 2.

_____

_____

Skill used:

_____

Child's reaction:

_____

My reaction:

_____

## III. A note I wrote:

_____

_____

## IV. Read Part II of "Engaging Cooperation."

*A Quick Reminder . . .*

## To Engage a Child's Cooperation

1. DESCRIBE WHAT YOU SEE, OR DESCRIBE THE PROBLEM.

   "There's a wet towel on the bed."

2. GIVE INFORMATION.

   "The towel is getting my blanket wet."

3. SAY IT WITH A WORD.

   "The towel!"

4. DESCRIBE WHAT YOU FEEL.

   "I don't like sleeping in a wet bed!"

5. WRITE A NOTE.

   (above towel rack)
   Please put me back so I can dry.
   Thanks!
   Your Towel

## PART II: COMMENTS, QUESTIONS, AND PARENTS' STORIES

### *Questions*

**1. Isn't "how" you say something to a child just as important as "what" you say?**

It certainly is. The attitude behind your words is as important as the words themselves. The attitude that children thrive on is one that communicates, "You're basically a lovable, capable person. Right now there's a problem that needs attention. Once you're aware of it, you'll probably respond responsibly."

The attitude that defeats children is one that communicates, "You're basically irritating and inept. You're always doing something wrong, and this latest incident is one more proof of your wrongness."

**2. If attitude is so important, why bother about words?**

A parent's look of disgust or tone of contempt can hurt deeply. But if, in addition, a child is subjected to words like "stupid" . . . "careless" . . . "irresponsible" . . . "you'll never learn," he's doubly wounded. Somehow words have a way of lingering long and poisonously. The worst part is that children sometimes pull out these words at a later date and use them as weapons against themselves.

**3. What's wrong with saying "please" to a child if you want him to do something?**

Certainly for requesting small favors like "please pass the salt" or "please hold the door," the word "please" is a common amenity—a way of taking the sting out of the otherwise crude commands: "pass the salt" or "hold the door."

We say "please" to our children to model a socially acceptable way to make a small request.

But "please" lends itself best to our more relaxed moments.

When we're really upset, a gentle "please" can lead to trouble.
Consider the following dialogue:

MOTHER:  (*trying to be nice*) Please don't jump on the sofa.
CHILD:   (*continues jumping.*)
MOTHER:  (*louder*) Please don't do that!
CHILD:   (*jumps again.*)
MOTHER:  (*suddenly slaps child hard*) I said "please," didn't I?

What happened? Why did this mother go from politeness
to violence in a few seconds? The fact is that when you've ex-
tended yourself and have been ignored, anger follows swiftly.
You tend to think, "How dare this kid defy me after I've been
so nice? I'll show him! Wham!"

When you want something done immediately, it's a good
idea to speak forcefully rather than to plead. A loud, firm
"Sofas are not for jumping on!" would probably stop the jumping a lot sooner. (If the youngster persists, he can always be
removed—swiftly, with a sternly repeated "Sofas are not for
jumping on!!")

## 4. Is there any way to explain the fact that sometimes my kids respond when I ask them to do something and sometimes I can't seem to get through?

We once asked a group of schoolchildren why they sometimes didn't listen to their parents. Here's what they told us:

"When I come home from school, I'm tired, and if my
mother asks me to do something I pretend I don't hear her."

"Sometimes I'm so busy playing or watching TV, I really
don't hear her."

"Sometimes I'm mad about something that happened in
school and I don't feel like doing what she tells me."

In addition to the children's thoughts, here are some questions you might want to ask yourself when you feel you're not
"getting through":

Does my request make sense in terms of my child's age and

ability? (Am I expecting an eight-year-old to have perfect table manners?)

Does he feel my request is unreasonable? ("Why does my mother bug me to wash behind my ears? Nobody looks there.")

Can I give her a choice about *when* to do something, rather than insisting upon "right now." ("Do you want to take your bath before your TV show or right after?")

Can I offer a choice about *how* something is done? ("Do you want to take your bath with your doll or your boat?")

Are there any physical changes that could be made in the house that would invite cooperation? (Could some hooks be placed low in the closet to eliminate the struggle with hangers? Would some additional shelves in a child's room make cleanup less overwhelming?)

Finally, are most of my moments with my child spent asking her to "do things?" Or am I taking out some time to be alone with her—just to "be together"?

**5. I must confess that in the past I've said everything to my daughter you're not supposed to. Now I'm trying to change and she's giving me a hard time. What can I do?**

The child who has had heavy doses of criticism may be supersensitive. Even a gentle "your lunch" may seem to her like one more indictment of her "forgetful nature." This child may need to have a lot overlooked and a great deal of approval before she can begin to hear anything resembling the slightest hint of disapproval. Later on in the book you'll find ways to help your youngster see herself more positively. In the meantime, there will very likely be a transition period in which she might react suspiciously and even with hostility to her parents' new approach.

But don't let your daughter's negative attitude discourage you. All the skills you've read about are ways of showing respect to another person. Most people respond to that eventually.

**6. Humor works best with my son. He loves it when I ask him to do something in a funny way. Is that all right?**

If you can reach your child's head through his funny bone, more power to you! There's nothing like a little humor to galvanize children into action and to perk up the mood in the household. The problem for many parents is that their natural sense of fun fizzles out from the daily irritation of living with kids.

One father said that a surefire way for him to put a spirit of play into the task ahead was to use another voice or accent. The kids' favorite was his robot voice: "This-is-RC3C. The next-person-who-takes-ice-and-doesn't-refill-tray-will-be-orbited-into-outer-space. Please-take-affirmative-action."

**7. Sometimes I find that I'm repeating myself about the same thing over and over again. Even though I use skills, I still sound as if I'm nagging. Is there any way to avoid this?**

Often what makes us repeat ourselves is a child who acts as if he hasn't heard us. When you are tempted to remind the child about something for the second or third time, stop yourself. Instead, *find out from him if you've been heard.* For example:

MOTHER:  Billy, we're leaving in five minutes.
BILLY:  (*doesn't answer and continues to read the comics.*)
MOTHER:  Would you tell me what I just said?
BILLY:  You said we're leaving in five minutes.
MOTHER:  Okay, now that I know you know, I won't mention it again.

**8. My problem is that when I ask for help my son says, "Sure, Dad, later," and then he never follows through. What do I do then?**

Here's an example of how one parent handled that problem:

| | |
|---|---|
| FATHER: | Steven, it's been two weeks since the lawn was mowed. I'd like it done today. |
| SON: | Sure, Dad, later. |
| FATHER: | I'd feel better if I knew just when you plan to get to it. |
| SON: | As soon as this program is over. |
| FATHER: | When is that? |
| SON: | About an hour. |
| FATHER: | Good. Now I know I can count on the lawn being done one hour from now. Thanks, Steve. |

### Comments, Cautions, and Anecdotes About Each Skill

**I. Describe.** Describe what you see, or describe the problem.

The best part of using descriptive language is that it takes out the finger-pointing and accusation, and helps everyone focus on what needs to be done.

"The milk spilled. We need a sponge."

"The jar broke. We need a broom."

"These pajamas are torn. We need a needle and thread."

You might want to try each of the above statements on yourself, only this time start each sentence with a "you." For example, "You spilled the milk . . . You broke the jar . . . You tore your pajamas." Notice the difference? Many people claim the "you" makes them feel accused and then defensive. When we describe the event (instead of talking about what "you did"), we seem to make it easier for the child to hear what the problem is and deal with it.

I was furious when my two young sons came to dinner covered with green watercolor paint, but I was determined not to lose my temper and scream at them. I turned to my list of skills that I had taped to the pantry door and used the first one I saw: Describe What You See. Here's what happened next.

ME: I see two boys with green paint on their hands and faces! They looked at each other and ran into the bathroom to wash up.

A few minutes later I walked into the bathroom and was ready to scream again. The tiles were covered with paint! But I hung on to my one skill.

ME: I see green paint on the bathroom walls!

My older boy ran to get a rag, saying, "To the rescue!" Five minutes later, he called me in to look again.

ME: (*sticking with description*) I see that someone helpful cleaned all the green paint off the bathroom walls.

My older boy beamed. Then the younger one piped up, "And now *I'm* going to clean off the sink!"

If I hadn't seen it, I wouldn't have believed it.

*Caution.* It is possible to use this skill in a way that can be irritating. For example, one father told us he was standing near the front door on a cold day and said to his son, who had just entered, "The door is open." The boy countered with, "So why don't you close it?"

The group decided that the boy experienced his father's descriptive statement as, "I'm trying to get you to do the right thing—hint, hint." The group also decided that descriptive statements work best when the child feels that his help is genuinely needed.

**II. Give information.** What we like about giving information is that, in a sense, you're giving the child a gift he can use forever. For the rest of his life he'll need to know that "milk turns sour when it's not refrigerated," that "open cuts need to be kept clean," that "fruit needs to be washed before eating," that "cookies get stale when the box is left open," and so on. Parents have told us that the skill of giving information isn't hard. What's hard, they say, is leaving off the insult at the end, such as "Dirty clothes belong in the laundry basket. You'll never learn, will you?"

We also like giving children information because the child seems to experience it as an act of confidence in him. He says to himself, "Grown-ups trust me to act responsibly once I have the facts."

Monique came home from her Brownie meeting and was wearing her uniform. She started to play in the garden. I must have yelled at her three or four times to change into a pair of slacks. She kept saying, "Why?"

I kept saying, "You'll rip your uniform."

Finally, I said, "Slacks are for playing in the garden; uniforms are for wearing to Brownie meetings."

To my amazement she stopped what she was doing and immediately went in to change.

A father shared this experience about himself and his newly adopted five-year-old Korean son:

Kim and I walked down the block together to visit a neighbor and return his ladder. As we were about to ring the bell, a group of kids who were playing in the street pointed to Kim and yelled, "He's a Chink! He's a Chink!" Kim looked confused and upset, even though he didn't know what the words meant.

A lot of thoughts rushed through my mind: "They haven't even got the right country, the little stinkers. . . . I'd like to give them hell and call their parents, but then they'd wind up taking it out on Kim. For better or worse this is his neighborhood, and he's got to find a way to live in it."

I walked up to the boys and very quietly said, "Name-calling can hurt feelings."

They seemed taken aback by what I said. (Maybe they thought they were going to be yelled at.) Then I went into my neighbor's house but left the door open. I didn't insist that Kim come inside. Five minutes later I looked out the window and saw Kim playing with the other kids.

• • •

I looked up to see three-year-old Jessica on her tricycle following her eight-year-old brother, who was cycling down the street. Luckily, no cars were in sight. I called out, "Jessica, two wheels can ride in the street. Three wheels belong on the sidewalk."

Jessica got off her tricycle, solemnly counted the wheels, and walked her tricycle onto the sidewalk, where she began to ride again.

*Caution.* Refrain from giving the child information she already knows. For example, if you were to tell a ten-year-old, "Milk turns sour when it's unrefrigerated," she might conclude either that you think she's stupid or that you're being sarcastic.

**III. The One-Word Statement.** Many parents have told us how much they appreciate this skill. They claim it saves time, breath, and boring explanations.

Teenagers we've worked with have told us they too prefer the single word, "Door" . . . "Dog" . . . or "Dishes," and find it a welcome relief from the usual lecture.

As we see it, the value of the one-word statement lies in the fact that instead of an oppressive command we give the child an opportunity to exercise his own initiative, and his own intelligence. When he hears you say, "The dog," he has to think, "What about the dog? . . . Oh, yeah, I didn't walk him yet this afternoon . . . Guess I'd better take him out now."

*Caution.* Don't use your child's name as your one-word statement. When a child hears a disapproving, "Susie," many times during the day, she begins to associate her name with disapproval.

**IV. Describe What You Feel.** Most parents are relieved to discover that it can be helpful to share their real feelings with their children, and that it's not necessary to be eternally patient. Children are not fragile. They're perfectly capable of dealing with statements like:

"This isn't a good time for me to look at your composition. I'm tense and distracted. After dinner I'll be able to give it the attention it deserves."

"It's a good idea to steer clear of me for the next little while. I'm feeling irritable and it has nothing to do with you."

One single mother who was raising two young children said that she used to be upset with herself because she often had no patience with them. Finally, she decided to try to be more accepting of her feelings, and let her children know about them—in terms they could understand.

She started saying things like "I have as much patience as a watermelon now." And a little later on, "Well, right now I have as much patience as a grapefruit." And still later she would announce, "It's about the size of a pea now. I think we ought to quit before it shrivels."

She knew the children took her seriously, because one evening her son said, "Mom, what size is your patience now? Could you read us a story tonight?"

Still others expressed concern about describing their feelings. If they shared their honest emotions, wouldn't that make them vulnerable? Suppose they said to the child, "That upsets me," and the child answered, "So, who cares?"

It's been our experience that children whose feelings are respected are likely to be respectful of adult feelings. But there could well be a transition period in which you might get a fresh "So, who cares?" If it comes to that, you can let the child know, "I do. I care about how *I* feel. And I care about how *you* feel. And I expect this to be a family where we are all caring about each other's feelings!"

*Caution.* Some children are very sensitive to their parents' disapproval. For them, strong statements like "I am angry" or "That makes me furious" are more than they can bear. In retaliation they'll belligerently answer, "Well, then, I'm angry at you, too!" For those children it's best just to state your expectations. For example, instead of "I'm angry at you for pulling the cat's tail," it would be more helpful to say, "I expect you to be kind to animals."

**V. Write a Note.** Most children love receiving notes—both those who can read and those who can't. Little ones are usually thrilled to receive a printed message from their parents. It encourages them to write or draw notes back to their parents.

Older children also like receiving notes. A group of teenagers we worked with told us that a note can make you feel good—"as if you were getting a letter from a friend." They were touched that their parents cared enough to take the time and trouble to write to them. One young man said that what he appreciated most about notes was that "they didn't get any louder."

Parents report that they too like using notes. They say it's a quick, easy way to get through to a child, and one that usually leaves a pleasant aftertaste.

One mother told us that she keeps a pad and an old coffee mug filled with a dozen pencils on her kitchen counter. Several times a week she finds herself in a situation where either the children have heard her make the same request so often they've tuned her out or she's about to give up on them and do the chore herself.

At those moments, she says it takes less out of her to pick up a pencil than to open her mouth.

Here's a sample of some of her notes:

DEAR BILLY,
   I HAVEN'T BEEN OUT SINCE THIS MORNING.
GIVE ME A BREAK.
      YOUR DOG,
      HARRY

DEAR SUSAN,
   THIS KITCHEN NEEDS TO BE PUT BACK
IN ORDER.

PLEASE DO SOMETHING ABOUT:
  1. BOOKS ON STOVE
  2. BOOTS IN DOORWAY
  3. JACKET ON FLOOR
  4. COOKIE CRUMBS ON TABLE
THANKS IN ADVANCE.
     MOM

NOTICE:
  STORY TIME TONIGHT AT 7:30 P.M.
  ALL CHILDREN WHO ARE IN PAJAMAS
  WITH TEETH BRUSHED ARE INVITED.
     LOVE,
     MOM AND DAD

A light touch with notes isn't necessary, but it can certainly help. Sometimes, however, the situation is not funny and humor would be inappropriate. We're thinking of the father who told us that his daughter ruined his brand-new CD by leaving it on the floor, where it got stepped on. He said that if he hadn't been able to vent his anger in writing he would have punished her. Instead, he wrote:

Alison,
  I'M BOILING!!!
  My new CD was taken without my
permission and now it's full of scratches
and doesn't play anymore.
     MAD DAD

A little later the father received this note back from his daughter:

Dear Dad,
  I'm *really sorry*. I'll buy you
another one this Saturday and whatever
it costs you can take it out of my
allowance.
     Alison

We never cease to marvel at how children who cannot read manage to "read" the notes their parents write to them. Here's the testimony of a young working mother:

> The worst time for me when I get home from work is that twenty minutes of trying to prepare dinner while the kids are running back and forth between the refrigerator and the breadbox. By the time the food is on the table, they have no appetite left.
>
> Last Monday night I put a crayoned note up on the door:

KITCHEN CLOSED
UNTIL DINNER

> My four-year-old immediately wanted to know what it said. I explained each word. He was so respectful of that note, he wouldn't even put his foot in the kitchen. He just played with his sister outside the door until I took the note down and called them in.
>
> The next night I put the note back up again. While I was making the hamburgers, I heard my son teaching his two-year-old sister what each word meant. Then I saw her point to each word and "read": "Kitchen . . . Closed . . . Until . . . Dinner."

The most unusual use of a note was told to us by a mother who was a part-time student. Here's her story:

> In a weak moment I volunteered to have a meeting at my home for twenty people. I was so nervous about having everything ready on time that I left school early.
>
> When I got home, I took one look around the house and my heart sank. The place was a mess—piles of newspapers, mail, books, magazines, dirty bathroom, beds unmade. I had a little over two hours to get everything into shape and I was starting to feel hysterical. The kids were coming home any minute, and I knew that I didn't have it in me to cope with a single demand or any of their fighting.

But I didn't want to have to talk or explain. I decided to write a note, but there wasn't an uncluttered surface in the house to put anything down on. So I grabbed a piece of cardboard, punched two holes in it, stuck in a string, and hung a sign around my neck:

*HUMAN TIME BOMB*
IF IRKED OR IRRITATED
WILL EXPLODE!!!!
COMPANY COMING
HELP URGENTLY NEEDED!

Then I went to work like a fury. When the kids came home, they read my sign and *volunteered* to clear their books and toys. Then, without another word from me, they made their beds—*and mine!* Unbelievable.

I was about to tackle the bathroom when the bell rang. I panicked for a moment, but it was only the man delivering the extra chairs. I motioned for him to come in and wondered why he didn't move. He just kept staring at my chest.

I looked down and saw the sign still there. As I started to explain, he said, "Don't worry, lady. Calm down. Just tell me where you want the chairs and I'll set them up for you."

People have asked us, "If I use these skills appropriately, will my children always respond?" Our answer is: We would hope not. Children aren't robots. Besides, our purpose is *not* to set forth a series of techniques to manipulate behavior so that children always respond.

Our purpose is to speak to what is best in our children— their intelligence, their initiative, their sense of responsibility, their sense of humor, their ability to be sensitive to the needs of others.

We want to put an end to talk that wounds the spirit and search out the language that nourishes self-esteem.

We want to create an emotional climate that encourages children to cooperate because they care about themselves, and because they care about us.

We want to demonstrate the kind of respectful communication that we hope our children will use with us—now, during their adolescent years, and, ultimately, as our adult friends.

# 3 | Alternatives to Punishment

As you began to use some of the skills for engaging cooperation, did you find that it took thought and self-control not to say some of the things you usually say? For many of us sarcasm, lectures, warnings, name-calling, and threats were all woven into the language we heard as we were growing up. It isn't easy to give up the familiar.

Parents have often told us how upset they were because, even after attending a session, they'd still find themselves saying things to their children they didn't like. The only difference was that now they heard themselves. Actually hearing yourself represents progress. It's the first step toward making changes.

I know for myself the process of change didn't come easily. I'd hear myself using the old, unhelpful ways—"What's wrong with you kids? You never remember to turn off the light in the bathroom." Then I'd get annoyed with myself. I'd resolve never to say that again. Then I'd say it again. Remorse. "I'll never learn this stuff . . . How else could I have said that? . . . I know . . . I should have said, 'Children, the light's on in the bathroom.' Or, better still, 'Kids, the light!'" Then I'd worry that I'd never have the chance to say it.

I had nothing to worry about. They always left the light on in the bathroom. But the next time I was ready for them: "Kids, the light." Someone ran and turned it off. Success!

Then there were the times when I'd say all the "right things" and nothing seemed to work. The kids would either ignore me or—even worse—defy me. When that happened, there was only one thing I wanted to do—PUNISH THEM!

In order to understand more deeply what happens between people when one person punishes another, please read the next two scenes and answer the questions that follow them.

*Scene One:*

MOTHER: Stop running up and down the aisles . . . I want you to stay close to me while we shop . . . Why are you touching everything? Put those bananas back . . . No, we are not buying them; we have plenty at home . . . Stop squeezing the tomatoes! I'm warning you, if you don't listen to me you are going to be sorry . . . Get your hand out of there, will you? *I'll* pick out the ice cream . . . You're running again. Do you want to fall?

Okay, that does it!! Do you know you nearly knocked over that old lady? You are going to be punished. You are not going to have a single spoonful of this ice cream I bought for tonight. Maybe that'll teach you not to behave like a wild animal!

*Scene Two:*

FATHER: Billy, were you using my saw?

BILLY: No.

FATHER: Are you sure?

BILLY: I swear, I never touched it!

FATHER: Well, then, how come I found it lying outside, full of rust, next to that go-cart you and your friend are making?

| BILLY: | Oh, yeah! We were using it last week and then it started to rain so we went inside, and I guess I forgot. |
|---|---|
| FATHER: | So you lied! |
| BILLY: | I didn't lie. I really forgot. |
| FATHER: | Yeah, the way you forgot my hammer last week and my screwdriver the week before! |
| BILLY: | Gee, Dad, I didn't mean to. Sometimes I just forget. |
| FATHER: | Well, maybe this will help you remember. Not only are you never going to get a chance to use my tools again, but for lying to me on top of it, you'll stay home when we all go to the movies tomorrow! |

**Questions.** 1. What motivated the parents in each scene to punish their children?

Scene I

_____

_____

Scene II

_____

_____

2. What do you think might be the feelings of the children who were punished?

Scene I

_____

_____

Scene II

_____

_____

To punish or not to punish?

Whenever that question comes up in a group, I usually ask, "Why? Why do we punish?" Here are some of the answers parents have given:

"If you don't punish them, kids will try to get away with murder."

"Sometimes I get so frustrated, I don't know what else to do."

"How will my child learn that what he did was wrong and not to do it again if I don't punish him?"

"I punish my son because it's the only thing he understands."

When I asked parents to remember their own feelings when they were punished, I got the following responses:

"I used to hate my mother. I'd think, 'She's such a bitch,' and then I'd feel so guilty."

"I used to think, 'My father's right. I am bad. I deserve to be punished.'"

"I used to fantasize that I'd get very sick and then they'd be sorry for what they did to me."

"I remember thinking, 'They're so mean. I'll fix them. I'll do it again, only next time I won't get caught.'"

The more these parents talked, the more aware they became that punishment could lead to feelings of hatred, revenge, defiance, guilt, unworthiness, and self-pity. Nevertheless, they still worried:

"If I give up punishment, won't I be putting my children in the driver's seat?"

"I'm afraid of losing my final method of control and leaving myself powerless."

I understood their concerns. I remember asking Dr. Ginott, "At what point is it all right to punish a child who ignores or defies you? Shouldn't there be consequences for a child who misbehaves?"

He answered that a child *should* experience the consequences of his misbehavior, but not punishment. He felt that in a caring relationship there was no room for punishment.

I pressed him further: "But suppose a child continues to disobey you. Isn't it all right to punish him then?"

Dr. Ginott said that the problem with punishment was that it didn't work, that it was a distraction, that instead of the child feeling sorry for what he has done and thinking about how he can make amends, he becomes preoccupied with revenge fantasies. In other words, by punishing a child we actually deprive him of the very important inner process of facing his own misbehavior.

This way of thinking—that punishment doesn't work because it's a distraction—was very new to me. But it left me with another question: What could I do instead?

Take some time now to think about how else the parents could have handled the two situations you read about. See what ideas you come up with.

1. What are some possibilities—other than punishment—for handling the child in the supermarket?

_____

_____

_____

_____

_____

2. What are some possibilities—other than punishment—for handling the child who took his father's tools and didn't return them?

_____

_____

_____

_____

_____

## Alternatives to Punishment

I'm always impressed by the ingenuity of parents. Give them a little quiet and some time in which to think, and they usually come up with a variety of ways to handle problems other than by punishment. For example, look at the suggestions that came from just one group:

Mother and child could have a rehearsal at home in a "pretend" store with props. As they playact together, Mother can review the finer points of supermarket decorum.

They could write a simple book together, with drawings, called *Johnny Goes to the Supermarket*. The book could include Johnny's responsibilities as an active member of the shopping team—the one who helps to push the cart, load, unload, and sort.

Or Johnny, with Mother's help, could work out a shopping list—in words or pictures—of groceries that he would be in charge of finding and putting in the basket.

Father and son could work out a library card system whereby each tool is checked out and must be returned before the next is borrowed.

Father might buy his son a starter set of tools for his next birthday. Or the son could start saving for his own set.

Notice, all of these suggestions stress prevention. Wouldn't it be wonderful if we could always forestall problems by planning ahead? For those times when we have neither the foresight nor the energy, here are some alternatives to punishment that can be used on the spot.

### Alternatives to Punishment

1. Point out a way to be helpful.
2. Express strong disapproval (without attacking character).
3. State your expectations.
4. Show the child how to make amends.
5. Offer a choice.
6. Take action.
7. Allow the child to experience the consequences of his misbehavior.

# ALTERNATIVES TO PUNISHMENT

*Instead of*

Point out a way to be helpful.

*Instead of*

Express strong disapproval
(*without attacking the
child's character*).

# ALTERNATIVES TO PUNISHMENT

*Instead of*

Offer a choice.

*Instead of*

Take action (*remove or restrain*).

But suppose he behaves so badly that Mother is forced
to leave the store. What then? On the following day,
without lecturing or moralizing, she can let him experience
the consequences of his misbehavior.

# LET HIM EXPERIENCE THE CONSEQUENCES.

# ALTERNATIVES TO PUNISHMENT

*Express your feeling strongly.*

*State your expectations.*

*Show the child how to make amends.*

For many children any of these approaches would be enough
to encourage them to act more responsibly.

## ALTERNATIVES TO PUNISHMENT
But suppose the child continues borrowing and forgetting?

*Offer a choice.*

And if he still continues . . . ?

*Take action.*

## Alternatives to Punishment

Now let's look at another way that parents can handle a persistent disciplinary problem. At the end of one workshop a mother described the difficulties she was having getting her son, Bobby, to come home on time. She told us about his constant excuses, his broken promises, and his broken watches. From the groans of recognition when she spoke, it was clear that her problem was not uncommon.

Before our next session I prepared an exercise for the group. I took the original situation and restated it from what I thought might be Bobby's point of view. Then I wrote three possible ways that parents might handle Bobby's chronic lateness.

Please try this same exercise for yourself now. After reading Bobby's story and each parent's reaction to it, write down how you think Bobby might feel.

*Bobby's story:* I like to play after school with my friends in the school playground. I know I'm supposed to be home by 5:45, but sometimes I forget. Yesterday and the day before, I came home late. My mother was so mad at me that today I made sure to ask my friend the time. I didn't want my mother to scream at me like that again. My friend told me that it was 6:15. I stopped playing right away and ran all the way home. I explained to my mother that I *did* remember to ask the time, but it was already too late, and I ran home as fast as I could.

*First Parent's Response:*

"I've had enough of your excuses! I see now you can't be trusted. Well, this time you're going to be punished. Every day next week you'll come home after school and *stay* home. And don't think you'll sit around watching TV either, because even if I'm not home I'm telling the sitter that there'll be no television for you. You can go straight to your room now, because dinner is over."

What might Bobby say to himself?

_____

_____

_____

_____

*Second Parent's Response:*
"Oh dear, you're all overheated from running. Let me get a washrag and wipe your face. Promise me you won't ever be late again.

"You're making a nervous wreck of me. Now go in and wash your hands, and please hurry, because your dinner is getting cold. . . . Oh, maybe Mommy will warm it up for you."

What might Bobby say to himself?

_____

_____

_____

_____

*Third Parent's Response:*
"You're telling me you made an effort and I'm glad to hear it. But I'm still upset. I don't want to have to go through that kind of worry again. I expect that when you say you'll be home at 5:45, I'll be able to count on it.

"We've eaten already. There's no more chicken left, but if you like you can make yourself a sandwich."

What might Bobby say to himself?

_____

_____

_____

_____

Obviously there is no way of determining what the real Bobby would say to himself, but you might be interested in hearing the thoughts of the parents in the group who did this exercise. They felt that the first parent was too punitive. (The child would think, "She's mean. I'll get back at her.") The second parent was a doormat. (The child would think, "I can get away with anything with her.") The third parent was "just right." She was assertive without being punitive. (Her child might think to himself, "Mom was really mad. I'd better get home on time from now on. Besides, she has confidence in me. I can't let her down. . . . And I didn't like having to make myself an old sandwich.")

With this exercise in mind, the real mother went home and tried this last approach. And it worked—for three weeks. Then Bobby went back to his old habit. The mother was at her wits' end. As she described her frustration, many questions arose in the group: "What can be done in a case like this?" . . . "Suppose you really have tried everything, and the problem goes on and on?" . . . "What can we do when there seems to be nothing left to do but punish?"

When a problem persists, we can usually assume that it is more complex than it originally appeared. For a complex problem, a more complex skill is needed. Parent educators, labor negotiators, marriage counselors have worked out some excellent detailed methods for resolving difficult conflicts. Here's the version that I presented to the group.

*To Problem-Solve*

Step I.  Talk about the child's feelings and needs.

Step II.  Talk about your feelings and needs.

Step III.  Brainstorm together to find a mutually agreeable solution.

Step IV.  Write down all ideas—without evaluating.

Step V.  Decide which suggestions you like, which you don't like, and which you plan to follow through on.

# PROBLEM-SOLVING

## Step I.
Talk about the child's feelings and needs.

## Step II.
Talk about your feelings and needs.

# PROBLEM-SOLVING

### Step III.
Brainstorm to find a mutually agreeable solution.

### Step IV.
Write down all ideas without evaluating.

# PROBLEM-SOLVING

## STEP V.

Decide which suggestions you like,
which you don't like,
and which you plan to follow through on.

# Alternatives to Punishment

After outlining to the group the steps of the problem-solving approach, we decided that it would be helpful if we role-played the situation. I played the mother and the real mother played her son, Bobby. Here's the script of the dialogue we had together, taken from the tape recorder that was on that evening. As you can see, the mother threw herself into her son's role wholeheartedly:

MOTHER: Bobby, there's something I'd like to talk about. Is this a good time for you?

BOBBY: (*suspiciously*) It's okay. What is it?

MOTHER: It's about the business of getting home on time for dinner.

BOBBY: I told you, I've been trying; but I always have to leave when we're right in the middle of a game!

MOTHER: Oh?

BOBBY: Nobody else has to go as early as me. Nobody!

MOTHER: Hmm.

BOBBY: And I have to keep asking everybody the time, cuz my stupid watch is broken, and they always tell me to "Shut up, pest!"

MOTHER: Oooh, that can hurt.

BOBBY: Yeah! Then Kenny calls me a baby.

MOTHER: That, too! . . . So what I hear you saying is that you're under a lot of pressure from the other kids to stay.

BOBBY: That's right!

MOTHER: Bobby, do you know how it is from my point of view?

BOBBY: Yeah, you want me home on time.

MOTHER: That's part of it, but mainly I worry when you're late.

BOBBY: Then don't worry!

MOTHER: I wish I didn't. . . . Look, let's put our heads together and take a fresh look at this problem and

|  |  |
|---|---|
| | see whether we could come up with some ideas that would be good for both of us. (*Mother takes out pencil.*) You start. |
| BOBBY: | I'll come home late, but you won't worry. |
| MOTHER: | All right, I'll write that down. What else? |
| BOBBY: | I dunno. |
| MOTHER: | Hey, I have a thought. I could come to the playground and pick you up. |
| BOBBY: | No . . . that's no good. |
| MOTHER: | We're writing down all our ideas. Later we'll decide which we like and which we don't like. What else? |
| BOBBY: | (*long pause*) I guess I could get my watch fixed. |
| MOTHER: | (*writes "Get watch fixed"*) Anything else? |
| BOBBY: | Why do we always have to eat together? Can't you just leave my dinner for me? |
| MOTHER: | (*writes "Leave dinner"*) The days are getting longer now. I suppose we could have dinner fifteen minutes later. |
| BOBBY: | Only fifteen minutes! |
| MOTHER: | You'd like it to be more. Hmm. (*writes "Eat 15 minutes later"*) Any other ideas or should we look at our list now and see what we want to cross out and what we want to keep? |
| BOBBY: | Let's look. |
| MOTHER: | (*reads*) *Possible Solutions* |
| | Bobby comes home late. Mother doesn't worry. |
| | Pick up Bobby at playground. |
| | Get watch fixed. |
| | Leave dinner in oven. |
| | Eat fifteen minutes later. |
| BOBBY: | Cross out where you pick me up every day. Kenny would really tease me if you did that. |
| MOTHER: | Okay . . . Well, I have to cross out. "Come home late," because the fact is I do worry. But let's look |

at this next one. I suppose I could move dinner to six fifteen. Would fifteen extra minutes help?

BOBBY: No . . . Well, maybe a little.

MOTHER: And I suppose I could leave dinner in the oven for you occasionally, if I knew ahead of time.

BOBBY: Yeah, and leave in "Get watch fixed."

MOTHER: Well, the problem with that is that this is the second time the watch has been broken, and I think I'd resent having to pay for the repairs again.

BOBBY: I have money saved. Almost four dollars. Would that be enough to get it fixed?

MOTHER: Not really . . . but it would certainly help. I suppose Dad and I might pay the rest.

BOBBY: I'll be careful, I swear. I'll take it off if me and Kenny do arm wrestling. . . . And I'll look at it while I'm playing so I know when to leave.

MOTHER: You will? . . . Hmm. (*looks at list*) Well, let's see what we've decided so far. I'll move dinner up to six fifteen. That'll give you fifteen extra minutes to play. We'll put our money together and get your watch repaired. And occasionally, if you let me know in advance, I can keep your dinner warm for you. How does all that hit you?

BOBBY: Good!

At our next session everyone immediately asked Bobby's mother, "Did you try problem-solving? . . . What happened?"

She smiled and told us that she had tried it that same night, and that Bobby was intrigued with the idea. "It was almost funny," she said. "What our whole discussion boiled down to was that he hated wearing a watch, but that if the family could eat fifteen minutes later he'd listen for the six o'clock whistle from the firehouse and that would be his signal to start for home.

"And so far," she said, "he's kept his word!"

Doesn't sound too hard, does it? But it is. And the hardest part is not the learning of the separate steps. With a little study, that can be accomplished. The hardest part is the shift we have to make in attitude. We have to stop thinking of the child as a "problem" that needs correction. We have to give up the idea that because we're adults we always have the right answer. We have to stop worrying that if we're not "tough enough" the child will take advantage of us.

It requires a great act of faith to believe that if we take the time to sit down and share our real feelings with a young person, and listen to his feelings, together we'll come up with solutions that will be right for both of us.

There is an important message built into this approach. It says, "When there is conflict between us, we no longer have to mobilize our forces against each other and worry about who will emerge victorious and who will go down in defeat. Instead, we can put our energy into searching for the kinds of solutions that respect both our needs as individuals." We are teaching our children that they needn't be our victims or our enemies. We are giving them the tools that will enable them to be active participants in solving the problems that confront them—now, while they're at home, and in the difficult, complex world that awaits them.

## ASSIGNMENT

I.  This coming week, use an alternative to punishment. What alternative did you use? What was your child's reaction?

_____

_____

_____

_____

_____

_____

II.  Think of a problem that comes up regularly in your home that might be eased by the problem-solving approach. Find a time that is good for both of you, a place where you won't be interrupted, and problem-solve with your child.

III. Read Part II of Alternatives to Punishment—Comments, Questions, and Parents' Stories.

*A Quick Reminder . . .*

---

## Instead of Punishment

1. EXPRESS YOUR FEELINGS STRONGLY—WITHOUT ATTACKING CHARACTER.

   "I'm furious that my new saw was left outside to rust in the rain!"

2. STATE YOUR EXPECTATIONS.

   "I expect my tools to be returned after they've been borrowed."

3. SHOW THE CHILD HOW TO MAKE AMENDS.

   "What this saw needs now is a little steel wool and a lot of elbow grease."

4. OFFER A CHOICE.

   "You can borrow my tools and return them or you can give up the privilege of using them. You decide."

5. TAKE ACTION.

   Child: "Why is the toolbox locked?"
   Father: "You tell me why."

6. PROBLEM-SOLVE.

   "What can we work out so that you can use my tools when you need them, and so that I'll be sure they're there when I need them?"

---

## PART II: COMMENTS, QUESTIONS, AND PARENTS' STORIES

### *Questions About Punishment*

## 1. If a small child who doesn't talk yet touches something he shouldn't, isn't it all right to slap his little hand?

Just because children aren't talking doesn't mean they aren't listening or understanding. Little children are learning every minute of every day. The question is, *what* are they learning? The parent has a choice here. She can repeatedly slap the child's hand, thus teaching him that the only way for him to learn what not to do is to be slapped. Or she can treat the child as a dignified, small human being by giving him information he can use now and for the rest of his life. As she removes the child (or the object), she can tell him firmly and clearly:

"Knives are not for licking. You can lick this spoon if you like."

"This china dog can break. Your stuffed dog won't break."

She may need to repeat the same information many times, but repeated information conveys a far different message from repeated slaps.

## 2. What is the difference between punishment and natural consequences? Aren't they just different words for the same thing?

We see punishment as the parent deliberately depriving a child for a set period of time or inflicting pain on him, in order to teach that child a lesson. Consequences, on the other hand, come about as a natural result of the child's behavior. A father in one of our groups once shared an experience that to us sums up the difference between punishment and consequences. Here it is in his words:

My teenage son asked to borrow my navy blue sweater, because he said it would look "neat" with his new jeans. I told him, "Okay, but be careful," and forgot about it after that. A week later when I wanted to wear it, I found it under a pile of dirty laundry on the floor of his room. The back was covered with chalk and the front was spattered with something that looked like spaghetti sauce.

I was so mad, because this wasn't the first time, that I swear if he had come in at that moment I would have told him that he could forget about going to the ball game with me on Sunday. I'd give his ticket to someone else.

Anyway, when I saw him later I had calmed down a little, but I still bawled him out. He told me he was sorry and all that, but darned if he didn't ask me for it again a week later. I said, "Nothing doing." No lectures. No speeches. He knew why.

Then, a month after that, he asked for my plaid shirt for a school field trip. I told him, "Look, before I lend anything again, I need some reassurance—in writing—that my shirt will be returned in the same condition in which it was borrowed." That night I found a note on my pile of mail. It said:

Dear Dad,
    If you let me borrow your shirt, I'll do everything I can to keep it clean.
    I won't lean against the blackboard. I won't put my ball point pen in the pocket. And when I eat lunch I'll cover myself with paper napkins.

Love,
Mark

Well, I was very impressed with the note. I figured that if he took the trouble to write it he'd probably take the trouble to do what he said.

P.S. The shirt was returned to me the next night on a hanger, and it was clean!

To us, that story showed natural consequences in action. One natural consequence of returning borrowed property in damaged condition is the owner's displeasure. Another natural consequence is the owner's reluctance to lend you anything again. It's also possible that the owner might change his mind if he gets some concrete evidence that it won't happen again. But the responsibility to change is clearly the borrower's. The owner doesn't have to do anything to you to teach you a lesson. It's a lot easier to learn from the hard realities of people's real reactions than from a person who decides to punish you "for your own good."

3. **Last week I found a pile of orange peels and pits on the sofa. When I asked my boys, "Who did it?" each one pointed to the other. If it isn't a good idea to find out which child is guilty and then punish him, what can I do?**

The question "Who did it?" usually leads to an automatic, "Not me," which in turn leads to "Well, one of you must be lying." The more we try to get at the truth, the more loudly the children protest their innocence. When we see something that angers us, it's more helpful to express that anger than to locate the culprit and punish him:

"I get furious when I see food on our sofa! Orange peels can stain it permanently."

At this point you may hear a chorus of "But I didn't do it." . . . "He made me" . . . "The dog did it" . . . "It was the baby."

This is your opportunity to let everyone know:

*"I'm not interested in knowing who did it. I'm not interested in blaming anyone for what happened in the past. I am interested in seeing improvement in the future!"*

By not blaming or punishing, we free the children to focus on taking responsibility, rather than on taking revenge.

"Now I'd like both of you to help clear the sofa of all peels and pits."

**4. You say that one alternative to punishment is to express your disapproval. When I do that my child looks so guilty and is so miserable for the rest of the day that I get upset. Is it possible that I'm overdoing it?**

We can understand your concern. Dr. Selma Fraiberg in her book *The Magic Years* says, "A child needs to feel our disapproval at certain times, but if our reaction is of such strength that the child feels worthless and despised for his offense, we have abused our power as parents and have created the possibility that exaggerated guilt feelings and self-hatred will play a part in this child's personality development."

That's why we feel that whenever possible, along with our disapproval, we should point the way toward helping a child to make amends. After his initial remorse, the child needs a chance to restore his own good feeling about himself and to see himself as a respected, responsible family member once again. As parents, we can give him that chance. Here are some examples:

"I'm furious! The baby was playing happily until you took her rattle away. I expect you to find some way to end her crying now!"

(Instead of "You made the baby cry again. Now you're going to get a smack.")

"It really upsets me to come home to a sink full of dirty dishes when you gave your word they would be done. I'd like them washed and put away before bedtime!"

(Instead of "You can forget about going out tomorrow night. Maybe that will teach you to keep your word.")

"A whole box of soap powder emptied on the bathroom floor! It makes me so angry to see such a mess. Soap powder is not for playing with! We need a bag, a broom, and a dustpan. Quick, before it gets tracked all over the house."

(Instead of "Look at the work you made for me. No TV for you tonight!")

Statements like these say to the child, "I don't like what you did, and I expect you to take care of it." We hope that later on in life, as an adult, when he does something he regrets, he'll think to himself, "What can I do to make amends—to set things right again?," rather than "What I just did proves I'm an unworthy person who deserves to be punished."

**5. I don't punish my son anymore, but now when I scold him for doing something wrong he says, "I'm sorry." Then the next day he does the same thing again. What can I do about it?**

Some children use "I'm sorry" as a way of placating an angry parent. They're quick to apologize and just as quick to repeat their misbehavior. It's important for these youngsters to realize that if they're genuinely sorry their feelings of remorse should be translated into action. The "repeat offender" can be told any of the following:

"Sorry means behaving differently."

"Sorry means making changes."

"I'm glad to hear you're sorry. That's the first step. The second step is to ask yourself what can be done about it."

### The Experts Speak Out on Punishment

Every once in a while an article appears singing the praises of punishment and telling us how to do it. ("Explain the punishment ahead of time" . . . "Punish as promptly as possible" . . . "Let the punishment fit the crime.") Often, to angry, beleaguered parents this kind of advice seems to make good sense. What follows are quotes from a variety of professionals in the mental-health field who have another point of view about punishment.

Punishment is a very ineffective method of discipline . . . for punishment, strangely enough, often has the effect of teaching the child to behave in exactly the opposite way from the way we want him to behave! Many parents use punishment simply because no one has ever taught them better ways of disciplining their children.

(*How to Father*, Dr. Fitzhugh Dodson, Signet, 1974)

The act of disciplining a child can be a frustrating one. However, at the outset it needs to be stressed that discipline means *education.* Discipline is essentially programmed guidance that helps people to develop internal self-control, self-direction, and efficiency. If it is to work, discipline requires mutual respect and trust. On the other hand, punishment requires external control over a person by force and coercion. Punishing agents seldom respect or trust the one punished.

("The Case Against Spanking," Brian G. Gilmartin, Ph.D., in *Human Behavior*, February 1979, vol. 8, no. 2)

From a review of the literature it is concluded that physical punishment by parents does not inhibit violence and most likely encourages it. Punishment both frustrates the child and gives him a model to imitate and learn from.

(*Violence and the Struggle for Existence*, Work of the Committee on Violence of the Department of Psychiatry, Stanford University School of Medicine, Edited by David N. Daniels, M.D., Marshall F. Gilula, M.D., and Frank M. Ochberg, M.D., Little, Brown & Company, 1970)

Confused and bewildered parents mistakenly hope that punishment will *eventually* bring results, without realizing that they are actually getting nowhere with their methods.

The use of punishment only helps the child to develop a greater power of resistance and defiance.

(*Children: The Challenge*, Rudolf Dreikurs, M.D., Hawthorn, 1964)

There are a number of other possibilities in learning which spanking provides, none of which are intended by parents. The child may learn how to avoid successfully any guilt feelings for bad behavior by setting up a cycle in which the punishment cancels the "crime" and the child, having paid for his mischief, is free to repeat the act another time without attendant guilt feelings.

The child who does everything possible to provoke a spanking is a child who is carrying a secret debt on the "sin" side of the ledger which the parent is invited to wipe out by means of a spanking. A spanking is just what the child does *not* need!

(*The Magic Years,* Selma H. Fraiberg, Scribners, 1959)

Researchers believe that one in five parents have suffered . . . abuse at the hands of their children, an expression perhaps of the adolescent turmoil that can bubble over: objects lobbed at their heads, shoving, pushing, furious verbal abuse . . . there is "stark evidence" that physical abuse of the parent is actually learned at the knee of the parent.

(*Newsday,* August 15, 1978)

### *Instead of Punishing*

#### (*Experiences Shared by Parents in Our Groups*)

My four-year-old daughter, Marnie, has always been a very difficult child. She gets me into such rages that I can't control myself. Last week I came home and found that she had scribbled on the wallpaper in her room with crayon. I was so furious, I gave her a good spanking. Then I told her I was taking her crayons away, which I did.

The next morning I woke up and thought I'd die. She had taken my lipstick and scrawled all over the bathroom tile. I wanted to strangle her, but stopped myself. Very calmly I asked, "Marnie, did you do this because you were mad at me for taking away your crayons?"

She nodded her head.

I said, "Marnie, I get very, very upset when the walls are written on. It's a lot of work for me to have to wash them off and get them clean again."

Do you know what she did? She took a washrag and started to try to wipe the lipstick off. I showed her how to use soap and water and she worked on the tile for about ten minutes. Then she called me in to show me that most of the lipstick was off. I thanked her and then I gave her back her crayons and some paper to put in her room for whenever she wanted to draw.

I was so proud of myself, I called my husband at work to tell him what I did.

It's been over a month now, and Marnie hasn't written on the walls since.

No sooner had I walked in through the door after last week's session than I received a phone call from Donny's math teacher. She sounded very angry. She told me that my son was falling behind in his work, that he was a disruptive influence in class, that he still didn't know his times table, and that maybe what he needed was more "discipline" at home. I thanked her for calling, but inside I was shaking. My first thought was "He should be punished. He'll watch no television at all until he learns those multiplication tables and starts to behave himself in class."

Luckily, I had an hour to cool off before he came home from school. When Donny came home, we had the following conversation:

ME: Mrs. K. called today and sounded very upset.

DONNY: Oh, she's always upset about something.

ME: I consider it a very serious matter when I get a call from the school. She said you were disruptive in class and you didn't know your times table.

## Alternatives to Punishment

DONNY: Well, Mitchell keeps hitting me on the head with his notebook. So I hit him back with mine.

ME: You feel you have to retaliate?

DONNY: What's retaliate?

ME: Get back at him.

DONNY: That's right. And sometimes he writes me a note and cracks me up. And then he kicks my chair until I answer him.

ME: No wonder no work gets done.

DONNY: I know my table up to six. I just don't know my sevens and eights.

ME: Hmm . . . Donny, do you think it would help your concentration in class if you and Mitchell didn't sit near each other?

DONNY: I dunno . . . Maybe . . . I could get the sevens and eights if I studied.

ME: I feel Mrs. K. should know that. Suppose we write her a letter. Okay with you? (*Donny nodded.*) I took out my pencil and wrote:
"Dear Mrs. K.,
  I discussed our phone conversation with Donny and he says—" Donny, what shall I tell her?

DONNY: Tell her to change my seat away from Mitchell.

ME: (*writing*) "He says he would like his seat to be changed so he doesn't sit so close to Mitchell." Is that right?

DONNY: Yeah.

ME: Anything else?

DONNY: (*long pause*) Tell her I'll write out my seven and eight times table and say it out loud to myself.

ME: (*I write and read to him.*) "He also plans to write out his seven and eight times table and drill himself." Anything else?

DONNY: No.

ME: I'll close by saying, "Thank you for bringing this matter to our attention."

121

I read the entire letter to Donny again. We *both* signed it and he brought it to school the next day. I know something must have changed, because when he came home the first thing he told me was that Mrs. K. had changed his seat and was "nice to him today."

This story was reported by a mother who had sat grimly through our first few sessions shaking her head. On the fourth session she came in and claimed the floor to tell us the following:

I didn't believe anything here could be applied to my child. Van is so stubborn, so unmanageable, the only thing he understands is punishment. Last week I almost fainted when my neighbor told me she had seen him cross a busy intersection that he had been strictly forbidden to cross. I didn't know what to do. I had already taken away his bicycle, his television, his allowance . . . what was left? In desperation, I decided to try some of the things you've been talking about in the group. When we came home I said, "Van, we have a problem. Here is how I think you feel. You want to get to the other side of the street when you want to without having to ask someone to cross with you. Is that right?" He nodded his head. "Here's how I feel. I worry when I think about a six-year-old boy crossing a dangerous intersection where there have been so many accidents.

"When there is a problem, we need a solution. Think about it and tell me what your ideas are at supper."

Van immediately started to talk. I said, "Not now. It's a very serious problem. I'd like us both to give it a lot of thought. We'll talk at supper when Daddy is here."

That night I prepared my husband in advance to "just listen." Van washed his hands and was in his seat promptly. As soon as his father came into the room he said very excitedly, "I have a solution! Every night, when Daddy comes home, we'll go to the corner, and he'll teach me how to look at the lights and when to cross." Then he paused, and said, "And on my seventh birthday I'll cross by myself."

My husband almost fell out of his chair. I guess we've both been underestimating our son.

Nicky, ten, reported in an offhand way (while I was rushing to make dinner and go out) that three of his textbooks were missing and I had to send in nine dollars. I totally blew up. My first impulse was to hit him or punish him. But, even though I was over the edge with anger, I somehow managed to get hold of myself and start my sentences with the word "I." I think I was screaming as loud as is humanly possible:

"I am furious! I am enraged! Three books are lost and now *I* have to cough up nine dollars for it! I'm so angry I feel like I'm going to explode! And to hear this when I'm rushing to make dinner and go out, and now I have to stop and take the time to write down the homework problems over the phone!! *I AM BOILING!*"

When I stopped screaming, the most concerned little face appeared in the doorway and Nicky said, "Mom, I'm sorry. You don't have to cough up the nine dollars. I'll cough it up out of my allowance."

I think the biggest grin I've ever grinned appeared on my face. I have surely *never* stopped feeling angry so fast and so completely. What are a few lost books to a person who has a son who really *cares* about her feelings!

### PART III: MORE ABOUT PROBLEM-SOLVING

#### *Before Problem-Solving*

We've discovered that for the problem-solving process to work, we have to, as the kids would say, "psych ourselves." We tell ourselves:

"I'm going to be as accepting and tuned in to my child

as possible. I'm going to listen for information and feelings I might not have heard before."

"I'll steer clear of judgments, evaluations, and lectures. I won't try to persuade or convince."

"I'll consider any new ideas—no matter how far-out."

"I won't be pressured by time. If we can't come up with an immediate solution, it may mean we have to do more thinking, more investigating, more talking."

The key word is *respect*—for my child, for myself, and for the unlimited possibilities of what can happen when two people of good will put their heads together.

### *Cautions About Each Step of the Problem-Solving Process*

Before you begin, ask yourself, "Am I still seething with emotion, or am I calm enough now even to begin this whole process?" (You can't problem-solve when you're boiling.) Then check out your child's mood. "Is this a good time for *you* to talk?" If she says "yes," then:

1. *Talk about the child's feelings.* ("I imagine you must be feeling . . .")
Don't rush this part. Let your attitude be: "I'm really trying to get clear on how *you* feel about all this." Only when the child feels heard and understood will she be able to consider your feelings.

2. *Talk about your feelings.* ("Here's how I feel about it.")
Keep this part short and clear. It's hard for a child to listen to a parent who goes on and on about his worry, his anger, or his resentment.

3. *Invite the child to work on finding a mutually acceptable solution.*

If possible, let the child come up with the first few ideas. The crucial point here is to refrain from evaluating or commenting on any of those ideas. The instant you say, "Well, that's no good," the whole process ends and you've undone all your work. All ideas should be welcomed. Very often the most unlikely ones can lead to some fine, workable solutions. The key sentence is "We're writing down all our ideas." It's not essential to write, but somehow putting each idea in writing gives great dignity to each contribution. (One child was overheard saying, "My mother is so smart. She writes down all my ideas.")

4. *Decide which ideas you like, which you don't like, and which ideas you want to put into action.*

Watch out for "put-down" statements ("That's a dumb idea"). Instead, describe your personal reactions:

"I wouldn't be comfortable with that because . . ." or

"That sounds like something I could do."

5. *Follow through.*

The danger here is getting so carried away with your good feelings at having come up with a workable solution that you don't bother to make a specific plan to follow through. It's important to add:

"What steps do we have to take to get this plan into motion?"

"Who'll be responsible for what?"

"By when shall we have it done?"

6. *Don't permit the child to blame or accuse you at any point.*

CHILD:    Yeah, but that wouldn't work because you always . . . You never . . .

It's important that the parent be firm when this happens.

PARENT:    No accusations or talk about the past. What we're trying to do now is focus on a solution for the future!

## *Questions About Problem-Solving*

### 1. Suppose the plan you and your child agree upon works for a while and then falls through. What then?

These are the times that test our determination. We can either go back to lecturing and punishing or we can go back to the drawing board. For example:

PARENT: I'm disappointed that our approach isn't working anymore. I find myself doing your job, and that's unacceptable to me. Shall we give the old plan another chance? . . . Shall we talk about what's getting in the way? . . . Or shall we work out another solution?

As adults, we realize that few solutions are permanent. What would work for the child when he was four may not work for him now that he is five; what worked in the winter may not work in the spring. Life is a continual process of adjustment and readjustment. What's important for the child is that he continue to see himself as part of the solution rather than as part of the problem.

### 2. Do you always have to go through all the steps to resolve the problem?

No. A problem can be resolved at any step along the way. Sometimes a simple description of your conflicting needs can lead to a very quick solution. For example:

MOTHER: We have a real problem here. You want me to take you for sneakers now. I want to finish sorting all the laundry and then I have to start supper.

CHILD: Maybe I could finish the laundry while you get ready to go, and then when we come home I'll help you make supper.

MOTHER: I think that would work.

**3. Suppose we go through all the steps and still don't come up with a solution we can both agree on. What then?**

That can happen. But nothing has been lost. By discussing the problem, each of you has become more sensitive to the other's needs. In a difficult situation this is often the best that can be hoped for. And sometime it's just a matter of needing more time to think, to "let the beans cook," before a solution can be reached.

**4. Suppose a child refuses to sit down and problem-solve with you. What then?**

There are some children who are uncomfortable with this approach. For these youngsters, a note, based on the same principle, can be an effective substitute.

> Dear Johnny,
>     I'd like your ideas on solving the problem of . . . You probably (want, need, feel . . . )
>     I (want, need, feel . . . )
>     Please let me know of any solutions you can think of that we might both agree on.
>
> Love,<br>Dad

**5. Isn't this an approach that works best for older children?**

Parents of young children have reported great success with this approach. On the following pages you'll find stories in which parents used problem-solving skills with children of various ages.

## *Problem-Solving in Action*

*Situation:* The cradle I lent to a friend was just returned to me. I put it in the bedroom. Brian, age two, examines it and is fascinated by the swinging basket.

BRIAN:    Mommy, I go up in cradle.

MOMMY:    Sweetheart, you're much too big for that cradle.

BRIAN:    Yes, I go up in cradle. (*begins to climb into it*)

MOMMY:    (*restraining him*) Brian, Mommy said you're too big. The cradle might break if I put you in it.

BRIAN:    *Please,* Mommy! I go up in cradle—*NOW!* (*begins to whine*)

MOMMY:    I said, *NO!!* (Poor move on Mommy's part. I realized it as soon as I said it, and as Brian's whining turned into a minor tantrum. I decided to try problem-solving with him.)

MOMMY:    Sweetie, I can see how much you want to get into the cradle—right now. It probably looks like lots of fun to swing in. I'd like to swing in it, too. The problem is that it won't hold me, and it won't hold you. We're too big.

BRIAN:    Mommy too big—just like Briney. (Brian leaves the room and comes back with Goover, his stuffed bear, and puts him in the cradle. He begins to rock the basket back and forth.)

BRIAN:    See, Mommy? Briney rocking Goover, okay?

MOMMY:    (Whew!) Goover is just the right size.

• • •

After much frustration with the whole toilet-training process, I decided to try the problem-solving technique with my son, who was three at the time. We sat down together at the table and I said, "David, I've been thinking about how hard it is for a little boy to learn how to use the toilet. I'll bet sometimes you're so busy playing that you don't even notice that you have to 'go.'"

Alternatives to Punishment

He looked at me with his big eyes but didn't say anything. Then I said, "I'll bet that sometimes even when you do notice it's hard to get to the bathroom in time and climb onto that toilet."

He nodded his head, "Yes."

Then I asked him to bring me paper and crayon so that we could write down all the ideas that we could think of that might help. He ran into his room and brought me a yellow paper and a red crayon. I sat down with him and began to write.

I started by listing two ideas.

Buy a step stool like the one Jimmy has in his bathroom.

Mommy will ask David if he needs to "go."

Then David piped up, "Barbara and Peter will help me." (Peter is his friend, who is trained, and Barbara is his mother.)

Then he said, "Peter wears 'big-boy pants.'"

I wrote, "Get big-boy pants for David."

The next day I ran out and bought him a step stool and a pile of training pants. David was delighted with both and showed them to Peter and Barbara, who were reassuring.

We talked again about recognizing when he has to "go"— the pressure in his tummy—the need to get to the bathroom and get his pants off in time.

He knew that I was sympathetic to the difficulties involved.

Anyway, it's been about three months now and he's just about completely trained. And is he proud of himself!

• • •

I waited impatiently for our next session; I had something exciting to share with the group. I had been liberated! And so had my three-and-a-half-year-old daughter, Rachel. It started early Tuesday morning when the telephone rang.

"Susie, could you take Danielle for me this afternoon?"

"Sure," I said.

We hung up, and I realized I had shopping to do and now I would have to drag *two* children around with me. Or—Rachel had been attending a forty-five-minute morning outdoor preschool group. However, she would go only if I sat on the bench outside within view. Other mothers dropped their kids off and left. I stayed!

I said to Rachel, "I must go shopping today while you're in preschool. Danielle will be with us all afternoon, and I won't have time to shop."

Tears from Rachel. Here was my opportunity to use my problem-solving skills. I said to Rachel, "I see you're sad. How can we solve this problem? Let's write this all down."

Rachel's eyes lit up as I wrote:

*Problem:* Rachel doesn't want Mommy to leave and Mommy has to buy milk. She doesn't have time after preschool, so she has to do it during preschool.

*Suggestions to solve problem:*

    (Mine) 1. Go during school and run back.

    (Rachel's) 2. Not buy milk.

    (Rachel's) 3. Go after school.

    (Mine) 4. While Mommy is shopping, Rachel could sing, draw, and play.

    (Mine) 5. Rachel will stay at preschool while Mommy is shopping.

    (Rachel's) 6. Mommy only buys one thing and will run back fast.

    (Rachel's) 7. Tomorrow we will buy gum together.

    (Rachel's) 8. If Rachel wants to cry, she will cry.

We read the list, and I explained that if I didn't buy milk Rachel and Daddy would be disappointed. So we crossed that off our list. I reexplained that I wouldn't have time to go after school—so that was crossed off, too. Rachel seemed content.

We walked to preschool. Rachel hugged and kissed me goodbye. She reminded me to go to one store only, and then sat down in the circle with the other children.

I dashed to the store and was back in plenty of time to see

Rachel happily engrossed in a game with her friends. School let out. Rachel greeted me with "Did you go?"

"I sure did. You must be proud of yourself—staying here by yourself."

Rachel nodded.

*Wednesday morning.*

RACHEL: *(looking tense)* Is there preschool today?

ME: *(expecting, "Are you staying?")* Yes.

RACHEL: Oh, Mommy . . . Well, if I want to cry, I'll cry. And if I don't want to cry, I won't!

ME: Let's write that down.

I did. She added that she would sit next to a friend. Then she said, "Mommy, when you come back, come back fast. So fast that you fall down. Run!"

I brought her to preschool. She gave me a hug, a kiss, and a reminder to run and run.

I returned forty-five minutes later.

ME: You stayed by yourself!

RACHEL: Yeah, I'm proud of myself!

*Friday morning:*

RACHEL: Mom, is there preschool today?

ME: Yes.

RACHEL: Well, write this down: I'll sit next to a friend.

Problem resolved. Rachel goes to preschool. Mommy shops! Now that I look back on it, I realize that it took a great deal of effort to discipline myself to spend the necessary time to sit with Rachel and work through our problem. I'm glad I did. Rachel is, too!

• • •

My son, Michael Howard, is five and a half and in kindergarten. He reads third- to sixth-grade books. He has a large vocabulary and has decided he wants to be a plastic surgeon. He likes it when I read to him from medical books on different parts of the body. Michael comes into my bed quite often at night. I have tried everything to keep him out without making him feel unwanted. I tried staying up until 2:30 A.M. When I was fast asleep he would come into my bed with his pillow, slippers, and robe and crawl under the covers in the middle of my king-size bed. I would find him there in the morning curled up next to me. He even suggested that I sleep in his bed and he would sleep in mine. After coming home from a workshop, I decided to try another way.

I asked Michael Howard what could be done so that he would not come into my bed at night. He said, "Let me think." He went into his room. About ten minutes later he was back with a yellow pad and a pen. He said, "Dad, take a memo." Then he told me what to write.

> DEAR MICHAEL,
> PLEASE DO NOT COME IN TONIGHT.
> LOVE,
> DAD

He left the room and returned with a yardstick and Scotch tape. He measured 44 inches (on the door outside my room), took the memo, and taped it to the door.

Michael said, "If you don't want me to come in, leave the note down. If it's okay to come in (tape was on back bottom of memo), tape the bottom over the top of the note. That would mean it's okay for me to come in."

I said, "Thanks."

At 6:02 A.M. Michael came into my bed. (I get up at approximately 6:00 A.M. on workdays.) Michael said, "See, Dad, I got up when it was dark and started into your room but your note was down and I couldn't see a thing, but in my mind I could read it. So I went back to bed. See, Dad, all you have to do is ask and I'll help you solve your problems."

This has been in effect for two weeks with very good results. This is the better way. Thanks.

## Alternatives to Punishment

### JENNIFER'S BEDTIME DILEMMA

Tuesday night, still fired up from last night's session, I broached the question to Jennifer (age five):

MOTHER: Do you have time to talk?

JENNIFER: Yes.

MOTHER: I'd like to talk about our "middle of the night" problem.

JENNIFER: Oh, okay.

MOTHER: Do you want to tell me how you feel about this situation that is making us both so unhappy?

JENNIFER: Something gets in me, Ma (*grimace on face, fists clenched*), and I can't stay in my room. I just want to come into your room.

MOTHER: Oh, I see . . .

JENNIFER: I know you hate it, right?

MOTHER: Well, let me tell you how I feel. After a long day I look forward to getting into bed, snuggling under the warm covers, and falling fast asleep. When I am awakened, I'm just not a very friendly mommy.

JENNIFER: I know.

MOTHER: Let's see if we can come up with a solution that can make us both happy, okay? (*taking out pad and pen*)

JENNIFER: You're going to write it? Is it going to be a list? (*vividly impressed*)

MOTHER: Yes. Can you start us off?

JENNIFER: I'd like to come into Mommy and Daddy's bed.

MOTHER: Okay (*writing*). Anything else?

JENNIFER: I could just wake you instead.

MOTHER: Mmm . . . (*writing*).

JENNIFER: I could read by my night-light if I scrunch down.

MOTHER: I bet you could . . .

JENNIFER: But if I had a lamp—could I have a lamp?

| | |
|---|---|
| MOTHER: | (*writing*) What would you do with a lamp? |
| JENNIFER: | (*getting excited*) I could read a book, play with my tongue depressors (*Father is a doctor*), write my letters . . . |
| MOTHER: | Somebody sounds excited. |
| JENNIFER: | Okay, what about number 4 (*on list*)? |
| MOTHER: | Have you any more ideas? |
| JENNIFER: | (*quickly*) I could ask for a drink. |
| MOTHER: | Mmm (*writing*). |
| JENNIFER: | And number 5 could be sneaking out to check if you're okay. |
| MOTHER: | We have some list! Let's go over it. |

Jen promptly put *x*'s next to the first and second solutions. She talked about buying a lamp, a pad, and crayons the next day. We picked out an atrocious orange lamp (*her* choice) to match (?) her red-and-white room. That night went beautifully, with me receiving a shoebox (her idea) full of drawings the next morning. It's been a whole week now that she's let me sleep. I'm keeping my fingers crossed.

• • •

Parents told us that once their children became accustomed to problem-solving, they were more able to work out their differences with their sisters and brothers. This was a big bonus for the parents. Instead of having to step in, take sides, play judge, and come up with a solution, they restated the problem and put it right back where it belonged—in the lap of the children. The statement that seemed to activate the children to take responsibility to resolve their own conflicts was: *"Kids, this is a tough problem, but I have confidence that you two can put your heads together and come up with a solution that you can both agree to."* This first example is from a father:

Brad (four) and Tara (two and a half) were outside. Brad was riding Tara's tricycle and Tara wanted to ride it. Tara started to get hysterical and Brad refused to get off.

134

Normally I wouldn't have hesitated to say, "Brad, get off. That belongs to your sister. You have your own bicycle!" But instead of taking Tara's side, I said, "I see you both have a problem. Tara, you want to ride your tricycle. Brad, you want to ride Tara's tricycle and she doesn't want you to." I then said to both of them, "I think you should try to find a solution to the problem that would be acceptable to both of you."

Tara continued to cry, and Brad thought for a moment. Brad then said to me, "I think Tara should stand on the back of the tricycle and hold on to my stomach while I ride."

I said, "This solution should be discussed with Tara, not me."

Brad then asked Tara and Tara agreed! They then both rode off into the sunset.

• • •

What never ceases to surprise us is the kinds of solutions children work out. They're usually completely original and far more satisfying than any suggestions the parents would have come up with.

When I returned home after our last session on problem-solving, my two children were in the midst of an argument about a red jacket they both wanted to wear. The jacket used to be worn by my six-year-old daughter and is now used by my three-year-old son. They were getting ready to go out and were fighting and screaming about who should wear the jacket.

I got their attention and said, "I see two children who want to wear the same red jacket.

"I see one child who used to own the jacket and still wants to have it.

"I see another child who wants to wear the red jacket because it belongs to him now.

"I believe you can both come up with a solution to this problem. I'll be in the kitchen when you're ready."

I went into the kitchen and my husband and I listened in amazement as we heard a discussion between them begin. Five minutes later they entered the room and said, "We came to a solution! Josh will wear the jacket to the restaurant. And when we leave the restaurant to go to the fair, I will wear the jacket and Josh can wear my new yellow one!"

• • •

This final story shows a young boy grappling with the problem of how to deal with his own strong emotions:

Scott (eight years old) has trouble getting out his feelings of anger. This particular evening, something set him off and he stormed away from the dinner table with fists clenched, not knowing of an acceptable way to get rid of all his fury.

On the way to his room, he accidentally knocked down one of my favorite vases. As I saw it smash and break on the floor, I became furious and, unfortunately, began screaming like a maniac. He ran into his room, slamming the door.

After my husband managed to glue the vase together and time had eased the angry feelings I had, I went to his door and knocked. When he said, "What?" I asked him if it was all right if I came in and was it a good time to talk.

He looked at me with gratitude and said, "Yes!" It was as if he was reassured, merely by my presence, that I still loved him and thought of him as a human being, not as a clumsy, uncontrolled child.

I began by asking him how he feels when he gets so-o-o angry. He told me that he wants to punch someone or break something, to storm around and to slam things as hard as he can. I told him that when he shows his anger that way I want to go into his room and take his favorite toy and tear it apart. Then we both looked at each other and kind of said, "Hmmm."

I asked him (with my paper and pencil in hand) if we could work out some way of showing or releasing anger that we could both live with, and he proceeded to give me suggestions:

Daddy could hang up my punching bag.

Put something on the wall to throw my ball at.

Hang up my beanbag chair.

Turn on my radio as loud as it goes.

Get a chin-up bar.

Smash a pillow over my head.

Slam doors.

Jump hard on the floor.

Jump on the bed.

Turn the light on and off.

Go out and run around the house ten times.

Rip up paper.

Pinch myself.

I said not a word, but wrote it all down. It was interesting that, after he said those things he knew he wouldn't be allowed to do, he giggled a bit, as if to let me know that this is what he'd *really* like.

As we went back over the list, I eliminated some things and explained to him why they wouldn't work for me. We settled on four possibilities.

Daddy would have to give a definite time that he would try to repair and hang up the punching bag.

The chinning bar would be used in the doorway to his room.

He would be able to run around the house only in the daylight.

When I questioned ripping up paper, I said, "There's only one problem with that."

He said, "Oh, I know. I'll pick it up afterward!"

By this time, we were sitting closely and touching and

talking very calmly. I finally said to him, "There's only one thing I'd like to add, and it's something that's always available to you when you feel so full of anger."

"I can talk about it," he said immediately.

We both went to bed feeling really good.

# 4 | Encouraging Autonomy

Most of the books on child-rearing tell us that one of our most important goals as parents is to help our children separate from us, to help them become independent individuals who will one day be able to function on their own without us. We're urged not to think of our children as little carbon copies of us or as extensions of ourselves but as unique human beings with different temperaments, different tastes, different feelings, different desires, different dreams.

Yet how are we to help them become separate, independent persons? By allowing them to do things for themselves, by permitting them to wrestle with their own problems, by letting them learn from their own mistakes.

Easier said than done. I can still remember my first child struggling to tie his shoelaces and me watching patiently for about ten seconds and then bending down to do it for him.

And all my daughter had to do was just mention that she was having a quarrel with a friend, and I'd jump in with instant advice for her.

And how could I let my children make mistakes and suffer failure when all they had to do was listen to me in the first place?

You may be thinking, "What's so terrible about helping children tie their shoelaces, or telling them how to resolve an argument with a friend, or seeing to it that they don't make mistakes? After all, children are younger and less experienced. They really are dependent on the adults around them."

Here's the problem. When one person is continually dependent on another, certain feelings arise. In order to get clear on what those feelings might be, please read the following statements and write down your reactions:

I. You are four years old. In the course of the day you hear your parents tell you:

"Eat your string beans. Vegetables are good for you."

"Here, let me zip that zipper for you."

"You're tired. Lie down and rest."

"I don't want you playing with that boy. He uses bad language."

"Are you sure you don't have to go to the bathroom?"

Your reaction:

_____

_____

_____

_____

II. You are nine years old. In the course of the day your parents tell you:

"Don't bother to try on that jacket. Green isn't your color."

"Give the jar to me. I'll unscrew the cap for you."

"I've laid your clothes out for you."

"Do you need help with your homework?"

Your reaction:

_____

_____

_____

_____

III. You are seventeen years old. Your parent says:

"It's not necessary for you to learn to drive. I'm much too nervous about accidents. I'd be happy to drive you wherever you want to go. All you have to do is ask."

Your reaction:

_____

_____

_____

_____

IV. You are an adult. Your employer says:

"I'm going to tell you something for your own good. Stop making suggestions about how to improve things around here. Just do your job. I'm not paying you for your ideas. I'm paying you to work."

Your reaction:

_____

_____

_____

_____

V. You are a citizen of a new nation. At a public meeting you hear a visiting dignitary, from a rich, powerful country, announce:

"Because your nation is still in its infancy and is as yet undeveloped, we are not unmindful of your needs. We plan to send you experts and materials to show you how to run your farms, your schools, your businesses, and your government. We'll also send professionals in family planning who will help you reduce your country's birthrate."

Your reaction:

_____

_____

It's probably safe to say that you wouldn't want your children feeling toward you most of the feelings you've just written down. And yet when people are placed in dependent positions, along with a small amount of gratitude they usually do experience massive feelings of helplessness, worthlessness, resentment, frustration, and anger. This unhappy truth can present a dilemma for us as parents. On the one hand, our children are clearly dependent on us. Because of their youth and inexperience, there's so much we have to do for them, tell them, show them. On the other hand, the very fact of their dependency can lead to hostility.

Are there ways to minimize our children's feelings of dependency? Are there ways to help them become responsible human beings who can function on their own? Fortunately, the opportunities to encourage our children's autonomy present themselves every day. Here are some specific skills that can help children to rely on themselves rather than on us.

### To Encourage Autonomy

1. Let children make choices.

2. Show respect for a child's struggle.

3. Don't ask too many questions.

4. Don't rush to answer questions.

5. Encourage children to use sources outside the home.

6. Don't take away hope.

# LET CHILDREN MAKE CHOICES.

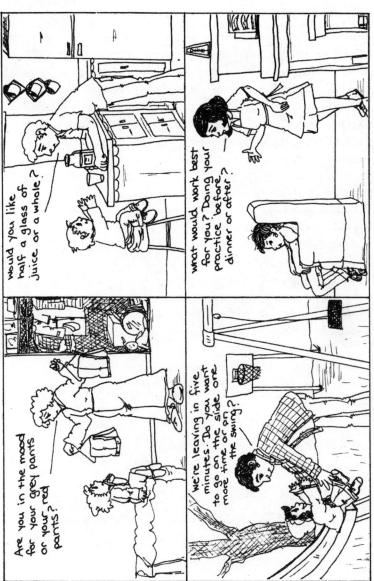

These are all choices that give a child valuable practice in making decisions. It must be very hard to be an adult who is forced to make decisions about career, lifestyle, mate without having had a good deal of experience in exercising your own judgment.

# SHOW RESPECT FOR A CHILD'S STRUGGLE.

When a child's struggle is respected, he gathers courage
to see a job through by himself.

# DON'T ASK TOO MANY QUESTIONS.

*Instead of*

*Instead of*

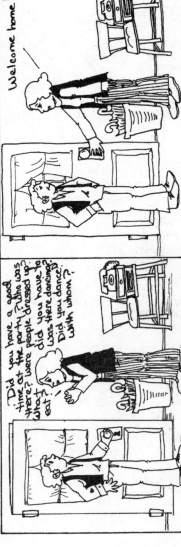

Too many questions can be experienced as an invasion of one's private life.

Children will talk about what they want to talk about when they want to talk about it.

DON'T RUSH TO ANSWER QUESTIONS.

*Instead of*

*Instead of*

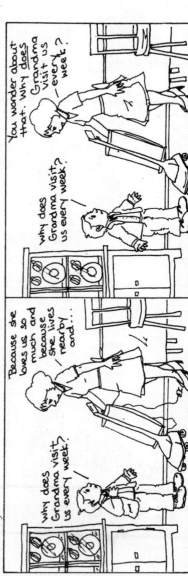

When children ask questions, they deserve the chance to explore the answer for themselves first.

ENCOURAGE CHILDREN TO USE SOURCES OUTSIDE THE HOME.

We want our children to know that they're not completely dependent on us. The world outside the home—the pet shop, the dentist, the school, an older child—can all be called upon to help them with their problems.

# DON'T TAKE AWAY HOPE.

*Instead of preparing children for disappointment,*        *let them explore and experience.*

By trying to protect children from disappointment,
we protect them from hoping, striving, dreaming,
and sometimes from achieving their dreams.

Even though many of these skills you just looked at may seem like common sense at first, there's nothing common about any of them. It takes some determination and practice to talk to children in ways that foster their independence.

In the following exercise you'll see six typical statements by parents. Please change each statement to one that will encourage a child's autonomy.

Parent originally says:

Revised statement that encourages autonomy:

1. Take your bath now.

1. (Offer a choice.)

_____

_____

_____

_____

_____

_____

_____

_____

_____

_____

2. Why are you having such a hard time putting your boots on? Here, put your foot up. I'll do it for you.

2. (Show respect for the child's struggle.)

_____

_____

_____

_____

3. Did you have fun at camp today? Did you swim? Did you like the other children? What's your counselor like?

3. (Don't ask too many questions.)

_____

_____

_____

_____

4. CHILD: Why does Daddy have to work every day?

PARENT: Daddy has to go to work every day so that we can have this nice house, good food, pretty clothing, and . . .

4. (Don't rush to answer questions.)

_____

_____

_____

_____

_____

_____

5. TEENAGER: I'm getting too fat. I want you to put me on a diet. What should I be eating?

PARENT: I've been telling you for years now to stop eating all that cake and candy and start eating fruit and vegetables.

5. (Encourage children to use sources outside the home.)

_____

_____

_____

_____

_____

_____

6. CHILD: Dad, I'm going to be a teacher when I grow up.

DAD: Don't count on it. Graduate schools are filled with teachers who can't get jobs when they get out of school.

6. (Don't take away hope.)

_____

_____

_____

_____

_____

_____

If you're thinking that the six skills you've just practiced aren't the only ones that encourage a child's autonomy, you'd be right. Actually, all the skills you've studied so far in this book help children see themselves as separate, responsible, competent people. Whenever we listen to children's feelings, or share our own feelings with them, or invite them to problem-solve with us, we encourage their self-reliance.

I know that for me the idea of encouraging the children to be in charge of the details of their own lives was revolutionary. I can still hear my grandmother saying admiringly of a neighbor, "She's the most wonderful mother. What she doesn't do for that child!" I grew up believing that good mothers "did" for their children. Only I took it one step further. I not only "did" for them, I thought for them as well. Result? Every day, over every trivial issue, there would be a contest of wills, ending with bad feelings all around.

When I finally learned to turn over to the children the responsibilities that rightfully belonged to them, everyone's disposition improved. Here's what helped me: Whenever I'd feel myself starting to get agitated or involved, I'd ask myself, "Do I have any choice here? . . . Must I take over? . . . Or can I put the children in charge instead?"

In this next exercise you'll see a series of situations that often get parents agitated, involved, or both. As you read each situation, ask yourself:

I. What can I say or do to keep my child dependent on me?

II. What could I say or do to encourage my child's autonomy?

*Some skills that might be helpful*

| *New Skills* | *Old Skills* |
| --- | --- |
| Offer a choice. | Accept your child's feelings. |
| Show respect for a child's | Describe what you feel. |
| struggle. | Give information. |

|        *New Skills*         |    *Old Skills*    |
| Don't ask too many questions. | Problem-solve. |

Don't ask too many questions.      Problem-solve.
Don't rush to answer questions.
Encourage use of sources
outside the home.
Don't take away hope.

CHILD: I was late for school today. You have to wake me up earlier tomorrow.
PARENT: (*keeping child dependent*)

_____

PARENT: (*encouraging autonomy*)

_____


CHILD: I don't like eggs and I'm tired of cold cereal. I'm not going to eat breakfast anymore.
PARENT: (*keeping child dependent*)

_____

PARENT: (*encouraging autonomy*)

_____


CHILD: Is it cold out? Do I need a sweater?
PARENT: (*keeping child dependent*)

_____

PARENT: (*encouraging autonomy*)

_____


CHILD: Oh heck, I can never get this button to button.
PARENT: (*keeping child dependent*)

_____

PARENT: (*encouraging autonomy*)

_____

CHILD: Know what? I'm going to start saving my allowance for a horse.

PARENT: (*keeping child dependent*)

---

PARENT: (*encouraging autonomy*)

---

CHILD: Betsy wants me to come to her party, but I don't like most of the kids who are going. What should I do?

PARENT: (*keeping child dependent*)

---

PARENT: (*encouraging autonomy*)

---

I suspect that some of the statements you wrote down came to you quickly and that others took considerable thought. It can be a challenge to find the language that engages a child's sense of responsibility.

The fact is, this whole business of encouraging autonomy can be quite complicated. As much as we understand the importance of our children being independent, there are forces within us that work against it. First, there's the matter of sheer convenience. Most of us today are busy and in a hurry. We usually wake the children ourselves, button their buttons, tell them what to eat and what to wear, because it seems so much easier and faster to do it for them.

Then we have to cope with our strong feelings of connectedness to our children. We have to fight against seeing their failures as our failures. It's hard to allow those so close and dear to us to struggle and make mistakes when we're certain that a few words of wisdom could protect them from pain or disappointment.

It also takes great restraint and self-discipline on our part not to move in with advice, particularly when we're sure we have the answer. I know that to this day whenever one of my children asks, "Mom, what do you think I should do?" I have to sit on myself not to tell them immediately what I think they should do.

But there's something even larger that interferes with our rational desire to help our children separate from us. I remember so well the deep satisfaction that came from being so totally needed by three small human beings. And so it was with mixed feelings that I discovered that a mechanical alarm clock could wake my kids more efficiently than all my motherly reminding. And it was also with mixed feelings that I gave up my job as reader of bedtime stories when the children finally learned to read by themselves.

It was my own conflicting emotions about their growing independence that helped me understand a story told to me by a nursery school teacher. The teacher described her efforts to convince a young mother that her son really would be fine if she wasn't sitting there in the classroom with him. Five minutes after the mother left, it became obvious that little Jonathan needed to head for the bathroom. When the teacher urged him to go, he mumbled unhappily, "Can't."

She asked, "Why not?"

"'Cause my Mommy isn't here," Jonathan explained. "She claps for me when I finish."

The teacher thought for a moment. "Jonathan, you can go to the bathroom and then clap for yourself."

Jonathan looked wide-eyed.

The teacher led him to the bathroom and waited. After a few minutes, from behind the closed door she heard the sound of applause.

Later that day the mother called her to say that the first words out of Jonathan's mouth when he came home were "Mommy, I can clap for myself. I don't need you anymore!"

"Would you believe it," the teacher exclaimed to me, "The mother said she was actually depressed about this."

I could believe it. I could believe that despite our feelings of pride in our children's progress and joy in their growing independence, there could also be the ache and the emptiness of no longer being needed.

It's a bittersweet road we parents travel. We start with total commitment to a small, helpless human being. Over the years we worry, plan, comfort, and try to understand. We give our love, our labor, our knowledge, and our experience—so that one day he or she will have the inner strength and confidence to leave us.

## ASSIGNMENT

1. Put into action at least two skills that would encourage your child's sense of himself or herself as a separate, competent, self-reliant person.

2. What was your child's reaction?

_____

_____

3. Is there anything you've been doing for your child that your child might start doing for himself or herself?

_____

_____

4. How could you shift this responsibility to your child without having him or her feel overwhelmed? (Most children do not respond well to "You're a big boy [or girl] now. You're old enough to dress yourself, feed yourself, make your own bed," etc.)

_____

_____

5. Read Part I of "Encouraging Autonomy."

*A Quick Reminder . . .*

---

## To Encourage Autonomy

1. LET CHILDREN MAKE CHOICES.

   "Are you in the mood for your gray pants, or your red pants?"

2. SHOW RESPECT FOR A CHILD'S STRUGGLE.

   "A jar can be hard to open. Sometimes it helps if you tap the lid with a spoon."

3. DON'T ASK TOO MANY QUESTIONS.

   "Glad to see you. Welcome home."

4. DON'T RUSH TO ANSWER QUESTIONS.

   "That's an interesting question. What do you think?"

5. ENCOURAGE CHILDREN TO USE SOURCES OUTSIDE THE HOME.

   "Maybe the pet shop owner would have a suggestion."

6. DON'T TAKE AWAY HOPE.

   "So you're thinking of trying out for the play! That should be an experience."

---

## PART I: COMMENTS, QUESTIONS, AND PARENTS' STORIES

### *Comments About Each Skill*

I. *Let Children Make Choices*

It might seem inconsequential to ask a child whether he wants a half glass of milk or a whole, his toast light or dark; but to the child each small choice represents one more opportunity to exert some control over his own life. There is so much a child must do that it's not hard to understand why he becomes resentful and balky.

"You must take your medicine."

"Stop drumming on the table."

"Go to bed now."

If we can offer him a choice about *how* something is to be done, very often that choice is enough to reduce his resentment.

"I can see how much you dislike this medicine. Would it be easier for you to take it with apple juice or ginger ale?"

"The drumming really bothers me. You can stop drumming and stay. You can drum in your own room. You decide."

"It's Mommy and Daddy's time to talk and your time to be in bed. Do you want to go to sleep now or do you want to play awhile in bed and call us when you're ready to be tucked in?"

Some parents feel uncomfortable about using this skill. They claim that a forced choice isn't much of a choice at all and becomes just another way to box a child in. An understandable objection. One alternative is to invite the child to come up with his own choice that would be acceptable to all parties. Here's what a father told us he did:

"My wife and I were about to cross the street with Tony— he's three—and the baby. Tony hates it when we hold his hand and struggles to get loose—sometimes in the middle of the street. Before we crossed I said, 'Tony, as I see it you have two choices. You can take hold of Mommy's hand or you can take my hand. Or maybe you have another idea that's safe.'

"Tony thought for a second and said, 'I'll hold the carriage.' His choice was fine with us."

II. *Show Respect for a Child's Struggle*

We used to think that when we told a child something was "easy," we were encouraging him. We realize now that by saying, "Try it, it's easy" we do him no favor. If he succeeds in doing something "easy," he feels he hasn't accomplished much. If he fails, then he's failed to do something simple.

If on the other hand we say, "It's not easy" or "That can be hard," he gives himself another set of messages. If he succeeds, he can experience the pride of having done something difficult. If he fails, he can at least have the satisfaction of knowing that his task was a tough one.

Some parents feel they're being phony when they say, "That can be hard." But if they were to look at the task from the point of view of an inexperienced child they would realize that the first few times you do anything new it really *is* hard. (Avoid saying, "That must be hard for *you*." A child might think, "Why for me? Why not for anyone else?")

Other parents complained that it was almost unbearable to stand there and watch a child struggle without offering more than just empathy. But rather than taking over and doing the job for the child, we suggest you give some useful information instead:

"Sometimes it helps if you push the end of the zipper all the way down into the little case before you pull it up."

"Sometimes it helps if you roll the clay into a soft ball before you try to make something."

"Sometimes it helps if you turn the knob of a lock a few times before you try the combination again."

We like the words "sometimes it helps," because if it doesn't help the child is spared feelings of inadequacy.

Does this mean that we must never do for our children what they can do for themselves? We trust each parent to sense when a child is tired or in need of extra attention, or even a little babying. At certain times there is great comfort that comes from having your hair brushed or your socks pulled on for you, even though you're perfectly capable of doing it yourself. As long as we, as parents, are aware that our basic direction is to help our children be in charge of themselves, we can comfortably enjoy "doing for them" occasionally.

III. *Don't Ask Too Many Questions*

The classic "Where did you go?" . . . "Out" . . . "What did you do?" . . . "Nothing" didn't come from nowhere. Other defensive tactics children use to fend off questions they aren't ready or willing to answer are "I dunno" or "Leave me alone."

One mother told us she felt she wasn't being a good parent if she didn't ask her son questions. She was amazed to discover that when she stopped bombarding him with questions and listened with interest when he did talk, he began to open up to her.

Does this mean you may never ask your child questions? Not at all. The important thing is to be sensitive to the possible effect of your questions.

*Caution:* One common parental inquiry that seems to be experienced as a pressure is "Did you have fun today?" What a demand to make upon a child! Not only did he have to go to the party (school, play, camp, dance) but the expectation is that he *should* enjoy himself. If he didn't, he has his own disappointment to cope with plus that of his parents. He feels he's let them down by not having a good time.

IV. *Don't Rush to Answer Questions*

In the course of growing up, children ask a bewildering variety of questions:

"What is a rainbow?"

"Why can't the baby go back to where she came from?"

"Why can't people just do whatever they want?"

"Do you have to go to college?"

Parents often feel put on the spot by these questions and search their minds for immediate, appropriate answers. The pressure they impose on themselves is unnecessary. Usually when a child asks a question she's already done some thinking about the answer. What she can use is an adult who will act as a sounding board to help her explore her thoughts further. There's always time for the adult to supply the "correct" answer later if it still seems important.

By giving our children immediate answers, we do them no favor. It's as if we're doing their mental exercise for them. It's much more helpful to children to have their questions turned back to them for further examination:

"You wonder about that."

"What do you think?"

We might even repeat the question.

"Why can't people just do whatever they want?"

We can credit the questioner:

"You're asking an important question—one that philosophers have asked for centuries."

There needn't be any hurry. The process of searching for the answer is as valuable as the answer itself.

### V. *Encourage Children to Use Sources Outside the Home*

One way to lessen a child's feelings of dependency on his family is to show him that there is a larger community out there with valuable resources waiting to be tapped. The world is not an alien place. There is help to be had when you need it.

Aside from the obvious benefit to the child, this principle also relieves the parent of having to be the "heavy" all the time. The school nurse can discuss sensible eating habits with the overweight child; the shoe salesman can explain what continual use of sneakers does to feet; the librarian can help a youngster wrestle with a tough research paper; the dentist can explain what happens to teeth that aren't brushed. Somehow all these outside sources carry more weight than volumes of talk from Mother or Dad.

VI. *Don't Take Away Hope*

Much of the pleasure of life lies in dreaming, fantasizing, anticipating, planning. By trying to prepare children for the possibility of disappointment, we can deprive them of important experiences.

A father told us about his nine-year-old daughter who had developed a passion for horses. One day she asked him if he would buy her a horse. He said it took some effort not to tell her that it was out of the question because of money, space, and town ordinances. Instead, he said, "So you wish you could have a horse of your own. Tell me about it." Then he listened as she went into long detail about how she'd feed her horse and groom him and take him for rides every day. Just talking about her dream to him seemed to be enough for her. She never pressed him again actually to buy the horse. But after that conversation, she took books out of the library about horses, drew sketches of horses, and started saving part of her allowance to buy land one day for her horse. A few years later she applied for a job helping out at a local stable, where she traded her services for occasional rides. By the time she was fourteen, her interest in horses had waned. One day she announced that she was buying a ten-speed bike with her "horse money."

## More Ways to Encourage Autonomy

I. *Let Her Own Her Own Body.*

Refrain from constantly brushing the hair out of her eyes, straightening her shoulders, dusting off lint, tucking her blouse into her skirt, rearranging her collar. Children experience this kind of fussing over them as an invasion of their physical privacy.

II. *Stay Out of the Minutiae of a Child's Life.*

Few children appreciate hearing, "Why do you write with your nose on the paper? . . . Sit up when you do your homework . . . Take your hair out of your eyes. How can you see what you are doing? . . . Button your cuffs. They look so sloppy hanging open . . . That old sweatshirt has got to go. Get yourself a new one . . . You spent your allowance on that? Well, I think it's a waste of money."

Many children react to this kind of talk with an irritable, "Ma-ah!" Or "Da-ad!" Translation: "Quit bugging me. Get off my back. It's my business."

III. *Don't Talk About a Child in Front of Him—No Matter How Young the Child.*

Picture yourself standing next to your mother as she tells a neighbor any of the following:

"Well, in the first grade he was unhappy because of his reading, but now he's doing better."

"She loves people. Everybody's her friend."

"Don't mind him. He's a little shy."

When children hear themselves discussed this way, they feel like objects—possessions of their parents.

IV. *Let a Child Answer for Himself.*

Over and over again the parent, in the presence of the child, is asked questions like:

"Does Johnny enjoy going to school?"

"Does he like the new baby?"

"Why isn't he playing with his new toy?"

The real mark of respect for the child's autonomy is to say to the inquiring adult, "Johnny can tell you. He's the one who knows."

V. *Show Respect for Your Child's Eventual "Readiness."*

Sometimes a child wants to do something very much but isn't emotionally or physically ready for it. She wants to use the bathroom like a "big girl" but can't yet. He wants to go swimming like the other kids, but he's still afraid of the water. She wants to stop sucking her thumb, but when she's tired it feels so good.

Instead of forcing, urging, or embarrassing a youngster, we can express our confidence in her ultimate readiness:

"I'm not concerned. When you're ready, you'll get into the water."

"When you decide to, you'll stop sucking your thumb."

"One of these days, you'll use the bathroom just like Mommy and Daddy."

VI. *Watch Out for Too Many "Nos."*

There will be many times as parents when we'll have to thwart our children's desires. Yet some children experience a blunt "No" as a call to arms, a direct attack on their autonomy. They mobilize all their energy to counterattack. They scream, have tantrums, call names, get sullen. They barrage the parent with "Why not?" . . . You're mean . . . I hate you!"

It's exhausting even for the most patient of parents. So what do we do? Give in? Say "Yes" to everything? Obviously not. That way lies the tyranny of the spoiled brat. Fortunately, we have some helpful alternatives that allow the parent to be firm without inviting a confrontation.

## SOME ALTERNATIVES TO "NO"

A. *Give Information* (and leave out the "No"):
CHILD: Can I go over to Suzie's to play now?
Instead of "*No*, you can't."
Give the facts:

"We're having dinner in five minutes."

With that information, a child might tell herself, "I guess I can't go now."

B. *Accept Feelings:*
CHILD: (At the zoo) I don't want to go home now. Can't we stay?
Instead of "*No*, we have to go now!"
Accept his feelings:

"I can see if it were up to you, you'd stay for a long, long time." (*As you take him by the hand to go*) "It's hard to leave a place you enjoy so much."

Sometimes resistance is lessened when someone understands how you feel.

C. *Describe the Problem:*
CHILD: Mom, can you drive me to the library now?
Instead of *"No,* I can't. You'll just have to wait."
Describe the problem:
   "I'd like to help you out. The problem is that the electrician is coming in the next half hour."

D. *When Possible, Substitute a "Yes" for a "No":*
CHILD: Can we go to the playground?
Instead of *"No,* you haven't had your lunch yet."
Substitute a "Yes":
   "Yes, certainly. Right after lunch."

E. *Give Yourself Time to Think:*
CHILD: Can I sleep over at Gary's house?
Instead of *"No,* you slept there last week."
Give yourself a chance to think:
   "Let me think about it."

This little sentence accomplishes two things: It takes the edge off the child's intensity (at least he knows his request will be seriously considered) and gives the parent time to think through her feelings.

It's true, the word "No" is shorter, and some of these alternatives seem much longer. But when you consider the usual fallout from "No," the long way is often the short way.

### More About Advice

The moment we mention to a group that giving advice to children may interfere with their autonomy, many parents are immediately up in arms. They feel, "Now that's going too far!" They cannot understand why they should be deprived of the right to share their parental wisdom. What follows are the questions of one persistent woman and a summary of the answers we gave her.

*Why shouldn't my child have the benefit of my advice when she has a problem? For example, my daughter, Julie, wasn't sure she should go to her friend's birthday party because she didn't like some of the other girls who were being invited. They "always whisper and call names." What's wrong with telling Julie that she should go anyway, because otherwise she'll be letting down her friend?*

When you give immediate advice to children, they either feel stupid ("Why didn't I think of that myself?"), resentful ("Don't tell me how to run my life!"), or irritated ("What makes you think I didn't think of that already?").

When a child figures out for herself what she wants to do, she grows in confidence and is willing to assume responsibility for her decision.

*Are you saying, then, that I should do nothing when my child has a problem? The few times I've told Julie, "It's your problem; you deal with it," she seemed very upset.*

Children do feel hurt and deserted when their parents ignore their problems. But between the extremes of ignoring completely or moving in with instant advice there's much a parent can do:

a) *Help her sort out her tangled thoughts and feelings.*

"From what you've been telling me, Julie, you seem to have two feelings about that party. You want to be with your friend on her birthday, but you don't want to have to contend with the girls you don't like."

b) *Restate the problem as a question.*

"So the question seems to be 'How do you find a way to

be at the party and deal with the name-calling of some of the girls?'"

It's a good idea to keep quiet after you've asked a question like this. Your silence provides the soil in which the child's solutions can grow.

c) *Point out resources your child can use outside the home.*

"I'll bet there are websites that have ideas on how to cope with name-calling and put-downs. You may want to see what they suggest."

*Suppose I do all that and then think of a solution that I'm sure Julie hasn't thought of. Can I mention it to her?*

After she's had time to become more clear about what *she* thinks and feels, she'll be able to give your idea a fair hearing—particularly if you introduce it in a way that shows respect for her autonomy:

"How would you feel about bringing a video to the party, like the one with that new comedian? Maybe the girls will be too busy laughing to start whispering."

When we preface our suggestion with "How would you feel about . . ." or "Would you consider . . . ," we acknowledge the fact that the advice that seems so "sensible" to us can be "not so sensible" to the child.

*But suppose I feel strongly that Julie should go to the party. Must I remain silent?*

*After* a child has explored her problem, it can be helpful for her to hear her parents' thoughts or convictions:

"It would bother me to think that you would have to miss the fun of a party because of the way some other girls act."

"I think it's important not to disappoint a good friend on her birthday, even if it entails some sacrifice."

A young person is entitled to know her parents' values. Even if she chooses not to act upon them just now, you can be sure you've given her something to think about.

## *When Parents Encourage Autonomy*

The week following one of our sessions on autonomy, the parents in our group had a great deal to tell one another.

I had two "firsts" this week with Danny. I let him work the bathtub faucet so that he could get the water temperature the way he likes it, and I let him make his own breakfast.

I always cut Rachel's food for her, because I didn't trust her with a knife. I finally bought her a little plastic knife, and now she feels very grown-up cutting her own meat.

When Shana was young and spilled anything, I always said, "Oh, Shana," and wiped it up for her. Now with Alyssa (fifteen months) I leave her cup on a small table. The first time she spilled, I pointed to the juice and showed her how to wipe it up with a paper towel. Now whenever she spills, she points to the paper towels and willingly cleans it up. Yesterday I left the towel out, and she took care of it herself, and then she showed me!

I can't stand it when the kids push food onto their forks with their fingers, or eat with their elbows on the table, or wipe their hands on their jeans instead of using their napkins. Yet I hate to constantly pick on them.

Last night I turned the problem over to them. Their solution: Three times a week we'd have "Manners Night," and the rest of the time they could eat the way they wanted, and I wouldn't say anything. (They even suggested that once a week we all "go natural," use no utensils, and eat everything with our fingers—including soup! But that was more than I could go along with.)

I told my son, "You have twenty minutes till bedtime. You can keep coloring and then go straight to bed or you can get ready for bed now and then have time to play with your circus lights in your bed." Immediate stampede to put pj's on, brush teeth, etc.

Nicole was crying and trying to button her blouse. She came to me and shoved the button in front of my nose. I said, "These small buttons are not easy to deal with. They can be so frustrating."

She backed away and kept trying herself. I was ready to give in and button it for her when she said, "There. I've done it!" and marched out.

I used to have clothing fights all the time with my four-year-old. Now I let her wear whatever she wants when there is no school. On school days I lay out two outfits on her bed and she decides.

I'm so proud of myself. I finally put an end to the daily hassles with my son over whether he should wear his sweater or his jacket. I told him, "Sam, I've been thinking. Instead of my telling you what to wear every day, I think you can tell yourself. Let's work out a chart and decide what clothing goes with what degree of temperature."

We drew up a chart together:

69 degrees and over . . . . . . no sweater

between 50 and 68 degrees . . . . . . sweater weather

49 degrees and under . . . . . . heavy jacket

Then I bought a large thermometer and he hung it outside on a tree. Now he looks at it every morning and there are no more arguments. I feel like a genius.

I didn't ask Howie any questions about what he did at camp. I allowed him to talk about what he wanted to, and he talked a blue streak.

Jody asked me, "Why don't we ever go anyplace good on vacation, like Bermuda or Florida?"

I almost started to answer her, but remembered not to. I said, "Why don't we?"

She stomped around the kitchen and said, "I know, I know . . . Because it's too expensive . . . Well, at least can we go to the zoo?"

I have to get used to the idea of not answering my son's questions for him. And I think he's going to have to get used to it, too. Here's what happened last week:

JOHN: Tell me how to make the atom bomb.

ME: That's an interesting question.

JOHN: Well, tell me.

ME: I'd have to think about it.

JOHN: Think about it now and tell me.

ME: I can't. But let's think about who or what could help us get the answer.

JOHN: I don't want to go to the library and look it up. Just tell me!

ME: I'm not able to answer that question without help, John.

JOHN: Then I'll ask Daddy. And if he doesn't know, then I'll ask William (a third grader). But it makes me mad that a third-grade kid knows more than a dummy mommy.

ME: No name-calling in this house!

Kevin told me he was going to sell the squash from his garden to the neighbors. I almost stopped him, because they were half the size of the ones in the supermarket and I didn't want him bothering the neighbors. But he was so excited that I let him. Besides, I didn't want to "take away hope."

He came back an hour later with a big smile on his face, seventy-five cents, and only one leftover squash. He said that Mrs. Greenspan told him he was an "enterprising young man" and "what did that mean?"

Jason told me he wants to be a policeman, a fireman, a fisherman, and an astronaut. I didn't foredoom him.

I'm doing better at staying out of the kids' fights. I tell them that I'm sure they can work it out themselves. And a lot of times they do.

These last few contributions were handed in at the end of the session:

... To this day my friends still remark at my independence. I am one of five children whose father worked six or seven days a week—depending upon how his retail business was going. I'm second from the oldest and became independent and self-reliant because I had to. My mother couldn't possibly "do" for five children and survive if she didn't teach us to do for ourselves.

However, I have ambivalent feelings about my childhood memories. I was proud that I didn't run to my mother and/or my dad to help with many problems and fears and needs, as did my friends. On the other hand, I would have liked it if it were also *my decision* about whether or not I wanted to confide in or be helped by a parent. (I knew my request would be denied on the basis of lack of time or whatever . . . so I stopped asking and did for myself.)

Children always want to be grown-up, but they still need to be children, need to grow gradually. I am proud of my mother's efficiency and capability in teaching us our routine, but I feel that there should have been the option to go to my parents when I needed them.

• • •

There is always so much for Kirk to do when he gets home from school that he never gets to any of it unless I keep after him. Finally, I wrote this note:

Dear Kirk,

Dad and I are unhappy because lately we seem to be fighting with you to do the things you know to do.

How long would you need to come up with a positive program for handling all you have to do? Twenty-four hours? More? We'd like to have a plan from you, in writing, by the end of the week that you think will work for you. It will need to include adequate time for:

—moving your arms 10 minutes, three times a day. (He broke his arm and hasn't been doing the exercises the doctor gave him.)
—walking the dog
—homework
—practicing
—fun and play

Love,
Mom

On Thursday night he presented us with a written schedule, and he's pretty much kept to it.

• • •

Paul was really worried about his report card. We were getting signals for days and days before it came. He'd say things like "I'm not gonna get such a good mark in math . . . I saw my mark in Mr. D's book. I wasn't supposed to see it."

In the evening after supper I said, "Paul, come over and let's look at your report card. He came over and his eyes were going every which way because he was anxious, but he sat down in my lap. He said, "Dad, you're not gonna like it."

ME: Well, let's see, Paul. It is your report card. How do you like it?

PAUL: Wait'll you see the math.

ME: Right now I'm not looking at the math. Let's start at the top. Let's see, there's a G (Good) in reading.

PAUL: Yeah, reading is okay.

ME: And I see a G in penmanship and you were having a lot of problems in penmanship. So you're coming along there . . . And you've got an E

(Excellent) in spelling! You were worried about it, too . . . This report card is looking good to me . . . English, an S.

PAUL: But I ought to be doing better in English.

ME: S is satisfactory.

PAUL: Yeah, but I should be doing better.

ME: Well now, math. What do I see there—an M (Minimum).

PAUL: I knew you were going to be mad!

ME: So this is the subject you're having some problems with.

PAUL: Oh yeah, I'm going to do much better in math.

ME: How are you going to do it?

PAUL: Well, I'll try harder.

ME: How?

PAUL: (*long pause*) I'll study harder and I'll do all my homework . . . And I'll finish my papers in school.

ME: Sounds as if you're setting goals for yourself. Let's get a piece of paper and write some of them down.

Paul got the paper and pencil and we listed all his subjects with the mark that he got next to it. In the second column, he wrote down the mark he would aim for on his next report card.

The surprising part is that I thought he was just going to zero in on the math and improve that. He decided to improve not only math but English, social studies, and science. When he got to math, he said he was going to improve all the way from an M to an E.

ME: Paul, that's quite a jump. Do you think you can do that?

PAUL: Oh yeah, I'm really going to work at math.

At the end of the report card, there's a space for a parent's comment and signature. I wrote: "I have discussed

Paul's report card with him, and he has decided to set new goals for himself. He plans to work harder—especially in math." Then I signed it and asked Paul to sign it, too.

The goal sheet was taped to his bedroom door so he could refer to it. For the next three days he came home with Es on his math papers! I couldn't believe it. I said, "Paul, when you set your mind to something there's no stopping you!"

● ● ●

I was raised in a very strict family. From the time I was small I was told what to do and when to do it. Whenever I asked "Why?" my father said, "Because I said so." I soon learned not to question.

When I had a son of my own there was one thing I was sure of. I didn't want to raise him that way. But I wasn't sure of what to do instead. The session on autonomy was very helpful to me. Here are some of the things that happened, which will give you an idea of what I mean.

When I became a single father I began to notice things I never did before. Robby was always stuffing himself with cookies. So I hid the cookie box and handed them out to him one at a time. The day after our last meeting, I came home with a box of cookies and put it on the table. I said, "Robby, I'm not going to be the cookie policeman anymore. This is the only box of cookies I'm buying this week. You can decide if you want to eat it all at once or if you want to make it last for the rest of the week. It's up to you." And that was it. I never had to say another word to him. He ended up taking two cookies every day and three on the weekend.

Also, I used to sit with him every night to help him with his homework, and we'd end up yelling at each other. One night I went into the living room and started to read the paper. Robby said, "Daddy, when are you going to help me?" I said, "I have confidence that if you give yourself time you'll be able to figure it out on your own." When I put him to bed that night he said, "I did all my homework myself. I love you, Daddy."

The next night he told me he wanted to talk something over with me. I said, "What is it?"

He said, "From now on, Daddy, I want to be my own man. Okay?"

I said, "It's okay with me."

Later on I told him, "Bedtime, Robby. Get into your pajamas and make sure you brush your teeth."

"I know that, Daddy," he said. "Remember, I'm my own man now!"

# 5 | Praise

Once upon a time there were two seven-year-old boys named Bruce and David. They both had mothers who loved them very much.

Each boy's day began differently. The first thing Bruce heard when he awakened in the morning was "Get up now, Bruce! You're going to be late for school again."

Bruce got up, dressed himself—except for his shoes—and came in for breakfast. Mother said, "Where are your shoes? Are you planning to go to school barefoot? . . . And look at what you're wearing! That blue sweater looks awful with that green shirt. . . . Bruce dear, what have you done to your pants? They're ripped. I want you to change them after breakfast. No child of mine is going school with torn pants. . . . Now watch how you pour your juice. Don't spill it the way you usually do!"

Bruce poured and spilled.

Mother was exasperated. As she mopped up the mess, she said, "I don't know what to do with you."

Bruce mumbled something to himself.

"What was that?" Mother asked. "There you go mumbling again."

Bruce finished his breakfast in silence. Then he changed his pants, put on his shoes, collected his books, and left for school. His mother called out, "Bruce, you forgot your lunch! If your head weren't screwed on to your shoulders, I bet you'd forget that, too."

Bruce took his lunch, and as he started out the door again, Mother reminded him, "Now, be sure to behave at school today."

David lived across the street. The first thing he heard in the morning was "Seven o'clock, David. Do you want to get up now or take five more minutes?" David rolled over and yawned. "Five more minutes," he mumbled.

Later he came to breakfast dressed, except for his shoes. Mother said, "Hey, you're dressed already. All you have left to put on are your shoes! . . . Uh-oh—there's a rip in the seam of your pants. Looks as if the whole side could split. Shall I sew it on you while you stand up or would you rather change?" David thought a second and said, "I'll change after breakfast." Then he sat down at the table and poured his juice. He spilled some.

"The cleanup rag is in the sink," Mother called over her shoulder as she continued making his lunch. David got the rag and wiped up the spill. They talked for a while as David ate his breakfast. When he was finished, he changed his pants, put on his shoes, collected his books, and left for school—without his lunch.

Mother called after him, "David, your lunch!"

He ran back to get it and thanked her. As she handed it to him she said, "See you later!"

Both Bruce and David had the same teacher. During the day the teacher told the class, "Children, as you already know, we'll be putting on our Columbus Day play next week. We need a volunteer to paint a colorful welcome sign on our classroom door. We also need a volunteer to pour and serve the lemonade for our guests after the play. And, finally, we need someone who will go around to the other third-grade classes and make a short speech inviting everyone to our play and telling them the time, day, and place."

Some of the children raised their hands immediately, some raised their hands tentatively, and some didn't raise their hands at all.

Our story stops here. That's all we know. About what happened afterward, we can only guess. But it certainly does leave us with food for thought. Take a moment now to consider these questions and answer them for yourself:

1. Would David be likely to raise his hand to volunteer?

2. Would Bruce?

3. What is the relationship between how children think of themselves and their willingness to accept challenges or risk failure?

4. What is the relationship between how children think of themselves and the kinds of goals they set for themselves?

Now that you've explored your own thoughts, I'd like to share mine with you. Granted, there are children who manage to brush off the belittling they get at home and still rise to the challenges of the outside world. And granted, there are some children who are treated with regard at home who still doubt their own abilities and shrink from challenge. However, it would seem logical that those children who grow up in families where their best is appreciated would be more likely to feel good about themselves, more likely to cope with the challenges of life, and more likely to set higher goals for themselves than those who don't.

As Nathaniel Branden has said in his book *The Psychology of Self-Esteem*, "There is no value judgment more important to man, no factor more decisive in his psychological development and motivation—than the estimate he passes on himself. . . . The nature of his self-evaluation has profound effects on a man's thinking processes, emotions, desires, values and goals. It is the single most significant key to his behavior."

If a child's self-esteem is so important, then what can we as parents do to enhance it? Certainly all the principles and skills we've talked about so far can help a child see himself as a person of worth. Each time we show respect for his feelings, each time we offer him a chance to make a choice, or give him a chance to solve a problem, he grows in confidence and self-esteem.

How else can we help our children build a positive and realistic self-image? Surely praising them would seem to be another part of the answer. But praise can be tricky business. Sometimes the most well-meant praise brings about unexpected reactions.

See for yourself if this is so. In the following exercise you'll find a description of four different hypothetical situations in which someone praises you. Please read each situation and jot down your reactions to the praise you received.

*Situation I:* You have an unexpected guest for dinner. You heat a can of cream of chicken soup, add some leftover chicken, and serve it over Minute Rice.

Your guest says, "You're a great cook!"

Your inner reaction:

_____

_____

_____

*Situation II:* You just changed out of your sweater and jeans into a new outfit to go to an important meeting.

An acquaintance approaches you, looks you over, and says, "You're always so beautifully dressed."

Your inner reaction:

_____

_____

_____

*Situation III:* You're taking an adult-education course. After a lively class discussion in which you participate, another student comes up to you and says, "You have a brilliant mind."

Your inner reaction:

_____

_____

_____

*Situation IV:* You've just started learning how to play tennis and, hard as you try, you still aren't making any progress with your serve. The ball usually goes into the net or off the court. Today you're playing doubles with a new partner, and your first serve lands where you hope it will.

Your partner comments, "Hey, you've got a perfect serve."

Your inner reaction:

_____

_____

_____

You've probably discovered for yourself some of the built-in problems of praise. Along with some good feelings can come other reactions:

Praise can make you doubt the praiser. ("If she thinks I'm a good cook, she's either lying or knows nothing about good food.")

Praise can lead to immediate denial. ("Always beautifully dressed! . . . You should have seen me an hour ago.")

Praise can be threatening. ("But how will I look at the next meeting?")

Praise can force you to focus on your weaknesses ("Brilliant mind? Are you kidding? I still can't add a column of figures.")

Praise can create anxiety and interfere with activity. ("I'll never be able to hit the ball like that again. Now I'm really uptight.")

Praise can also be experienced as manipulation. ("What does this person want from me?")

I remember my own frustrations whenever I tried to praise my children. They'd come to me with a painting and ask, "Is it good?"

I'd say, "What a beautiful painting."

They'd ask, "But is it *good*?"

I'd say, "Good? I told you it's beautiful . . . fantastic!"

They'd say, "You don't like it."

The more extravagantly I praised, the less I got through. I never understood their reactions.

After my first few sessions with Dr. Ginott, I began to realize why my children rejected my praise as fast as I gave it. He taught me that words that evaluate—good, beautiful, fantastic—made my children as uncomfortable as you probably felt in the exercise you just did. But, most important, I learned from him that helpful praise actually comes in two parts:

1. The adult describes with appreciation what he or she sees or feels.

2. The child, after hearing the description, is then able to praise himself.

I recall the first time I tried putting that theory into practice. My four-year-old came home from nursery school, shoved a page of penciled scribble under my nose, and asked, "Is it good?"

My first reaction was an automatic "Very good." Then I remembered. No, I've got to describe. I wondered, How do you describe scribble?

I said, "Well, I see you went circle, circle, circle . . . wiggle, wiggle, wiggle . . . dot, dot, dot, dot, dot, dot, dot, and slash, slash!

"Yeah!" he nodded enthusiastically.

I said, "How did you ever think to do this?"

He thought awhile. "Because I'm an artist," he said.

I thought, "It's a remarkable process. The adult describes, and the child really does praise himself."

On the next page you'll find more examples of how descriptive praise works.

## DESCRIPTIVE PRAISE.

*Instead of evaluating,*        *describe what you see or feel.*

*Describe*

*Describe*

I must confess that in the beginning I was dubious about this new method of praise. Even though it had worked for me once, the very thought of having to change to a descriptive style of praising irritated me. Why should I have to give up "Great . . . wonderful . . . terrific," which came so naturally to me, and find another way to express my honest enthusiasm?

But I tried anyway, dutifully at first, and after a while I noticed that the children really did begin to praise themselves. For example:

ME: (*instead of "Jill, you're terrific"*) You figured out that the cans of corn on sale—the three-for-a-dollar ones—are actually more expensive than the brands that aren't on sale. I'm impressed.

JILL: (*grinning*) I got "the smarts."

ME: (*instead of "Andy, you're great"*) That was a complicated phone message you took from Mrs. Vecchio. It was written so clearly, I knew exactly why the meeting was postponed, who I had to call, and what I had to tell them.

ANDY: Yeah, I'm a pretty dependable kid.

There was no doubt about it. The children were becoming more aware and appreciative of their own strengths. This alone was an incentive for me to continue making an effort. And it *was* an effort. It's a lot easier to say "Wonderful" about something, than to really look at it, and experience it, and then describe it in detail.

In this next exercise you'll have a chance to practice using descriptive praise. As you read about each situation take time out to picture in your mind exactly what it is your child has done. Then describe, in detail, what you see or what you feel. *Situation I:* A young child has just dressed herself for the first time. She stands in front of you, hoping you'll notice.

Praise unhelpfully:

_____

Praise by describing in detail what you see or feel:

_____

_____

_____

What might the child say to herself?

_____

_____


*Situation II:* You've been invited to see your child in a school play. He or she plays the part of king, queen, or witch. (Choose one.) After the show, your youngster comes running up to you and asks, "Was I good?"

Praise unhelpfully:

_____

_____

Praise by describing in detail what you saw or what you felt:

_____

_____

_____

What might the child say to himself?

_____

_____


*Situation III:* You notice that your child's schoolwork is improving in small ways. His compositions now have margins. He's been drilling himself on his vocabulary words until he knows them. His last report was finished one day ahead of time.

Praise unhelpfully:

_____

_____

Praise by describing in detail what you see or what you feel:

_____

_____

_____

What might the child say to himself?

_____

_____

*Situation IV:* You've been sick in bed for a few days. Your child has drawn you a get-well card decorated with balloons and hearts. She hands it to you and waits for your response.

Praise unhelpfully:

_____

_____

Praise by describing in detail what you see or what you feel:

_____

_____

_____

What might your child say to herself?

_____

_____

Having done this exercise, you're probably more clear now on how children experience evaluative praise:
"You're a good girl."
"You're a great actor."
"You're finally becoming an excellent student."

"You're so thoughtful."

You're probably also clear about how they feel themselves when they hear praise that describes their achievement:

"I see you put your shirt on with the tag in the back; you zipped your pants; you put on matching socks; and you buckled your shoes. What a lot of different things you did!"

"You were such a regal queen! You stood tall and straight, and when you gave your big speech your voice filled the auditorium."

"Seems to me you're putting extra effort into your schoolwork these days. I notice your compositions have margins, your reports are done ahead of time, and you've worked out a way to teach yourself vocabulary."

"I love these yellow balloons and red hearts. They cheer me up. I feel better already, just looking at them."

There is another way to praise that also uses description. The additional element here is that we add to the description one or two words that sum up the child's praiseworthy behavior.

# SUMMING UP IN A WORD

For your own practice, complete the sentence by filling
in the missing word or words in the drawings on this page.

1.

2.                                        3.

Some possible ways to complete the sentence in:

Drawing 1. "Determination" or "willpower" or "self-control."

Drawing 2. "Flexible" or "resourceful" or "adaptable."

Drawing 3. "Friendship" or "loyalty" or "courage."

There's nothing sacred about any of the words listed above. And again there are no right or wrong answers. The point is to find a word that will tell a youngster something about himself that he may not have known before—to give him a new verbal snapshot of himself.

What I personally like about this way to praise is that it's so "doable." It's a matter of really looking, really listening, really noticing, and then saying aloud what you see and what you feel.

One wonders how such a simple process can have such a profound effect. And yet day after day from our small descriptions our children learn what their strengths are: A child finds out that he can take a confusing mess of a room and turn it into a neat, orderly room; that he can make a gift that's useful and gives pleasure; that he can hold the attention of an audience; that he can write a poem that's moving; that he is capable of being punctual, of exercising willpower, of showing initiative, resourcefulness. All of that goes into his emotional bank, and it can't be taken away. You can take away "good boy" by calling him "bad boy" the next day. But you can't ever take away from him the time he cheered his mother with a get-well card, or the time he stuck with his work and persevered even though he was very tired.

These moments, when his best was affirmed, become life-long touchstones to which a child can return in times of doubt or discouragement. In the past he did something he was proud of. He has it within him to do it again.

## ASSIGNMENT

1. A quality I like about my child is:

_____

_____

_____

_____

2. Something he or she has done recently that I appreciated but never mentioned is:

_____

_____

_____

_____

3. What could I say to show my appreciation to him (or her), using the skills of descriptive praise?

_____

_____

_____

_____

_____

4. Read Part II of "Praise."

*A Quick Reminder ...*

---

**Praise and Self-Esteem**

Instead of Evaluating
("Good" ... "Great!" ... "Fantastic!"),
Describe.

1. DESCRIBE WHAT YOU SEE.

   "I see a clean floor, a smooth bed, and books neatly
   lined up on the shelf."

2. DESCRIBE WHAT YOU FEEL.

   "It's a pleasure to walk into this room!"

3. SUM UP THE CHILD'S PRAISEWORTHY BEHAVIOR WITH A WORD.

   "You sorted out your Legos, cars, and farm animals,
   and put them in separate boxes. That's what I call
   *organization!*"

---

## Part II: COMMENTS, QUESTIONS, AND PARENTS' STORIES

We've often noticed that parents in our groups will tell one another enthusiastically about something one of their children just did:

> "For three days now Donny has been setting his alarm and getting himself up in the morning. I'm so glad not to be involved anymore."
>
> "Recently Lisa has been calling home when she knows she's going to be late. I can't tell you how much that means to me!"

When we asked these parents whether their children were aware of their appreciation, they often looked blank.

It seems that praise for helpful behavior doesn't come readily. Most of us are quick to criticize and slow to praise. We have a responsibility as parents to reverse this order. Our children's self-esteem is too valuable to be left to chance or entrusted to strangers. You may have noticed yourself that the outside world doesn't rush in to offer praise. When is the last time another driver said to you, "Thank you for only taking up one parking space. Now I have room for my car"? Our efforts to be cooperative are taken for granted. One slipup, and condemnation is swift.

Let us be different in our homes. Let us realize that, along with food, shelter, and clothing, we have another obligation to our children, and that is to affirm their "rightness." The whole world will tell them what's wrong with them—loud and often. Our job is to let our children know what's right about them.

### *Some Cautions About Praise*

1. *Make sure your praise is appropriate to your child's age and level of ability.* When a very young child is told with pleasure, "I see you're brushing your teeth every day," he experiences

pride in his accomplishment. Were you to tell the same thing to a teenager, he might feel insulted.

2. *Avoid the kind of praise that hints at past weaknesses or past failures:*

"Well, you finally played that piece of music the way it should be played!"

"You look so nice today. What did you do to yourself?"

"I never thought you'd pass that course—but you did!"

It's always possible to rephrase your praise so that the focus is on the child's present strength:

"I really like the way you kept a strong, rhythmic beat going in that piece."

"It's a pleasure to look at you."

"I know you put in a lot of work to pass that course."

3. *Be aware that excessive enthusiasm can interfere with a child's desire to accomplish for herself.* Sometimes parents' continual excitement or intense pleasure in their child's activity can be experienced by the child as pressure. A young person who gets daily doses of "You're such a gifted pianist! You should be playing at Carnegie Hall" may think to herself, "They want it for me more than I want it for myself."

4. *Be prepared for a lot of repetition of the same activity when you describe what a child is doing appreciatively.* If you don't want him to blow the whistle five more times, then refrain from saying, "You certainly know how to make a big noise with that whistle!" If you don't want her to climb to the top of the jungle gym, don't tell her, "You really know how to use your climbing muscles." There's no doubt about it. Praise invites repetition and a great outpouring of effort. It's potent stuff. Use it selectively.

## *Questions*

### 1. I'm trying to learn to praise differently, but sometimes I forget and "great" or "fantastic" slips out. What can I do?

Please allow yourself your initial reaction. If you're feeling genuinely enthusiastic and find yourself exclaiming, "Great!" the child will hear the enthusiasm in your voice and experience it as an expression of your feelings. However, you can always enrich your initial reaction with the kind of description that helps a child know the extent of your appreciation: "There I was, tired out after a long day at work, and I came home to find the whole yard raked clean, with all the leaves bagged and put up front. I feel like a lucky dad!"

With a little specific description, you've just improved upon "Great."

### 2. How do you praise a child for finally doing what he should have been doing all along?

My older boy is usually so obnoxious when we go for a ride with the family that we're all miserable. Last week he behaved beautifully. I didn't want to tell him he was "good" or that he was "finally acting like a human being," and yet I did want to give him recognition for his behavior. How could I have done it without putting him down?

You're always on safe ground when you make a descriptive statement to a child about your own feelings. You can tell him, "I especially enjoyed our trip today."

He'll know why.

### 3. Is it all right to praise a child by saying, "I'm so proud of you"?

Suppose you had studied for a difficult and important test for a week. When the marks came back, you discovered that you not only passed but did very well. When you called a friend to tell her the good news, she said, "I'm so proud of you!"

What is your reaction? We suspect that you'd feel that somehow the emphasis had been shifted from your accomplishment to her pride. Chances are you'd much rather have heard something like "What an achievement! You must be so proud of yourself!"

**4. Last week when my son won a swimming award, I told him, "I'm not surprised. I knew all along you could do it." He looked at me strangely. I thought I was boosting his confidence; did I say something wrong?**

When a parent says, "I knew all along you could do it," he's giving credit to his own omniscience rather than to his child's achievements. The child might even think, "How come my father knew I'd win? I didn't know."

It would be more helpful to the child to hear *his* accomplishments described: "That award represents months of practice and a lot of determination!"

**5. My son gets plenty of praise from me, and yet he's still fearful of risking failure. He goes to pieces if something he attempts doesn't turn out right. Is there anything I can do?**

There are a number of ways that you could be helpful to him:

1. *When he's upset, don't minimize his distress.* ("There's nothing to be upset about.") Instead, bring out into the open what you think he might be feeling.

"It can be frustrating to work on a project for so long and not have it come out the way you want!"

When his frustration is understood, a child tends to relax inside.

2. *It helps when a parent can be accepting of his child's*

*mistakes and view them as an important part of the learning process.*

It can even be pointed out that a mistake can be a discovery. It can tell you something you never knew before:

"You found out that a soft-boiled egg can become hard just from sitting in hot water."

3. *It also helps if parents can be accepting of their own mistakes.*

When parents "beat up" on themselves ("I forgot my key again. What is the matter with me? That was such a dumb thing to do! How could I be so stupid? I'll never learn."), children conclude that this is the proper way to treat themselves when *they* make mistakes.

Instead, let us provide a more humane, solution-oriented model for our children. When we do something we wish we hadn't, let's seize the opportunity to say aloud to ourselves:

"Oh, heck, I wish I hadn't forgotten that key . . . It's the second time . . . What can I do to make sure it doesn't happen again? . . . I know, I'll have a duplicate key made up and keep it in a secret place."

By being kind to ourselves, we teach our children to be kind to themselves.

### When Parents Praise

One evening several parents were talking about how easy it was to take a child's good behavior for granted, and what an effort it required to make an appreciative comment. They decided to assign themselves the task of looking actively for, and commenting on, anything positive their children did, instead of letting it slip by. One mother came up with the following list of things she normally would never have mentioned to her five-year-old:

This week Paul learned the word "evaporation" and the concept of it.

He played with a seven-month-old infant with gentleness.

He gave me privacy and quiet after I told him how much I needed it.

He expressed his anger in words.

Another mother told us:

Yesterday Joshua (age three and three-quarters) wanted me to read a story to him as we were on our way out. When I told him I didn't have the time to read, because we had to leave, he said to me, "I didn't mean read to me *before* we go. I meant *after* we come home."

I said to him, "Joshua, you really know the difference between before and after!"

Joshua replied proudly, "Yup!" Then he thought awhile and said, "And I know when I want a cookie. *Before* dinner!"

Here's another example from a father who decided to start validating his seven-year-old daughter's strengths. One morning he told her:

"I see a girl who can get up in the morning all by herself, eat breakfast, get washed and dressed, and be ready for school on time. Now that's what I call self-reliance!"

A few days later when she was brushing her teeth, she called her father over and pointed to her mouth. "Now, that's what I call clean teeth!" she said.

Several parents also began to notice how often praise seemed to motivate their children to want to be more cooperative, to work harder than ever. Here are their experiences:

My husband and I wanted to sleep late on a Sunday morning, and our two children did not come in to wake us as usual. When I awoke I went in to them and said, "Brynn (she's six), it must have been so difficult for you to stay out of Mommy and Daddy's room. That took a lot of willpower!"

Brynn said to me, "I know what willpower is! That means when you want to wake up your mommy and daddy but you know you shouldn't. So you don't.

"Now I'm going to set the table and make breakfast!" And she did.

Michael called me in to show me that he made his bed for the first time. He was jumping up and down with excitement. I didn't have the heart to tell him that the spread didn't cover the pillows or that it was dragging on the floor on one side and short on the other. I just said, "Wow, you got the spread to cover most of the bed!"

The next morning he called me in again and said, "See, I got it to cover the pillow, too. And I made the sides even!"

It was amazing to me. I always thought that for a child to improve you had to point out what they did wrong. But by my telling Michael what he did right he seemed to want to improve on his own.

It bothered me that Hans never takes initiative for doing any job around the house. By the age of nine, I feel he should be taking more responsibility.

Tuesday night I asked him to set the table. Usually he needs constant prodding to finish a task, but this time he did it all with no reminders. I said to my husband, within earshot of Hans, "Frank, did you see what Hans did? He got the placemats out, the dishes, the salad bowl, the napkins, the silverware, and he even remembered your beer! That's really taking full responsibility." There was no apparent reaction from Hans.

Later when I went upstairs to put my younger son to bed, I asked Hans to come up in fifteen minutes. He said, "Okay."

In fifteen minutes he was up and in bed. I said, "I asked you to come up and be in bed in fifteen minutes and here you are—exactly on time. That's what I call being a person of your word." Hans smiled.

The next day Hans came into the kitchen before supper and said, "Mom, I came to set the table."

I was thunderstruck. I said, "You came before I called you. I really appreciate that!"

Since then I've been noticing scattered instances of change. One morning he made the bed without being asked; another morning he dressed before breakfast. It seems the more I look for the best in him, the easier it is for him to be better.

I used to operate on the reward system. Whenever I was worried that Melissa might not behave, I'd say, "If you're good, I'll buy you ice cream or a new toy or—whatever." Melissa would be good that one time, but then I had to promise her another reward for the next time.

Recently I've stopped saying, "If you're good, I'll . . ." Instead, I say, "Melissa, it would be helpful to me if . . ." And when she does do something helpful, I try to describe it back to her.

For example, last weekend I told her that it would be helpful if she made her grandparents feel welcome when they visited. When they came on Sunday, she was terrific with them. After they left I told her, "Melissa, you made Granny and Pop so happy when they were here. You told them jokes, offered them some of your trick-or-treat candy, and you showed them your gum-wrapper collection. That's what I call hospitality!" Melissa just glowed.

With the old way, she felt good for the moment because she got a reward. With this new way, she feels good about herself as a person.

Often children can use praise at the very times that we're least likely to give it to them—when they're *not* doing especially well. In these next two examples you'll see parents praising under difficult circumstances.

Last year (in third grade) Lisa's penmanship was awful. The teacher mentioned it to me. I felt as if I myself had been criticized. I began to point out to Lisa, every night, how sloppy her homework was and how poorly formed her letters were.

A few months later, Lisa wrote a note to the teacher saying how much she liked her. The note wasn't signed. When I mentioned to Lisa that she forgot to sign the note, she said, "The teacher will know it's from me, because of the bad handwriting."

My heart sank! The child said it so matter-of-factly, because she had accepted the fact that her writing was poor and nothing could be done.

After reading *Liberated Parents/Liberated Children*, I began all over. Each night that Lisa showed me her homework, instead of criticizing I would find one neat sentence, or one word, or at least one neat letter and comment on it. After a few months of no criticizing, and a little deserved praise, her handwriting has improved 100 percent!

This was one day I was glad for whatever skills I knew. I was driving home with my children—two, six, and nine years old. Jennifer, my six-year-old, decided to open up a big plastic bowl of popcorn—which, of course, she spilled all over the car. All kinds of responses went through my hassled brain: "Greedy kid . . . couldn't you wait till we got home . . . now look at what you've done!"

Instead, I just described the problem in a matter-of-fact voice. I said, "Popcorn is all over the car. That needs a vacuum."

When we arrived home, Jennifer immediately went into the house to get the vacuum cleaner out of my room. However, nothing ever goes smoothly. When Jennifer took out the vacuum cleaner, she knocked over a plant and there was dirt all over my bedroom. This was too much for a six-year-old to handle. She completely broke down in hysterical tears.

For a moment I didn't know what to do. Then I tried to reflect her feelings: "This is just too much! . . . How frustrating!" and so on, and so on. She eventually calmed down enough to tackle the car, but the thought of the bedroom was still too much.

She cleaned the car and called me out to see it. Instead of evaluating her, I observed, "There was popcorn all over the car and now I don't see one piece."

She was so pleased with herself, she said, "And *now* I'm going to clean your bedroom."

"Oh, I see," I said, rejoicing inside.

A few parents found that it was even possible to use praise at the most unlikely times—when their children did something they shouldn't. Instead of scolding the children, they inspired them to do better by reminding them of their past praiseworthy behavior. Here's one mother's account:

When Karen told me she lost her subway pass and that she thought it fell out of her pocket, my first impulse was to bawl her out for being so careless. But she looked so miserable that I said, "Come to think of it, Karen, you've held on to your subway pass for the last three and a half terms of high school. That's a lot of days of being responsible."

Karen said, "I guess so. But still I'm not taking any more chances. When I get my new one, I'm keeping it in my wallet."

Another dividend that came from descriptive praise was the courage it seemed to generate in some children. The following experiences illustrate what we mean:

Kristin is eight, and as far back as I can remember she

has always been afraid of the dark. She'd jump out of bed a dozen times after we put her to sleep to go to the bathroom, to get a drink of water, or just to make sure we were there.

Last week her report card arrived. It was full of praise. She spent the whole day admiring it and reading it over to herself again and again. Just before bedtime she said to me, quoting her report card, "A girl who is responsible, who works well with others, who obeys the rules, who is respectful of others, who reads fourth-grade books but is only in third grade—*she won't be afraid of what's not there!* I'm going to sleep."

She went to bed that night and I didn't see her until the next morning.

I can't wait to see the teacher on Open School Night to let him know what his words meant to one little girl.

Brian is nine years old and has always been shy and lacking in confidence. I've been listening to his feelings a lot lately, trying not to give him advice—the way I always do—and giving him lots of praise instead. Two days ago we had this conversation:

BRIAN: Mom, I'm having problems with Mrs. I. She's always picking on me and making remarks to the class about me.

MOM: Oh.

BRIAN: Yes, you know when I got my hair cut she said, "Look, class, we have a new boy in school."

MOM: Hmmm.

BRIAN: And then when I wore my new checkered pants she said, "Oh, look at Mr. Fancy Pants."

MOM: (*unable to resist*) Do you think you should have a talk with her?

BRIAN: I already did. I asked her, "How come you always seem to be picking on me?" She said,

"One more crack like that and I'll send you to the headmaster's office."

Mommy, I felt so low. What can I do? If I go to the headmaster and tell him, she'll really be on my back.

MOM: Hmmm.

BRIAN: Well, maybe I'll stick it out. There are only thirty more days left.

MOM: That's true.

BRIAN: No, I just can't stand it. I think you'd better go up to school with me.

MOM: Brian, I think you're mature enough to handle this situation. I have great confidence in you. Chances are you'll do the right thing. (*kiss and hug*)

The next day:

BRIAN: Mommy, I feel so *good* about myself. I went to the headmaster and he said I had courage to come to him, and he was glad that I was strong enough to, and he was glad I thought enough of him to share my problem with him. That's why he's there, you know!

MOM: You handled that difficult situation all by yourself!

BRIAN: (*looking ten feet tall*) Yeah!

This final example shows the inspirational effects a coach's descriptive praise had on a young soccer team. After each game, each member of the team of nine- and ten-year-olds would receive a letter from him. Here are excerpts from three of those letters:

September 16

Dear Tomahawks,

Sunday you were nothing short of a POWERHOUSE. On offense we exploded for six goals, the most for any game this year. On defense we kept the ball in their end of the field all game, with their only goal coming when the outcome of the game was no longer in doubt.

Practice will be Saturday, Willets Field, 10:00–11:15 A.M. See you then.

Sincerely,
Bob Gordon
Coach

October 23

Dear Tomahawks:

WHAT A GAME! WHAT A TEAM!
Not only did our "orange-crush" defense shut out one of the top scoring teams in the league, but you also held them to only a few good shots on goal. Our offensive attack was really balanced, with five players scoring goals. More importantly, many of these goals were the result of good passing and good position-playing. This victory was truly a team victory, with everyone making important contributions.
We are still in second place, one point behind the Poncas, with two games remaining. However, no matter how we finish, you can all be proud of the way you played this season.
We have our usual practice on Saturday at Willets Field, 10:00–11:15 A.M.
See you then.

Sincerely,
Bob Gordon
Coach

November 18

Dear *CHAMPIONS:*

This weekend's games were the most exciting I have ever seen. All during the year the Tomahawks have shown their great offense and their great defense. This weekend they showed their great heart and fighting spirit. Even though time appeared to be running out, you never gave up and you came away with a thrilling victory you so richly deserved.

Congratulations to all of you: you are champions one and all.

Sincerely,
Bob Gordon
Coach

# 6 | Freeing Children from Playing Roles

I remember the moment when my son, David, was born. Five seconds had gone by and he still hadn't breathed. I was terrified. The nurse slapped him on his back. No response. The tension was excruciating. She said, "He's a stubborn one!" Still no response. A moment later he finally cried—that piercing sound of the newborn. My relief was indescribable. But later on that day I found myself wondering, "Is he really stubborn?" By the time I brought him home from the hospital, I had put the nurse's comment in its place—foolish words from a foolish woman. Imagine putting a label on an infant less than half a minute old!

And yet every time during the next few years, when he kept on crying no matter how long I patted or rocked him, when he wouldn't try a new food, when he refused to take his nap, when he balked at getting on the bus to nursery school, when he wouldn't wear a sweater on a cold day, the thought would flit through my mind, "She was right. He is stubborn."

I should have known better. All the psychology courses I had taken had warned of the dangers of the self-fulfilling prophecy. If you labeled a child as a slow learner, he could begin to see himself as a slow learner. If you saw a child as mischievous, chances are he'd start showing you just how mischievous he could be. Labeling a child was to be avoided at all costs. I agreed completely, and yet I couldn't stop thinking of David as a "stubborn kid."

The only comfort I had was in knowing I wasn't alone. At least once a week, I'd hear some parent, somewhere, say something like:

"My oldest is my problem child. The youngest is a pleasure."

"Bobby is a born bully."

"Billy is a pushover. Anyone can take advantage of him."

"Michael is the lawyer in the family. He's got an answer for everything."

"I don't know what to feed Julie anymore. She's such a picky eater."

"It's a waste of money to buy anything new for Richie. He destroys everything he lays his hands on. The boy is just plain destructive."

I used to wonder how these children acquired their labels to begin with. Now, after years of hearing about what goes on inside families, I realize that the casting of a child in a role could start very innocently. For instance, one morning Mary says to brother, "Get me my glasses."

Brother says, "Get them yourself, and quit bossing."

Later she says to Mother, "Brush my hair and make sure you get out all the knots." Mother says, "Mary, you're being bossy again."

Still later, she says to Daddy, "Don't talk now. I'm watching my show." Daddy responds, "Listen to the big boss!"

And, little by little, the child who has been given the name begins to play the game. After all, if everyone calls Mary bossy, then that's what she must be.

You may be wondering, "Is it okay to think of your child as bossy as long as you don't call her by that name?" That's an important question. Can the way a parent even thinks about a child affect the way a child thinks about herself? In order to become more clear about the relationship between how parents see their children and how children see themselves, let's try this experiment now. As you read the next three scenes, imagine that you are the child in each of them.

*Scene I:* You're about eight years old. One evening you walk into your living room and find your parents working on a big jigsaw puzzle together. As soon as you see what they're doing, you ask if you can do the puzzle with them.

Mother says, "Did you do your homework yet? Were you able to understand it?"

You say, "Yes," and ask again if you can help with the puzzle.

Mother says, "Are you sure you understood all the homework?"

Father says, "I'll go over the math with you a little later."

Again, you ask to help.

Father says, "Watch carefully how Mom and I do the puzzle and then we'll let you see if you can put in one piece."

As you start to lower a piece into place, Mother says, "No, dear. Can't you see that piece has a straight edge? How can you put a straight edge in the middle of a puzzle!" She sighs heavily.

How do your parents see you?

_____

How does their view of you make you feel?

_____

_____

_____

*Scene II:* The same. You come into the living room and find your parents working on a puzzle. You ask to join them.

Mother says, "Don't you have something else to do? Why don't you go watch television?"

Your eye suddenly spots a piece for the chimney in the puzzle. You reach for it.

Mother says, "Watch out! You'll ruin what we've done."

Father says, "Can't we ever have a peaceful moment?"

You say, "Please, just this one piece!"

Father says, "You never give up, do you?"

Mother says, "Okay, *one* piece, but that's it!" She looks at Father, shakes her head, and rolls her eyes.

How do your parents see you?

_____

How does their view of you make you feel?

_____

_____

_____

*Scene III:* The same. As you see your parents working on a puzzle, you step closer to look at it.

You ask, "Can I help?"

Mother nods and says, "Sure, if you like."

Father says, "Pull up a chair."

You see a piece that you're certain is part of the cloud and lower it into place. It doesn't fit.

Mother says, "Almost!"

Father says, "Pieces with straight sides generally go on the edge."

Your parents continue to work on the puzzle. You study the picture for a while. Finally, you find the right place for your piece.

You say, "Look, it fits!"

Mother smiles.

Dad says, "You really persisted with that one."

How do your parents see you?

_____

How does their view of you make you feel?

_____

_____

_____

_____

Were you surprised at how easily you got the message of how your parents saw you? Sometimes it takes no more than a few words, a look, or a tone of voice to tell you that you're either "slow and stupid," "a pest," or a basically likable and capable person. How your parents think of you can often be communicated in seconds. When you multiply those seconds by the hours of daily contact between parents and children, you begin to realize how powerfully young people can be influenced by the way their parents view them. Not only are their feelings about themselves affected, but so is their behavior.

When you were doing this exercise and your parents saw you as "slow," did you feel your confidence begin to go? Would you even attempt to do more of the puzzle yourself? Did you feel frustrated because you weren't as quick as everyone else around you? Did you say to yourself, "Why even try?"

When you were seen as a "nuisance," did you feel that you had to assert yourself in order not to be pushed away? Did you feel rejected and defeated? Or did you feel angry—as if you wanted to mess up their stupid puzzle and get back at them?

When you were seen as a basically likable and competent person, did you feel as if you could behave in a likable and competent way? If you made a few mistakes, would you be tempted to give up or would you tell yourself to try again?

Whatever your reactions, it seems safe to conclude that the way parents see their children can influence not only the way children see themselves but also the way they behave.

But what if a child has already been cast in a role, for whatever reason? Does that mean he has to play out that part for the rest of his life? Is he stuck with it, or can he be freed to become whatever he's capable of becoming?

On the next few pages you'll see six skills that can be used by any parent who wants to liberate his child from playing out a role.

## To Free Children from Playing Roles

1. Look for opportunities to show the child a new picture of himself or herself.

2. Put children in situations where they can see themselves differently.

3. Let children overhear you say something positive about them.

4. Model the behavior you'd like to see.

5. Be a storehouse for your child's special moments.

6. When your child behaves according to the old label, state your feelings and/or your expectations.

# LOOK FOR OPPORTUNITIES TO SHOW THE CHILD A NEW PICTURE OF HIMSELF OR HERSELF.

# PUT CHILDREN IN SITUATIONS WHERE
# THEY CAN SEE THEMSELVES DIFFERENTLY.

Mischievous

Scatterbrain

All-thumbs

Greedy

# LET CHILDREN OVERHEAR YOU SAY
# SOMETHING POSITIVE ABOUT THEM.

Crybaby

Excitable

# MODEL THE BEHAVIOR YOU'D LIKE TO SEE.

Sore ~~loser~~

Disorganized

# BE A STOREHOUSE FOR
## YOUR CHILD'S SPECIAL MOMENTS.

Uncoordinated

# WHEN YOUR CHILD BEHAVES ACCORDING TO THE OLD LABEL, STATE YOUR FEELINGS AND/OR YOUR EXPECTATIONS.

 Greedy

 Whiner

The skills for helping a child view himself differently are not limited to the ones in this chapter alone. All the skills you worked on in this book can be useful to hold open the door to change. For example, one mother who used to call her son "a forgetter" wrote this note to help him think of himself as a person who could remember when he wanted to.

Dear George,
Your music teacher called today to tell me that you didn't have your trumpet for the last two orchestra rehearsals.
I trust you'll find a way to remind yourself to bring it from now on.

Mom

A father decided to problem-solve instead of calling his son a bully. He said, "Jason, I know it makes you angry when you're trying to concentrate on your homework and your brother whistles, but hitting is *out*. How else can you go about getting the quiet you need?"

Does it seem difficult to you—this whole idea of helping a child view himself differently? I don't know of any harder demand that can be made of a parent. When a child persistently behaves in any one way over a period of time, it requires great restraint on our part not to reinforce the negative behavior by shouting, "There you go again!" It takes an act of will to put aside the time to deliberately plan a campaign that will free a child from the role he's been playing.

If you can take the time now, ask yourself:

1. Is there any role my child might have been cast in—either at home, in school, by friends, or by relatives? What is that role?

---

2. Is there anything positive about the role? (For instance, a spirit of fun in the "mischief-maker"; the imagination of the "daydreamer.")

_____

_____

3. How would you like your child to think of himself or herself? (capable of being responsible, capable of seeing a job through to the end, etc.)

_____

_____

_____

_____

By answering these difficult questions, you've done the preliminary work. The real campaign lies ahead. Take a look now at the skills listed below. Then write down the actual words you might use to put each skill into action.

A. *Look for opportunities to show this child a new picture of himself or herself.*

_____

_____

_____

_____

B. *Put the child in a situation where he or she can see himself or herself differently.*

_____

_____

_____

_____

C. *Let the child overhear you say something positive about him or her.*

_____

_____

_____

_____

D. *Model the behavior you'd like to see.*

_____

_____

_____

_____

E. *Be a storehouse for your child's finest moments.*

_____

_____

_____

_____

F. *When he or she behaves according to the old label, state your feelings and your expectations.*

_____

_____

_____

_____

G. *Are there any other skills you can think of that might be effective?*

_____

_____

_____

_____

The exercise you just completed was one I did myself many years ago. What made me do it? One evening when I picked David up at his scout meeting, the scoutmaster signaled me to step into the next room with him. His expression was grim.

"What is it?" I asked nervously.

"I wanted to talk to you about David. We've been having our little problems."

"Problems?"

"David refuses to follow instructions."

"I don't understand. For what? You mean for the project he's working on now?"

He tried to smile patiently. "I mean for *all* the projects we've been working on since the beginning of the year. When your son gets an idea in his head, you can't budge him. He has his own way of doing things and he won't listen to reason. Frankly, the other boys are getting a little fed up with him. He takes up a lot of the group's time. . . . Is he stubborn at home, too?"

I don't remember what I answered. I babbled something, herded David into the car, and left quickly. David was quiet on the way home. I turned on the radio—grateful not to have to talk. My stomach was in such a knot, it ached.

I felt as if David had finally been "found out." For years I had been pretending to myself that he was just a little bit stubborn at home—with me, with his father, with his sister and brother. But now there was no running away from the truth. The outside world had confirmed what I had never been willing to face. David was rigid, obstinate, inflexible.

It was hours before I could fall asleep. I lay there blaming David for not being like the other kids and blaming myself for all the times I had called him a "mule" or a "stubborn ox." It wasn't until the next morning that I could put the scoutmaster's view of my son in perspective and begin to think about how to be helpful to David.

There was one thing I was sure of. It was important for me *not* to jump on the bandwagon and push David further into this role. My job was to look for and affirm his best. (If I didn't, who would?) Okay, so he was "strong-willed" and "determined." But he was also capable of being open-minded and flexible. And that's the part that needed validating.

I made a list of all the skills I knew for helping a child see himself differently. Then I tried to think of the kind of situation that had caused David to balk in the past. What could I say to him if anything like it happened again? Here's what I came up with:

A) *Look for opportunities to show the child another picture of himself.* "David, you agreed to come to Grandma's with us, even though you really wanted to stay home and play with a friend. That was 'giving' of you."

B) *Put the child in a situation where he can see himself differently.* "Each member of this family seems to want to go to a different restaurant. David, maybe you can come up with an idea that could break the deadlock."

C) *Let the child overhear you say something positive about him.* "Dad, David and I worked out a compromise this morning. He didn't want to wear boots. I didn't want him sitting around in school with wet feet. Finally, he thought of the idea of wearing his old sneakers to school and bringing along a pair of dry socks and his good sneakers to change into."

D) *Model the behavior you'd like to see.* "I'm so disappointed! I had my heart set on seeing a movie tonight, and Dad reminded me that we had agreed to go to a basketball game. . . . Oh well, I guess I can put the movie off for one more week."

E) *Be a storehouse for your child's special moments.* "I remember how at first you had some strong feelings against going to that Boy Scout camp. But then you began to think about it, and read about it, and talk to some of the other kids who went there. And eventually you decided to try it for yourself."

F) *When your child acts according to his old label, state your feelings and/or your expectations.* "David, to people at a wedding, old jeans seem like a mark of disrespect. To them it's as if you're saying, 'This wedding isn't important!' So, as much as you hate the thought of wearing a suit and tie, I expect you to dress appropriately."

G) *Are there any other skills that might be helpful?* More acceptance of David's negative feelings. More choices. More problem-solving.

This was the exercise that changed my direction with David. It made it possible for me to see him in a new light, and then to treat him as I had begun to see him. There were no dramatic overnight results. Some days went very well. It seemed the more I appreciated David's capacity to be flexible, the more flexible he was able to be. And some days were still pretty bad. My anger and frustration would drive me right back to square one, and I'd find myself in a shouting match with him all over again.

But over the long haul I refused to become discouraged. I hung on to my new attitude. This "determined" son of mine had an equally "determined" mother.

The little boy is grown now. Just recently when he wouldn't listen to reason (that is, my point of view), I became so upset that I forgot myself and accused him of being "pigheaded."

He seemed startled and was quiet for a moment.

"Is that how you see me?" he asked.

"Well, I . . . I . . ." I stammered with embarrassment.

"That's okay, Mom," he said gently. "Thanks to you, I have another opinion of myself."

*A Quick Reminder . . .*

---

### To Free Children from
### Playing Roles

1. LOOK FOR OPPORTUNITIES TO SHOW THE CHILD A NEW PICTURE OF HIMSELF OR HERSELF.

   "You've had that toy since you were three and it almost looks like new!"

2. PUT CHILDREN IN SITUATIONS WHERE THEY CAN SEE THEMSELVES DIFFERENTLY.

   "Sara, would you take the screwdriver and tighten the pulls on these drawers?"

3. LET CHILDREN OVERHEAR YOU SAY SOMETHING POSITIVE ABOUT THEM.

   "He held his arm steady even though the shot hurt."

4. MODEL THE BEHAVIOR YOU'D LIKE TO SEE.

   "It's hard to lose, but I'll try to be a sport about it. Congratulations!"

5. BE A STOREHOUSE FOR YOUR CHILD'S SPECIAL MOMENTS.

   "I remember the time you . . ."

6. WHEN YOUR CHILD ACTS ACCORDING TO THE OLD LABEL, STATE YOUR FEELINGS AND/OR YOUR EXPECTATIONS.

   "I don't like that. Despite your strong feelings, I expect sportsmanship from you."

---

## PART II: PARENTS' STORIES—
## PRESENT AND PAST

Here are the experiences of several parents who were determined to free their children from the roles in which they had been cast:

During the sessions on putting children in roles, I began to feel sick to my stomach. I thought of how disgusted I've been with Greg recently and about the awful things I've been saying to him:

"I wish you could see yourself. You're acting like such a jerk."

"Why are you always the one to hold everyone up?"

"I guess I shouldn't expect any more of you. I should know by now how nasty you are."

"You'll never have any friends."

"Act your age. You're behaving like a two-year-old."

"You eat so sloppy. You'll never learn to eat properly."

I thought of him as my "nemesis" and I never let up on him. To top it off I had a conference with his teacher this week and she complained that he was immature. Awhile ago, I probably would have agreed with her, but that day her words hit me like a ton of bricks. I figured the situation couldn't get much worse, so I decided to try some of the things from our sessions.

At the beginning I found I was too angry to be nice. I knew Greg needed some positive feedback, but I could hardly talk to him. So I wrote him a note the first time he did something right. I wrote:

Dear Greg:

I had a nice day yesterday. You made it easy for me to get out on time for the Sunday school car pool. You were up, dressed, and waiting for me.

Thanks.

Mom

A few days later I had to take him to the dentist. As usual he began running all over the office. I took off my watch and handed it to him. I said, "I know you can sit still for five minutes." He looked surprised, but he did sit down and was quiet until the dentist called him in.

After the dentist I did something I never did before. I took him out alone for a hot chocolate. We actually had a conversation. That night when I put him to bed I told him that I enjoyed the time we spent together.

I find it hard to believe that those few little things could have made a difference to Greg, but he seems to want to please me more, which encourages me. For instance, he left his book and jacket on the floor of the kitchen. Normally that would be my cue to scream at him. Instead, I told him that it made me mad to have to pick up after him but that I had confidence he'd remember from now on to put his things where they belong.

And at dinner I stopped criticizing his table manners every second. The only time I say anything is if he does something absolutely gross, and then I try to say it only once.

I'm also trying to give him more responsibility around the house in the hope that he will start behaving more maturely. I ask him to take clothes out of the dryer, to unload the groceries and put them away, and other things like that. I even let him scramble his own egg the other morning. (And I kept my mouth shut when some of the egg landed on the floor.)

I'm almost afraid to say it, but his behavior is definitely better. Maybe it's because I'm better with him.

•  •  •

Heather is adopted. From the first day she came to us, she was a joy. And she continued to grow into a sweet, adorable child. I thought of her not only as my pride and joy but I'd tell her a dozen times a day what happiness she brought to me. It wasn't until I read your chapter on roles that I wondered whether I might be placing too heavy a burden on her to be "good," to be "my pleasure." I also wondered whether there might be other feelings inside her that she was afraid to show.

My concern led me to try a number of things that were new. I suppose the most important thing I did was to think of ways to let Heather know that all her feelings were okay, that it was all right to be angry, upset, or frustrated. When I was a half hour late one day in picking her up from school I said, "It must have been irritating for you to have to wait so long for me." (This was instead of my usual "Thank you for being so patient, sweetheart.") Another time I told her, "I bet you felt like giving your friend a piece of your mind for breaking a date with you!" (Instead of my usual "Well, honey, other people just aren't as considerate as you.")

I also tried to model what I wanted for her. I began to allow myself to talk about my own negative feelings more often. The other day I told her, "I'm feeling crabby now and I'd like some time to myself." And when she asked to borrow my new scarf I told her that I didn't feel like sharing it just yet.

I tried to praise her differently. Instead of carrying on about how happy her schoolwork made me, I described what *she* had accomplished ("This is a clear and well-organized report"), and let it go at that.

The other morning was a first. Heather was in the shower and I was rinsing a few dishes. She banged on the wall and I turned the hot water down halfway. Later she came storming into the kitchen and yelled at the top of her lungs, "I *asked* you not to run the hot water. I had a freezing-cold shower!!"

If she had done that a month ago, I would have been shocked. I would have told her, "Heather, that's not like you to behave that way!"

This time I said, "I can hear how angry you are! And I'm making a mental note not to use any hot water *at all* the next time you're in the shower!"

I have the feeling Heather is going to be "expressing herself" a lot more in the future, and I'm sure I won't like everything I hear; but in the long run, I still think it's more important for her to be real than to have to continue being "mother's joy."

P.S. Now whenever I hear people telling me how "good" their children are, I'm a little suspicious.

• • •

Yesterday I was in the playground with my two daughters. About four times I heard myself call out to Kate, the older one (eight), "Keep an eye on Wendy." . . . "Hold on to her when she walks up the slide." . . . "Be sure to stay close to her."

I began to wonder if I was casting Kate in the role of Responsible Older Sister. It's true, I was giving her a lot of trust, but maybe I was giving her a lot of pressure, too. And yet, in practical terms, I often needed her help.

I also began to wonder if I was treating Wendy (five) as too much of a baby. I'm not planning to have any more children, so I guess I'm happy to treat her that way. After all, she *is* my baby.

The more I thought about it, the more I realized that Kate is probably resentful. She's been refusing to walk home with Wendy from summer play school, and she won't read to her anymore. I also realized that at Wendy's age Kate was doing things for herself that Wendy still isn't doing, like pouring her own milk.

I haven't done anything about it yet, but I'm slowly getting a conviction about what both my daughters need. Wendy needs to be helped to become more self-reliant, mostly for her own sake but also so there's less pressure on Kate. And Kate needs to have a choice about whether she wants to take care of her sister, except when I absolutely need her help. And maybe I can give Kate a little babying too, once in a while. It's been a long time since I've done that.

• • •

It was lucky for Neil that I made it to the group last week. When I came home that morning I got a call from my next-door neighbor. Her voice was shaking. She saw Neil pick three of her prize tulips on the way to school.

I was beside myself. I thought, "Here we go again!" He'll deny that he had anything to do with it, just the way he did when he took the clock apart. (Later, I found the pieces in his room.) And the way he did when he told me he skipped a grade. (When I called the teacher, she told me no one ever skips anymore.) He's been lying so much lately, even his brother has been saying, "Ma, Neil's lying again!"

I know I haven't handled it well. I always demand that he tell me the truth, and when he doesn't I usually call him a liar, or give him a lecture on lying, or punish him. I suppose I've just been making things worse, but honesty is so important to me and my husband. I can't understand how Neil could be this way.

Anyway, as I said before, I was lucky I had a session on roles, because even though I was very upset, I knew I didn't want to put Neil in the role of "liar" again.

When he came home for lunch, I didn't fence with him. ("Did you? Are you sure you didn't? Don't lie to me this time.") I got right to the point. I said, "Neil, Mrs. Osgood told me you picked her tulips."

"No, I didn't. It wasn't me!"

"Neil, she saw you. She was standing at the window."

"You think *I'm* a liar. *She's* the one that's a liar!"

"Neil, I don't want to talk about who's lying and who isn't. The thing is done. For some reason you decided to pick three of her tulips. Now we have to think about how to make amends."

Neil started to cry. "I wanted some flowers for my teacher."

I said, "Oh. So that was why. Thank you for telling me what happened. . . . Sometimes it's hard to tell the truth, especially if you think it might get you into trouble."

Then he really started to sob.

I put him on my lap. I said, "Neil, I can hear how sorry you are. Mrs. Osgood is very upset. What can be done?"

Neil burst into tears again. "I'm afraid to tell her I'm sorry!"

"Can you write it?"

"I don't know . . . Help me."

We made up a little note and he printed it (he's in first grade).

I said, "Do you think that's enough?"

He looked bewildered.

"How would you feel about buying her a pot of tulips to fill in the empty spot?"

Neil broke into a big smile. "Could we?"

Right after school we went to a florist. Neil picked out a pot with four tulips, and he delivered the pot and his note to Mrs. Osgood's doorstep. Then he rang the bell and ran home.

I don't think he'll pick her flowers again, and somehow I don't think he'll lie so much anymore. I just know he'll be more open with me from now on. And when he isn't (I guess I've got to be realistic) I won't put him in the role of liar. I'll find a way to make it possible for him to tell me the truth.

• • •

One day, toward the end of a session on roles, a father started us reminiscing. He said, "I remember when I was a kid I used to come to my dad with all kinds of crazy schemes. He'd always listen to me very seriously. Then he'd say, 'Son, you may have your head in the clouds, but your feet are rooted in the ground.' Now, that picture he gave me of myself—as someone who dreams, but also someone who knows how to deal with reality—has been one that's helped me through some pretty rough times. . . . I was wondering whether anyone else here had that kind of experience."

There was a thoughtful silence as each of us began to reach into the past to look for the messages that had marked our lives. Slowly, together, we began to remember aloud:

"When I was a little boy, my grandmother always used to tell me I had wonderful hands. Whenever I'd thread a needle for her or untie the knots in her wool, she'd say I had *goldeneh hendt.*' I think it's one of the reasons I decided to become a dentist."

"My first year of teaching was overwhelming for me. I used to tremble whenever my chairman dropped in to observe a lesson. Afterward, he'd give me one or two pointers, but then he'd always add, 'I never worry about you, Ellen. Basically, you're self-correcting.' I wonder if he ever knew what an inspiration those words were to me. I hung on to them every day. They helped me believe in myself."

"When I was ten, my parents bought me a unicycle. For a month I mostly fell off it. I thought I'd never learn to ride the thing, but one day there I was pedaling along, keeping my balance! My mother thought I was remarkable. From then on, whenever I was worried about learning something new—like French, for instance—she'd say, 'Any girl who can ride a unicycle will have no trouble with French.' I knew she was being illogical. What did riding a unicycle have to do with learning a language? But I loved hearing it. That was almost thirty years ago. And, to this day, whenever I'm faced with a new challenge I hear my mother's voice: 'Any girl who can ride a unicycle . . .' I may laugh, but that image still helps me."

Almost everyone in the group had a memory to share.

When the session ended, we just sat there and looked at one another. The father who had started us all remembering shook his head in wonderment. When he spoke, he spoke for all of us. "Never underestimate the power of your words upon a young person's life!"

# 7 | Putting It All Together

Parents have pointed out to us that the process of freeing children from playing out roles is a complicated one. It involves not only a whole change of attitude toward a child but also requires a working knowledge of many skills. One father told us, "To change a role, you've really got to be able to put it all together—feelings, autonomy, praise, alternatives to punishment—the works."

In order to illustrate the contrast between the well-intentioned parent and the parent who relates with skill as well as love, we've written two scenes (based on characters in *Liberated Parents/Liberated Children*). In each of these, seven-year-old Susie tries to play out the role of "The Princess." As you observe how Mother copes with her daughter in this first scene, you might want to ask yourself, "What else could she have done?"

### The Princess—Part I

MOTHER: I'm home, everybody! . . . Hi, Susie! . . . Don't you say hello to your mother? (*Susie glances up sullenly and continues to color, ignoring her mother.*)

MOTHER: (*putting down her packages*) Well, I think I'm almost ready for tonight's company. I've got rolls, fruit, and (*dangling a paper bag in front of her daughter, trying to coax a smile from her*) a little surprise for Susie.

SUSIE: (*grabbing the bag*) What'd you get me? (*pulling things out one at a time*) Crayons? . . . That's good . . . pencil case . . . (*indignantly*) a blue notebook! You know I hate blue. Why didn't you buy me a red one?

MOTHER: (*defending herself*) It just so happens, young lady, that I went to two stores for you and neither of them had red notebooks. The supermarket was all out, and so was the stationery store.

SUSIE: Why didn't you try the store near the bank?

MOTHER: I didn't have time.

SUSIE: Well, go back. I don't want the blue.

MOTHER: Susie, I'm not going to make another trip just for a little notebook. I've got a lot to do today.

SUSIE: I won't use the blue notebook. You just wasted your money.

MOTHER: (*sighing*) Boy, are you spoiled! Always have to have everything your own way, don't you?

SUSIE: (*turning on the charm*) No I don't, but red is my favorite color. And blue is so yucky. Oh please, Mommy, please!

MOTHER: Well . . . Maybe I can go back later.

SUSIE: Oooh good. (*Goes back to coloring.*) Mommy?

MOTHER: Yes?

SUSIE: I want Betsy to sleep over tonight.

MOTHER: Now *that's* out of the question. You know Daddy and I are having dinner company tonight.

SUSIE: But she *has* to sleep over tonight. I already told her she could.

MOTHER: Well, call her back and tell her she can't.

SUSIE:     You're mean!

MOTHER:    I'm not mean. I just don't want children under-
           foot when I'm having company. Remember the
           way you two carried on last time?

SUSIE:     We won't bother you.

MOTHER:    (*loud*) The answer is no!

SUSIE:     You don't love me! (*starting to cry*)

MOTHER:    (*distressed*) Now, Susie, you know perfectly well
           I love you. (*cupping her chin tenderly*) Come on,
           who's my little princess?

SUSIE:     Oh please, Mommy, pretty please? We'll be so
           good.

MOTHER:    (*weakening for the moment*) Well . . . (*shaking
           her head*) Susie, it won't work out. Why do you
           always make it so hard for me? When I say "no"
           I mean "no!"

SUSIE:     (*throws coloring book on floor*) I hate you!

MOTHER:    (*grimly*) Since when do we throw books? Pick
           it up.

SUSIE:     I won't.

MOTHER:    Pick it up this instant!

SUSIE:     (*Shrieks at the top of her lungs and throws new
           crayons on the floor one at a time.*) No! No! No!
           No!

MOTHER:    Don't you dare throw those crayons!

SUSIE:     (*throwing another crayon*) I will if I want to.

MOTHER:    (*slapping Susie on the arm*) I said stop it, you
           little brat!

SUSIE:     (*shrieks*) You hit me! You hit me!

MOTHER:    You broke the crayons I bought you.

SUSIE:     (*crying hysterically*) Look! You made a mark.

MOTHER:    (*Very upset, she rubs Susie's arm.*) I'm so sorry,
           sweetheart. It's just a tiny scratch. It must have
           been my nail. It'll be better in no time.

SUSIE:     You *hurt* me!

| MOTHER: | You know I didn't mean it. Mommy wouldn't hurt you for the world. . . . You know what? Let's call up Betsy and tell her she can come tonight. Will that make you feel better? |
|---|---|
| SUSIE: | (*still teary*) Yeah. |

As you can see, there are times when love, spontaneity, and good intentions are simply not enough. When parents are on the firing line, they need skills, too.

As you read this next scene you'll see the same mother with the same child. Only this time she uses all her skills to help her daughter behave differently.

### *The Princess—Part II*

| MOTHER: | I'm home, everybody! . . . Hi, Susie. I see you're busy coloring. |
|---|---|
| SUSIE: | (*not looking up*) Yeah. |
| MOTHER: | (*putting down her packages*) There, I think I'm set for tonight's company. By the way, I picked up some school supplies for you while I was out. |
| SUSIE: | (*grabbing the bag*) What'd you buy me? (*pulling things out*) Crayons . . . that's good . . . pencil case . . . (*indignantly*) a blue notebook! You know I hate blue. Why didn't you buy me a red one? |
| MOTHER: | Why didn't I? |
| SUSIE: | (*hesitating*) Because the store didn't have a red one? |
| MOTHER: | (*crediting Susie*) You guessed it. |
| SUSIE: | Then you should have gone to another store. |
| MOTHER: | Susie, when I go out of my way to buy something special for my daughter, what I'd like to hear is: "Thanks, Mom . . . Thank you for the crayons . . . Thank you for the pencil case . . . Thank you for getting me a notebook—even if it isn't the color I like." |

SUSIE:      (*grudgingly*) Thank you . . . but I still think blue is yucky.

MOTHER:     No doubt about it, when it comes to color you are a person of definite taste!

SUSIE:      Yeah! . . . I'm making all the flowers red . . . Mom, can Betsy sleep over tonight?

MOTHER:     (*considering the request*) Daddy and I are having company tonight. But she's certainly welcome another night. Tomorrow? Next Saturday?

SUSIE:      But she *has* to sleep over tonight. I already told her she could.

MOTHER:     (*firmly*) As I see it, Susie, the choice is tomorrow night or next Saturday. Whichever you prefer.

SUSIE:      (*her lip quivering*) You don't love me.

MOTHER:     (*pulling up a chair next to her*) Susie, now is not the time to talk about love. Now we're trying to decide the best night for your friend to visit.

SUSIE:      (*teary*) The best night is tonight.

MOTHER:     (*persistently*) We want to find a time that meets your needs and my needs.

SUSIE:      I don't care about your needs! You're being mean to me! (*Throws coloring book on floor and starts to cry.*)

MOTHER:     Hey, I don't like that! Books are not for throwing! (*Picks up book, dusts it off.*) Susie, when you feel strongly about something, tell me your feelings with words. Tell me, "Mom, I'm angry! . . . I'm very upset! . . . I was counting on Betsy sleeping over tonight."

SUSIE:      (*accusingly*) We were going to make chocolate chip cookies together and watch television!

MOTHER:     I see.

SUSIE:      And Betsy was going to bring her sleeping bag and I was going to put my mattress on the floor next to her.

MOTHER: You had the whole evening worked out!

SUSIE: We did! We were talking about it all day in school today.

MOTHER: To look forward to something and then to have to change your plans can be pretty frustrating.

SUSIE: That's right! So can she come tonight, Mommy, please . . . please . . . pretty please?

MOTHER: I wish tonight were good for me because you want it so much. It isn't. (*Stands up.*) Susie, I'm going into the kitchen now—

SUSIE: But, Mommy . . .

MOTHER: (*as she leaves*) And while I'm preparing dinner I'll be knowing how very disappointed you are.

SUSIE: But, Mommy . . .

MOTHER: (*calling out from kitchen*) As soon as you decide what other night you want Betsy to visit, please let me know.

SUSIE: (*Picks up the phone and calls friend.*) Hello, Betsy. You can't come tonight . . . My parents are having some dumb company. You can come tomorrow or next Saturday.

In this second dramatization, Mother had the skills she needed to keep Susie from playing out the role of "Princess." Wouldn't it be wonderful if in real life we too were able to always come up with the kind of responses that were helpful to our children and helpful to ourselves?

But life isn't a neat little script that can be memorized and performed. The real-life dramas that children engage us in every day don't give us time for rehearsal or careful thought. However, with our new guidelines, though we may do and say things we regret, we have a very clear direction to which we can return. There are basic principles we can depend on. We know that we can't go too far wrong if we take time to listen to our children's feelings, or talk about our own feelings, or work in terms of future solutions, rather than past blame. We may be thrown off course temporarily, but chances are we'll never lose our way completely again.

One final thought: Let's not cast ourselves in roles either— good parent, bad parent, permissive parent, authoritarian parent. Let's start thinking of ourselves as human beings first, with great potential for growth and change. The process of living or working with children is demanding and exhausting. It requires heart, intelligence, and stamina. When we don't live up to our own expectations—and we won't always—let's be as kind to ourselves as we are to our youngsters. If our children deserve a thousand chances, and then one more, let's give ourselves a thousand chances—and then two more.

# What's It All About, Anyway?

Just by reading this book you've asked a great deal of yourself. There have been new principles to absorb, new skills to put into practice, new patterns to learn, and old patterns to unlearn. With so much to sort out and make your own, it's sometimes hard not to lose sight of the larger picture. So once again, for the last time, let's take a look at what this method of communication is all about.

We want to find a way to live with one another so that we can feel good about ourselves and help the people we love feel good about themselves.

We want to find a way to live without blame and recrimination.

We want to find a way to be more sensitive to one another's feelings.

We want to find a way to express our irritation or anger without doing damage.

We want to find a way to be respectful of our children's needs and to be just as respectful of our own needs.

We want to find a way that makes it possible for our children to be caring and responsible.

We want to break the cycle of unhelpful talk that has been handed down from generation to generation, and pass on a different legacy to our children—a way of communicating that they can use for the rest of their lives, with their friends, their coworkers, their parents, their mates, and one day with children of their own.

# Afterword

# Many Years Later

Dear Reader,

When *How to Talk* . . . was first published back in 1980, we had our fingers crossed. We weren't at all sure how people would react. The format was so different from our first book. *Liberated Parents/Liberated Children* was the story of our personal experiences. This book was basically a version of the workshops we had been giving around the country. Would parents find it helpful?

We knew how people responded when we worked with them directly. Whenever we'd present a two-part program (evening lecture followed by a morning workshop), we'd find that even before the morning session began parents would be waiting for us—eager to tell how, overnight, they had tried a new skill and how pleased they were with the results.

But that happened because we were there in person—role-playing with the audience, answering their questions, illustrating each principle with examples, using all our energies to drive home our convictions. Would readers be able to "get it" from the pages of a book?

They did. In numbers that astonished us. Our publisher informed us they were printing additional copies to meet the demand. An article in the *New York Times* reported that of the hundreds of parenting books flooding the market, *How to Talk* . . . was one of the "top ten sellers." PBS produced a six-part series based on each chapter. But the biggest surprise came from the amount of mail that filled our boxes. Letters arrived in a steady stream, not only from the United States and Canada but from countries all over the globe, some so small or unfamiliar we had to look them up in an atlas.

Most people wrote to express their appreciation. Many described, in some detail, just how our book had touched their lives. They wanted us to know exactly what they were doing differently now—what was working with their children and what wasn't. It seemed that parents everywhere, no matter how different the culture, were dealing with similar problems and searching for answers.

There was another theme that emerged in the letters. People spoke of how hard it was to change old habits: "When I remember to use my skills everything goes better, but too often I revert, especially when I'm under pressure." They also expressed a desire for additional help: "I want this approach to be a more natural part of me. I need practice and support. Do you have any materials my friends and I can use to study these methods together?"

We understood their needs. As young mothers, we had sat in a room with other parents and discussed each skill, and struggled together to come up with the most respectful, effective ways to deal with the endless challenges presented by children. It was because we knew how valuable the group experience could be that we conceived the idea of writing a series of do-it-yourself workshops based on our book. We felt sure that if parents were given an easy-to-follow, step-by-step program they could learn and practice the skills together, on their own, without the help of a trained leader.

Our "master plan" worked. Parents organized groups, ordered our workshop materials, and really were able to use them successfully. But what we hadn't anticipated was the number of professionals requesting and using the *How to Talk* . . . program. We heard from psychiatrists, psychologists, social workers, educators, ministers, priests, and rabbis.

We were also surprised by the variety of organizations using

our materials—domestic-violence crisis centers, drug and alcohol rehabilitation units, juvenile probation departments, the
Boy Scouts, state prisons, schools for the deaf, Head Start, and
military bases in the United States and abroad. Eventually,
more than 150,000 groups around the world had used or were
using our audio and video programs.

All during this time, we would receive a persistent request,
mostly from social-service agencies, "Parents desperately need
communication skills. Do you have any materials that could
help us train volunteers to go out into the community and run
your *How to Talk* . . . program?"

What an interesting idea! We wished we did. Maybe at
some time in the future we could write a . . .

A phone call came from the University of Wisconsin Cooperative Extension. They had done it! Unbeknownst to us, and
in partnership with the Wisconsin Committee for the Prevention of Child Abuse, they had obtained a federal grant to create a leadership training manual for our How to Talk So Kids
Will Listen Group Workshop program. It seems they had already used it to teach more than a hundred volunteers how to
run our workshops for over seven thousand parents in thirteen
counties. With great enthusiasm they described the success of
their project and their dream of replicating it in every state.
Would we look at their manual, make any necessary changes,
and join them in a broader publishing venture?

After recovering from the shock of this "too good to be true"
offer, we made plans to meet with them and work together.
The training manual has just been published.

So here we are today on another anniversary of the book
we launched with some trepidation so long ago. No one could
have predicted then, certainly not us, that it would have such
staying power or that it would take on a life of its own and re-
cast itself into so many different shapes and forms.

Nevertheless, once again we found ourselves with questions. Would *How to Talk* . . . continue to withstand the test of

time? After all, several decades had gone by. In addition to all the mind-boggling technological advances, the whole family picture was changing. There were more single, divorced, and stepparents, more nontraditional families, more homes where both mother and father were out in the workforce, more children in day care. Were these methods of communicating as relevant in today's harder, harsher, faster world as they were a generation ago?

As we reread our book with an eye on the current scene, we both came to the same conclusion. The principles were more important than ever. Because parents, whatever their status, were more stressed and more guilty than ever—torn between the competing demands of work and family, pushing themselves to fit forty-eight hours into a twenty-four-hour day, trying to do everything for and be everything to all the important people in their lives. Add to that a consumer culture that bombards their children with materialistic values; television that exposes them to explicit sexual images; websites that offer them instant, sometimes unsavory companionship; video games that desensitize them to violence; movies that stimulate them with multiple murders in the name of fun and entertainment, and it's not hard to understand why so many of today's parents feel shaken and overwhelmed.

We know full well this book is not a total answer. There are problems that cannot be solved by communication skills alone. Nevertheless, we believe that within these pages parents will find solid support—strategies that will help them cope with the built-in frustrations of raising children; clear methods that will enable them to set limits and impart their values; concrete skills that will keep families close and connected despite pernicious outside forces; language that will empower parents to be firm and nurturing—nurturing to themselves as well as to their children.

We are delighted at the opportunity this anniversary edition presents. It gives us a chance to share with you our current thinking and some of the feedback we've received over the years—the letters, the questions, the stories, the insights of other parents.

We hope that somewhere in this mix you'll find an additional kernel of information or inspiration to help you carry on with the most important job in the world.

Adele Faber
Elaine Mazlish

# I. The Letters

It's always a great pleasure to hear from our readers, but the letters that are most gratifying are those where people share how they actually used the principles in *How to Talk* . . . and applied them to the complexities of their lives.

> Your book has given me the hands-on tools I've been desperately searching for. I don't know how I would have handled all the hurt and anger my nine-year-old son felt about his father and me getting a divorce if I hadn't read *How to Talk*. . . .
>
> Most recent example: Tommy returned from his day with his father all down-in-the-mouth because his dad called him a "turkey."
>
> It took all my willpower not to bad-mouth my "ex" and tell Tommy his father was the one who was the "turkey." Instead I said, "Oh boy, that must have hurt. Nobody likes to be called names. You wish Daddy would just tell you what he wants without putting you down."
>
> I could see by Tommy's expression that what I said helped. But I'm not going to let this drop. I'm going to have a talk with his father. I just have to figure out how to do it without making things worse.
>
> Thank you for my newfound confidence.

• • •

I bought your book for four dollars in a used bookstore, and by now I can honestly say it was the best investment I ever made. One of the first skills I tried was "Describe what you see." When I got positive results, I almost fell out of my chair. My son, Alex (four), is a very strong-willed child (my parents call him "bullheaded"), which gives me many opportunities to use the ideas in your book.

Here's how the chapters on "Roles" and "Problem-Solving" helped me: Whenever I participated in Alex's preschool co-op program, I noticed the teacher getting more and more annoyed with him, especially when he wouldn't join the group for singing or anything else that didn't interest him. If Alex is bored or restless, it's hard for him to sit still. He rolls around, runs around, walks around. His teacher kept saying his name—"Alex, sit down . . . Alex, stop that! . . . Alex!!!" I saw him being put in the role of "troublemaker."

One day after school I talked to him about what he didn't like about the program and what he did. It turned out that he was tired of singing "Old McDonald" and having to listen to some of the same stories. But he really enjoyed the crafts and the games.

Then I told him how hard it was for the teacher to teach songs or tell stories to all the children when one child was running around disturbing the class. I was about to ask him to list some solutions when, out of the blue, he said, "Okay, Mom. I'll be wild in the playground *after class!*"

I gulped and said, "Sounds good to me." And since then the teacher hasn't had anything to complain about. The more I use my skills with my son, the more positive changes I see in him. It's as though a new little person has stepped out.

• • •

The elementary school counselor recommended *How to Talk* . . . when we were having behavior problems with our six-year-old son.

After reading the book, borrowing the videos from the Michigan State University Extension Office nearby, and teaching myself the parenting skills, several of my friends noticed such a change in our son that they asked what I was doing that made such a difference in his behavior and in my relationship with him. (He went from saying, "I hate you. I wish I wasn't your son" to "Mom, you're my bestest pal.")

After telling my friends about the book, they asked me to teach them. I was able to get all the necessary materials from the Extension Office—the video series and the workbooks—and gave a six-week course to my class of twelve parents (including my husband!). Sometime later, the Extension office asked me if I would give it again and open it to the public, which I did. I've been teaching the series for several years now and have seen some incredible changes for the better in the lives of the children whose parents attended the workshops.

Lately, I notice it takes some parents a little longer to catch the spirit of the program. They're under so much pressure; they want fast answers. Also, maybe they've been influenced by all the recent advice out there telling them that if they don't get tough (punish, spank) to make their kids mind they're not doing their job, not being responsible. But once they start actually using your approach and seeing for themselves how it works and how in the long run the kids are so much more cooperative, they become enthusiastic about the program.

As for me, when I look back I see that our son was becoming an angry and rebellious little boy. Finding your materials, learning and applying the skills in *How to*

*Talk* . . . , has literally saved our family life and improved our relationship with our son one hundred percent. I firmly believe that as long as these skills are a part of our lives we can help prevent our son from becoming the type of teenager who could make some very deadly choices out of anger and rebellion.

Thank you for presenting what you had learned in such a clear way that it can be self-taught.

• • •

I found *How to Talk* . . . in our local library and must say it is the most worn-out book I have ever seen. In fact, I'm sure the only thing holding it together is the soundness of its contents.

It's been extremely helpful to me in dealing with my ten-year-old daughter, who has recently developed an attitude. I don't know where it comes from—her friends or TV—but she's taken to saying things like "You never buy anything good to eat" or "How come you got me such a dumb video game? It's for little kids."

Thanks to you, I no longer defend myself or try to be understanding. Now when she gets "mouthy," I stop her right in her tracks. I'll say something like "Lisa, I don't like being accused. If there's something you want or don't want, you need to tell me in another way."

The first time I did this, I could see she was taken aback. But now I notice that when she starts out being fresh I don't even have to say anything. Sometimes I just give her "a look," and she'll stop and actually make an effort to be civil.

• • •

Your book is the greatest thing to come along since the dishwasher and the microwave! Just this morning I was rushing to get the baby ready for day care and reminded Julie (four) that she needed to use her Nebulizer machine for her asthma before she got dressed for school. She ignored me and started playing with her Barbie doll. Normally I would have screamed at her and taken the doll away, which would have led to her having a tantrum and me being frantic and late for work.

Instead, I took a deep breath and said, "I can see how much you want to play with Barbie. I'm sure she wants to spend time with you, too. Would *you* like to turn on your Nebulizer or do you think Barbie would like to turn it on?" She said, "Barbie wants to turn it on," at which point she walked over to the machine, let the doll "turn it on," completed her treatment, and then got dressed.

Thank you from the bottom of my frazzled nerves.

### *From Parents of Teenagers*

We're frequently questioned about the "best" age to start using these skills. Our standard reply is "It's never too early and never too late." Here's what parents of teenagers had to tell us:

People are always asking me how come my kids are so wonderful. I give my wife most of the credit, but I also tell them about *How to Talk* . . . because it's helped me really "live" what I believe in. I explain that it's not just a matter of saying or doing any one particular thing. It's about a way of living together with real respect. And when you get that respect going, that's what gives you whatever power or influence you have when they get to be teenagers.

I know there are no guarantees, and I'm not saying it's easy. Recently Jason, my fourteen-year-old, asked me for money to go to the movies. It turned out he wanted to see this R-rated film that I had read about and didn't think was appropriate for him. I gave him my objections, including the fact that he was underage. He said his friends were all going and he didn't want to miss out. I repeated my position. He said I couldn't really stop him because he was tall and could pass for seventeen, and if not, someone on line would get him in.

I said, "I know I can't stop you, but I'm hoping you won't go. Because from everything I've read, this movie is all about connecting sex with violence, and I think that is a sick connection. Sex shouldn't have anything to do with one person hurting or using another. It has to do with two people caring about each other."

Well, I didn't give him the money and I hope he didn't go. But even if he did, I have a feeling he'll be sitting there with my voice in his head. Because of our relationship, there's a good chance he'll at least consider my point of view. And that's the only protection I can give him against all the garbage out there in the world.

• • •

I want to let you know that your book has changed my life and thinking . . .

. . . and my children's lives

. . . and my relationship with my husband

. . . and his with the kids

. . . and, most especially, our relationship with our teenage daughter, Jodie.

One of the things we used to get into fights over was curfew. No matter what time we set, she always managed to be late and nothing we said or did made any difference. It was a real worry, because in our town a lot of kids go to parties where there's no supervision. Once the police were called in because a party attracted a lot of uninvited kids and neighbors complained about noise and beer bottles thrown on their lawns. Even when the parents are home, half the time they go upstairs to watch TV or sleep and have no idea what's going on downstairs. One Saturday morning, my husband and I sat down with Jodie to see if we could solve the problem together. He told her if he had his way he'd move the family to a desert island for the next two years until she went to college. But since that wasn't practical we'd have to think of something else.

I said, "Seriously, Jodie, you have a right to enjoy a night out with your friends. And Dad and I have a right to a worry-free evening. We need to figure out something that will satisfy all of us."

Well, we did. Here's what we finally agreed to: We'll be responsible for checking to make sure there's an adult in the house. Jodie will be responsible for coming home sometime between eleven-thirty and midnight. Since we go to bed early, I'll set the alarm for twelve-fifteen—just in case something unexpected comes up. The second Jodie gets home, she'll turn off the alarm. That way she'll have her fun and her parents will have a peaceful night's sleep. But if the alarm goes off, all our alarms will go off, and we'll have to start tracking her down.

Our agreement held. Jodie has kept her part of the bargain and made it her business to "beat the clock" every time.

Thank you for your life preserver of a book!

### *Not for Children Only*

Our purpose in writing *How to Talk* . . . was to help parents have better relationships with their children. We never expected that some people would use the book to change their relationship with their own parents or with themselves:

I was raised with no praise and lots of verbal abuse. After several years of escaping life through drugs and alcohol, I sought therapy to try to change my destructive behavior. My therapist recommended your book and it has been a terrific help to me—not only with the way I talk to my eighteen-month-old son but in the way that I now talk to myself.

I try not to belittle myself anymore. I'm starting to appreciate and give myself credit for all I do to make a life for me and my son. I'm a single mom and was terrified at the thought of repeating my upbringing, but now I know I won't. Thank you for helping me believe in myself.

• • •

*How to Talk . . .* , my "Bible," has helped me break a cycle of five generations of negating persons and feelings. It's taken me a long time, but I've finally learned I don't have to choke back my feelings—even the bad ones. I'm okay as I am. I hope my four children (seventeen, fourteen, twelve, and ten) can at some point appreciate the effort it took on my part (years of going to your parenting classes) to be able to raise the next generation of people willing and able to communicate instead of negate, negate, negate. P.S. I got your book when my seventeen-year-old was one. It's been my salvation!

• • •

I am a forty-year-old mother of two boys. What has affected me most deeply about your book is the realization that I have been terribly damaged by my parents' attitude toward me. My father still manages to say something hurtful to me every time we see each other. Since I've had children, these remarks are all nasty little digs about what a hopeless mother I am and what a mess I am making of my boys' upbringing. I realize now that even though I'm an adult, part of me is still a child suffering from lingering wounds of doubt and self-hatred.

The weird thing is that I am a conscientious, hard worker, who has had relative success as an artist. Yet my father always paints a picture of a person who is completely the opposite of me.

After reading your book, I found the courage to begin to stand up to my father. Recently, when he told me I was lazy, I replied that he might see me that way but that I had another picture of myself. (He was nonplussed by that.) I have new hope now that I can heal the child inside me by giving it the parenting it never had.

# The Letters

## *From Teachers*

At almost every conference, one or two teachers would take us aside to tell us how our books had affected them, not only personally but professionally as well. Some put their experiences in writing:

> I read *How to Talk So Kids Will Listen . . .* nine years ago when I first started teaching. I was used to working with adults and hadn't yet had children of my own. Your book may have saved my life. It has certainly helped me be a much better teacher to my seventh and eighth graders and a much happier person.
>
> The most helpful shift in my thinking came from no longer asking myself how to "make" the kids learn or behave. Now I ask myself how I can motivate my students to take ownership of the problem. My most recent success came with Marco, a self-appointed class clown, who disrupted the other students and got zeros on tests. One day after class, I stopped him. I said, "Marco, I need to talk to you. What do you think would help you to learn?"
>
> My question stunned him. I think he expected to be sent to the principal's office. After a long silence he said, "Maybe I should take notes."
>
> The next day Marco not only began taking notes but he raised his hand and talked in class. One of the other boys said, "Hot damn, Marco. You know something!"
>
> Over the years I have recommended, lent, and discussed your book with literally hundreds of parents and teachers. I usually keep a copy on my nightstand. Conscious attention to its precepts also helps me be the kind of father, husband, and friend that I want to be more often.

• • •

> My students have all benefited from your chapter on praise. I have one boy who has ADD. In nine months he

had turned in only three math assignments. After reading *How to Talk . . .* , I began to use descriptive language to point out his positives. I started saying things like "You figured it out" or "Oh, you caught your own error" or "You persisted until you got the right answer." The next week he turned in *every single assignment.* He is so proud of his work he wants me to tell his mother at the next parent conference.

I have another student who has handwriting that is so bad even he can't read what he's written. His spelling grades have all been in the fifty-percent area. He goes to another teacher for extra help. I shared my book with her, and together we have stormed him with praise. We both described *whatever was right* about his handwriting and spelling. ("You remembered to put the silent 't' in *often.*") Today he burst into my room and announced that he got nineteen spelling words right out of twenty. It was his first A in spelling ever.

• • •

I am an educational diagnostician in a large school district in Texas. After years of training teachers and experimenting with a variety of different methods—behavior modification, reinforcement theory, increasingly severe punishments, loss of recess time, detention, suspension—my colleagues and I have come to the same conclusion: The principles and skills you write about in all your books are the skills we need to use and teach our teachers to use. We are convinced that when our classrooms really work, they work because relationships are working. And relationships work when communication is humane and caring.

### Response from Abroad

We were fascinated by the feedback we received from foreign countries. That our work would be meaningful to people in cultures so very different from our own was a continuing source of amazement to us. When Elaine spoke at the International Book Fair in Warsaw, she asked the audience to explain the passionate response to our work in Poland (*How to Talk . . .* was a bestseller there). A father told her, "For years we have been under Communist rule. Now we have political freedom, but your book shows us how to be free within ourselves—how to give respect to ourselves and respect to our families."

• • •

From China, a woman wrote:

I am a teacher of English in Guangzhou, China. While I was a visiting college student in New York, I was also a babysitter of Jennifer, a little girl of five years old. Before me, she had a babysitter from another country who was unkind to her. She was hit and locked in a dark room from time to time for being naughty. As a result, Jennifer grew to be more eccentric and unsociable. What is more, she often burst into hysterical cries.

For my first few weeks, I applied to Jennifer the traditional Chinese methods, which tend to tell children how they should behave. Yet such methods did not turn out to be effective. The little girl burst into hysterical cries more often, and she even hit me.

Jennifer's mother was so sympathetic with me that she went to a psychological doctor for advice. He recommended to her your book *How to Talk So Kids Will Listen & Listen So Kids Will Talk*. The mother and I read it eagerly and tried our best to use the knowledge we learned from it. It has proved to be a success. Jennifer began to talk more, and we gradually became good friends. "Xing Ying, you are so good at dealing with Jennifer," said the grateful parents.

I am now back in China and have become a mother of a little boy myself. I have been applying the methods I learned from your book to deal with him and they have proved to be effective. Now my desire is to assist other Chinese parents to become more effective and happier in relation to their children.

• • •

From Victoria, Australia, a mother wrote:

I have used some of your suggestions with my children and found that they, especially my two elder, taciturn children, are talking to me more frequently. When they come home from university or school and I greet them with "I'm glad to hear you come in the door," or something along those lines (and not "How was school/uni today?"), I get a smile. My elder daughter is actually instigating conversation with me and not avoiding me.

• • •

A social worker who ran our *How to Talk* . . . program in Montreal, Quebec, wrote to describe a visit to her in-laws in Capetown, South Africa:

I met with the head of a parenting centre in the area to see what work they are doing. The centre offers classes both for the middle-class people who live nearby and for the residents of the sprawling shantytown called Kayelisha, on the outskirts of town. In Kayelisha, families live in small tin houses, each house about the size of a bedroom—no electricity, no running water, no sanitation facilities. The people from the centre hold classes there, using *How to Talk* . . . as a basis and translating the cartoons into Afrikaans so the residents can understand. They said they have about ten copies of the book in their lending library, and that they are all worn out and dog-eared from use.

I will also be sending a copy of your newest book, *How to Talk So Kids Can Learn*, to a friend from Johannesburg who runs education programs for teachers who work far away from cities in tiny communities.

Thought you'd like to know the scope of your influence!

### *Parents Under Duress*

Most of the examples in *How to Talk . . .* showed people dealing with everyday, run-of-the-mill problems. When a woman approached us after a lecture and described, with tear-filled eyes, how her relationship with her son, who had Tourette's syndrome, had gone from hopeless and hostile to upbeat and loving as a result of our book, we were overwhelmed. Since then we have heard from a number of mothers and fathers who have used our work to cope with especially stressful or serious problems.

Almost always the writers credit us for the changes they've made. As we see it, the credit belongs to them. Anybody can read a book. It takes a person of great determination and dedication to study the words on a page and use them to triumph over heartache. Here's what some parents had done:

> My home is sometimes like World War III. My daughter (seven) is ADHD. When she takes her medication, she is for the most part manageable. But when it wears off we have this out-of-control child. (I know a lot of parents of kids with ADHD who have to go to "tough love.")
>
> When I read your book, I wondered if these skills would work with an ADHD child. Well, they do. Now I notice that if I talk to her in this new way when she's on her medication, it helps her all through the day—particularly with her social skills. I feel sure that if I keep on this way, it will help her later in life as well. Thank you for your book.

• • •

> My husband and I are both psychologists. Our son, eight, has recently been diagnosed with ADHD. We have

had many troubling times with him. A friend introduced us to your books *Liberated Parents/Liberated Children* and *How to Talk So Kids Will Listen* . . . and we found them to contain the most useful approach we have come across to date.

We were both trained primarily in the use of behavioral methods, which were extremely counterproductive with our son. Your approach, based on mutual respect and understanding, has gradually helped us to get what we want from him without trying to control everything that happens. It has been a most welcome relief!

I feel that my knowledge of effective interaction patterns is only in its infancy, but I have been busy sharing what I have learned in my clinical practice. Your methods are effective in a wide variety of settings and with a wide variety of populations.

Thank you for your willingness to share all of your experiences and admit your weaknesses. It has helped your readers to admit their own.

• • •

My son, Peter, was discovered to have amblyopia at the ripe old age of six. His doctor made it clear that we had six months to work on "patching" with glasses or Peter would run the risk of severely impaired eyesight in his right eye. He was required to wear the patch four hours per day, during school hours.

Needless to say, Peter was embarrassed and uncomfortable. He tried to get out of doing it every day, and I was at my wits' end. He complained that it gave him a headache and that he could see worse than ever and that it "hurt." I acknowledged his feelings and was firm all at once, but his attitude did not improve.

At last, after five or six days of this, I was worn down. I said, "Look, Pete, I'll put the patch on for four hours so

I'll know just what it's like and then we can figure out ways to make it work better." I only said this out of pity for him; I didn't realize that it was going to have the effect it did.

Within twenty minutes I had a terrible headache. I lost depth perception, so that trying to do ordinary things like open a cabinet door, get the laundry out of the dryer, let the cat go out, or even walk upstairs were all incredibly difficult. By the end of four hours, I was a miserable, exhausted wreck who *fully understood* what this child was going through.

We talked. Although I couldn't change the requirements, Peter and I recognized that we had experienced the same things. My affirming how hard it was and my obvious inability to handle it as well as he did was apparently all that he needed. From that point on, he was able to wear the patch religiously every day during school for the four hours. His sight was saved and he didn't even have to wear glasses.

The lesson to me was, sometimes it's not enough just to give lip service to what a child is feeling. Sometimes you have to go an extra step to "see things through his eyes."

• • •

I have been running your *How to Talk* . . . group workshops for many years now. Since I picked up your first book in 1976 I have been an advocate of your work. At that time my first child, Alan, had just been born. He is twenty-two years old now and suffers from severe mental illness. This disease is a brain disorder that is hereditary in my family. Because of the skills I learned and teach, Alan's prognosis is so much better than that of most of the other sufferers, and I am able to help him in his grief and acceptance of his disability. Also, I am able to manage the ups and downs of his emotional roller coaster that comes with the disease by using my skills.

As I attend support groups for other parents who have similarly disabled children, I realize that your methods have made my whole situation much more positive in outlook and manageability. Hopefully, we will be able to help Alan to continue to make progress in his life and, more important, prevent him from relapse and hospitalization, which so often occur.

I am so grateful for the seventeen years' experience I have using these principles. Alan's siblings suffer as well, from fear of getting the disease to the terrible imbalance of resources in our family in managing the disability. The skills help my husband and me to be empathetic and aware of their plight. Your work has been a great gift to our family.

# II. Yes, but . . . What if . . . How about . . . ?

Not all the feedback we received was positive. Some people were disappointed at not finding more help for children who had serious or complex problems. Others were unhappy at not having their particular questions answered. Still others were frustrated because they had made a genuine effort to say or do things differently with little or no success. Their common refrain was "I tried it, but it didn't work."

When we asked what actually happened and heard the details of their experience, it was almost always easy to see what went wrong and why. Evidently, there were some ideas we needed to develop more fully. Here are some of the comments and questions we heard, along with our responses:

### About Choices

**I gave my teenager a choice and it backfired. I told him he could either get a haircut and come to Thanksgiving dinner or he could have Thanksgiving dinner in his room and that it was up to him.**

**He said, "Fine, I'll have it in my room." I was shocked. I said, "What?! You would do that to me! And to your family?" He just turned his back on me and walked away. Maybe choices don't work with teenagers.**

Before you offer a child of any age a choice, it helps to ask yourself, *"Are both of these options acceptable to me and likely to be acceptable to my child?"* Or are these choices really threats in disguise? Will he experience me as using a technique to try to manipulate him? At its best, the subtext of a choice should be "I'm on your side. There's something I want you to do (or not do), but rather than giving you an order I'd like to give you some say in the matter."

What choice could you have given your teenage son about his hair? Chances are, none. Most teenagers experience almost any parental comment about their hair—the style, the color, the length, the cleanliness or lack thereof as an invasion of their personal space.

But suppose you can't contain yourself? If you're willing to risk moving into this sensitive area, approach with caution: "I know it's none of my business; however, if you could consider the possibility of allowing the barber to remove just enough hair so that we could see your eyes, you'd have a thankful mother on Thanksgiving."

Then make a quick exit.

**What do you do if you give your child two choices and she rejects both of them? The doctor prescribed a medicine for my daughter that she hates, and I did exactly what you suggested. I told her that she could have it with apple juice or ginger ale. She said, "I don't want either one," and clamped her mouth shut.**

When children have strong negative feelings about doing something, they're not likely to be receptive to any choices. If you want your daughter to be open to the options you offer, you need to start by giving her full respect for her negative feelings: "Boy, I can see by the way you're wrinkling your nose how much you hate even the thought of taking that medicine." A statement like that can relax her. It says, "Mom understands and is on my side." Now your daughter is more emotionally ready to consider your words. "So, honey, what could make it less awful for you—taking it with juice or ginger ale? Or can you think of something that would help—even a little." Actually, the possibilities for choices are endless:

Do you want to take it fast or slow?
With your eyes open or closed?
With the big spoon or the little spoon?
Holding your nose or your toes?
While I sing or while I'm quiet?
Should I give it to you or would you rather take it yourself?

The point is, some things are easier to swallow if someone understands how hard it is for you, and if you have a small say in how it goes down.

### *About Consequences*

Another communication breakdown occurred when consequences were included in the problem-solving process. One parent told us how disappointed she was when the one time she tried to work out a solution with her children they all ended up in a big fight.

**I called a family meeting and told the kids what the vet said about our dog being seriously overweight and not getting enough exercise. We were going through all the problem-solving steps together and making good progress, deciding who would be responsible for what and at what time, when my middle son asked what the consequence would be if someone didn't do his job. My oldest suggested no TV for one night. The other two said that wasn't fair. To make a long story short, we all wound up in this big argument about what a fair consequence should be, with everybody mad at one another and no plan about what to do for the dog. I can only conclude that my boys just aren't mature enough for problem-solving.**

It is not a good idea to bring up consequences when you're trying to solve a problem. The whole process is geared toward creating trust and goodwill. As soon as the idea of a consequence for failure is introduced, the atmosphere is poisoned. Doubt is created, motivation is killed, and trust is destroyed.

When a child asks what the consequence would be if he doesn't do his part, the parent can respond, "I don't want us even to think about consequences. Right now we need to figure out how to make sure our dog gets healthy and stays healthy. It will take all of us working together to make that happen.

"We understand there will be times when we won't feel like doing our part. But we'll do it anyway, because we don't want to let one another or our dog down. And if someone gets sick or there's an emergency we'll take turns getting the job done. In this family, we all look out for one another."

### Alternatives to "But"

A number of parents complained that when they acknowledged their children's feelings the children became even more upset. When we asked exactly what they said, the problem became clear. Each of their empathic statements included a "but." We pointed out that the word *but* tends to dismiss, diminish, or erase all that went before. Here is each parent's original statement, with our suggested revision that eliminates the "but."

**Original statement:** "You sound so disappointed about missing Julie's party. But the fact is you have a bad cold. Besides, it's only one party. There will be plenty of other parties in your life."

**Child thinks:** "Dad just doesn't understand."

**Revised statement:** (Instead of "butting away" the feeling, give it full value.) "You sound so disappointed about missing Julie's party. You were looking forward to celebrating your friend's birthday with her. The last place on earth you wanted to be today was in bed with a fever."

If Dad is feeling expansive, he can express what his daughter might wish: "Don't you wish someone would finally discover a cure for the common cold?"

**Original statement:** "I know how much you hate the thought of having a sitter again, but I need to go to the dentist."

**Child thinks:** "You always have a reason to leave me."

**Revised statement:** (Delete "but." Substitute *"The problem is . . ."*) "I know how much you hate the thought of having a sitter again. *The problem is* I need to go to the dentist."

What's the difference? As one father commented, *"'But'* feels like a door slammed in your face. *'The problem is'* opens the door and invites you to consider a possible solution." The child might say, "Maybe while you're at the dentist I could play at Gary's house." Mom might say, "Maybe you could come with me and read a book in the waiting room." Then again, there might not be a solution that satisfies the child. Nevertheless, by acknowledging that there is a problem we make it easier for him to deal with it.

**Original statement:** "Holly, I can see how unhappy you are about your haircut. But you'll see, it will grow. In a few weeks you won't even notice it."

**Child thinks:** "No kidding. Like I couldn't figure that out for myself."

**Revised statement:** (Delete *"but."* Substitute *"And even though you know."*) "Holly, I can see how very unhappy you are about your haircut. *And even though you know* it will grow, you still wish somebody would have listened to you when you said you wanted only an inch taken off."

By prefacing your statement with *and even though you know*, you credit your daughter's intelligence and make your point without dismissing hers.

### *"Why Did You ... ?" "Why Didn't You ... ?"*

Some parents complained because they felt that they went out of their way to be understanding of their children only to be met with a hostile response.

**As a new stepmother I'm well aware of how important it is not to be critical of the children. I leave the discipline up to their father. But when he was out of town and the teacher sent a note saying my stepson's report was overdue, I knew I had to handle it. I was very calm. I just asked him, in a friendly way, why he didn't get his report in on time, and he exploded at me. Why?**

Any sentence that begins with *Why did you* or *Why didn't you* can feel like an accusation. The question forces a youngster to think about his shortcomings. Beneath your friendly *"Why didn't you,"* he may hear, "Isn't it because you're lazy, disorganized, irresponsible, and a hopeless procrastinator?"

Now he's on the spot. How shall he answer you? He's left with two untenable choices. He can either own up to his inadequacies or he can try to defend himself and make excuses for them: "Because the assignment wasn't clear . . . Because the library was closed, etc." In either case, he becomes more upset with himself, more angry at you, and less likely to think about how to remedy the situation.

What might you substitute that would lead to a nondefensive reaction? You can turn the problem over to your stepson and offer your support. As you hand him the note from his teacher, you can say:

"This was addressed to Dad and me, but you're the person who will know how to take care of it. If there's anything getting in the way of starting or finishing the report, or if you want someone to bounce some ideas off, I'm here."

### *About Time-Out*

Several parents were disappointed at reading the book from cover to cover and not finding anything about "time-out." Initially, we were puzzled by the comment. We had raised six children between us without ever sending anyone to time-out. Then, little by little, we began to notice a groundswell of books and magazine articles advocating time-out as a new disciplinary method, a humane alternative to spanking, and instructing parents on precisely how to carry out the procedure successfully.

How could we not consider it? The explanation seemed almost reasonable. By sending the misbehaving child into another space or place, with nothing to distract him—no books, toys, or games—and insisting that he sit there for a specified amount of time, one minute for each year of his life—the child will soon see the error of his ways and return chastened and well behaved.

But the more we thought about it and the more we read about it in all its variations, the less we liked it. To us it seemed that time-out was not new or innovative but an updated version of the outdated practice of making a "naughty" child stand in the corner.

We wondered, suppose Billy hits his little sister because she keeps pulling on his arm while he's trying to draw and Mom, in a fury, sends him to "do-time" in his time-out chair. She claims that's better than hitting Billy for hitting his sister. But what might be going on in Billy's mind as he's sitting there? Is he thinking, "Now I've learned my lesson. I must never hit my sister again, no matter what she does." Or is he feeling, "No fair! Mom doesn't care about me. She only cares about my stupid sister. I'll fix her when Mom's not looking." Or is he concluding, "I'm so bad, I deserve to be sitting here all by myself."

It is our conviction that the child who is misbehaving does not need to be banished from the members of his family, even temporarily. However, he does need to be stopped and redirected: "Billy, no hitting! You can tell your sister, *with words*,

271

how mad it makes you feel when she pulls on your arm while you're trying to draw."

But suppose Billy tells her and suppose she continues pulling? And suppose Billy hits her again? Doesn't that call for time-out?

Sending Billy to "solitary" might stop the behavior for the moment, but it doesn't address the underlying problem. What Billy needs is not time *out* but private time *with* a caring adult who will help him deal with his feelings and figure out better ways to handle them. Mom might say, "It's not easy to have a little sister who's always pulling at you to get your attention. Today she made you so angry that you hit her. Billy, I can't allow either one of my children to hit the other. We need to make a list of things you can do instead if she bothers you again when you're trying to draw."

What are some alternatives to hitting?

- Billy could yell "Stop!" in her face—very loud.
- He could push her hand away—gently.
- He could give her her own piece of paper and a crayon.
- He could give her something else to play with.
- He could draw when his sister is napping.
- He could draw in his room with the door closed.
- If nothing else works, he can call Mom for help.

Billy can post his list of solutions wherever he likes and consult it whenever the need arises. He no longer sees himself as someone who acts so bad when he's mad that he needs to be sent away but as a responsible person who has many ways to cope with his anger.

### About Spouses and Significant Others

A number of our readers shared a common frustration. They found nothing in the book about how to get through to a resistant spouse.

**I'm trying to change the way I talk to the children, but I'm being undermined by a husband/wife/partner who doesn't go along with my new approach. Do you have any suggestions for me?**

When the same question arose at one of our lectures, we asked people in the audience what they had done. Here are their responses:

- I talk to my husband about the changes *I'm* trying to make. That way, he feels included in the process but doesn't feel any pressure to have to change himself.
- We keep the book in the car. Whoever isn't driving reads a little bit aloud and then we talk about it.
- My husband won't read books on parenting. He's from the "what's the difference what you say, as long as your kids know you love them" school. Finally, I told him, "Look, when we decided to have children we knew we wanted to do right by them. We wouldn't think of dressing them in rags or giving them a diet of junk food. Well by the same token, why would we talk to them in ways that aren't healthy—especially if there are better options out there? Our kids deserve the best—from both of us."
- I try to involve my husband by asking his advice about the best way to handle certain situations with our two sons. I'll say something like "Honey, I need to bounce this off you. This is an area where I have no experience, since I was never a little boy. Now, what would make you more likely to want to cooperate—if your mother said this to you or if she said that?" Usually, he answers right away, but sometimes he'll think about it and come up with a suggestion I never would have thought of.
- My wife hates it when I tell her what to say or how to say it. It's best if I just use the skills myself and say nothing. Something must be rubbing off on her, because the other morning as we were rushing to get out, my daughter

refused to put on her jacket. Instead of arguing, my wife gave her a choice. She asked her if she wanted to wear it *regular* or *backward.* My daughter giggled, picked *backward,* and off we went.

### The Power of Playfulness

Several parents took us to task for not including a chapter on humor. In our defense, we explained that when we were writing the chapter on "Engaging Cooperation" we actually did debate the pros and cons of including humor. We knew how doing anything offbeat or unexpected could change the mood in seconds from mad to glad. But how could we ask parents, with everything else they had to do, to "be funny." So we limited ourselves to two short paragraphs about humor. Big mistake. Parents, we discovered, are funny. Even those who don't believe they can be. Anytime we had a workshop, anywhere in the country, and asked the very serious, grown-up parents to get in touch with the playful, funny, silly, zany, kid part of themselves, they did. They came up with the most delightful examples of what could be done or what they had done to raise their own spirits and melt their children's resistance.

Sometimes my three-year-old refuses to get dressed because he wants me to do it for him. When he gets in this mood, I put his underwear on his head and try to put his socks on his hands. He, of course, tells me I'm doing it wrong and then puts his underwear on and his socks on his feet. Then he says, "See, Mommy, this is how it goes." I act completely surprised and try to put his pants on his arms or his shirt on his legs. The game always ends with laughter and hugs.

• • •

To get my son to brush his teeth we invented germs— Geraldine and Joe—who would be hiding. So we would brush each spot while they would sing, "We're having a party in Benjamin's mouth." Then they would scream when he brushed them and yell when he spit them down the drain. They would call out, "We'll be back!"

The challenge of maintaining a semblance of order in any home with children of any age seemed to generate the most creative solutions. Here's what some parents did to motivate their children to help around the house or clean up after themselves.

We're trying to establish some traditions to encourage our new "blended" family—her three (seven, nine, and eleven) and my two (ten and thirteen)—to get along better. Arguing about who does what chores has been a real sore point. Now every Saturday morning we write down all the jobs that have to be done on separate pieces of paper. Then we fold them, put each one in a different color balloon, blow them up, and throw all the balloons into the air. Each child grabs one, breaks it, does the job, comes back, and breaks the next. On it goes until all the jobs are done and we congratulate one another on our great teamwork!

• • •

I'm an at-home dad who recently came up with a new way to deal with all the mess the kids make. I take out my special deck of cards with all the high numbers removed. Then each boy picks a card that tells him how many things he has to put away. There's lots of excitement as they count what they put away and rush back to see what their next card will be. The last time I did it, the whole cleanup was finished in twenty minutes and the kids were disappointed that the game was over.

• • •

SCENARIO: One room with two girls. Pieces from three puzzles all over the floor.

MOM: "Okay, kids, this is called *Can you beat the music?* I'm going to play this new album and the idea is to see if you can get all the puzzle pieces back in their original boxes before the first song ends."

They went for it and finished the job in two and a half songs.

• • •

I've got four boys. At least fifty times a day I'm yelling at them to put their shoes away. The first thing they do when they come home is take off their shoes and drop them in the middle of the floor, and I'm always tripping over eight shoes.

INSPIRATION: I write *shoes* on a piece of paper, put a string through it, and hang it over the entrance to the kitchen, low enough so they'll run into it when they come home.

Kevin, my eight-year-old, is the first to arrive. The note brushes his hair as he enters the kitchen.

KEVIN: What's this?
ME: Read it.
KEVIN: Shoes? What's that supposed to mean?
ME: What do you think?
KEVIN: Are we going to get new shoes today?
ME: No.
KEVIN: (*thinking hard*) Do you want us to put our shoes away?
ME: You guessed it.

Kevin puts shoes away! Comes back and explains the note to the next three kids *who put away their shoes!!!*

KEVIN: You should make a sign like that for washing your hands.

• • •

My teenagers hate cleaning the bathroom. ("Ma, it's gross!") I didn't argue. I just posted a note on the mirror over the sink. Here's the poem that did the trick:

Grab the Comet and a rag
Scrub-a-dub—Oh, what a drag!
Edges, ledges, nooks, and crannies
Don't forget where sit the fannies
Yes, it does, it takes some time
But work well done is so sublime!

Thanks.

Love,
Mom

• • •

The mother who gave us this story titled it "Nothing Lasts Forever":

I wanted all the trains and tracks cleared out of the den, so I walked into my son's room and pretended to call him on the phone. Ring. Ring.

He pretended to pick it up and said, "Hello."

I said, "Is this the Reilly Construction Company?"

He said, "Yes."

I said, "I have this big job of removing some heavy trains and tracks to another location and I heard your company was the best."

He came in and picked everything up. I tried it a second time and it worked again. Then one day I rang him up and asked, "Is this Reilly Construction?"

My son answered, "He's out of business."

# III. Their Native Tongue

Our mentor, Dr. Haim Ginott, wasn't born in the United States. He came to this country from Israel as a young adult. It was here that he studied for his doctorate, published his books, and ran parent guidance groups. When we first joined one of his groups, we remember complaining to him about how hard it was to change old habits: "We find ourselves starting to say something to the kids, stopping, tripping over our own tongues." He listened thoughtfully and then replied, "To learn a new language is not easy. For one thing, you will always speak with an accent. . . . But for your children it will be their native tongue!"

His words were prophetic. Not only as they applied to our children but to our readers' children as well. We heard from many parents how their youngsters were using this new language in the most natural way. Here are their experiences as told or written:

I'm a working mother and have a very tight schedule. My three-year-old hates to get up and is usually very irritable. So I usually say, "You're feeling cranky this morning, aren't you?" He says, "Yah," and feels better and is more cooperative.

One morning I woke up feeling irritable because I was running late. He looked at me with concern and said, "Are you feeling cranky, Mommy? I still love you so much." It amazed me that he was so perceptive. He made me feel better and my day was great!

• • •

My four-year-old, Megan, said to her brother, "Justin, I don't like it when you kick me." (Usually she kicks him back.) He said, "Okay, Megs." And that was it! Then Megan came and told me she used her new skill and it worked. She was surprised and proud of herself.

• • •

I would have been institutionalized by now without your magic spells. Just to let you know how much I use your methods, my daughter (age almost five) recently said, upon being told it was bedtime, "But, Mommy, what are my choices?" (She loves it when I ask her if she wants to walk to bed or hop to bed.)

The other day we were playing and she was being the mommy and she said to me, "Sweetheart, here are the choices: You can have a Jeep or a sports car—pick one!"

• • •

My four-year-old son, Danny, is sitting on the floor with his friend Christopher. They're playing with toy animals and having a pretend fight. Suddenly it turns into a real fight.

CHRISTOPHER:   Danny, stop! You're hurting my hand!

DANNY:   You're hurting me!

CHRISTOPHER:   I had to! You were pressing my hand down.

DANNY:   I had to, because you were pressing *my hand* down.

ME:   (Thinking I should intervene, but not sure what to say.)

DANNY: Wait a minute. (*sits back on his heels and thinks*) Christopher, here are our choices: We can play with the animals and *not* press each other's hands down . . . or we can *not play* with the animals and play a different game. Which do you *choice*?

CHRISTOPHER: Let's play another game.

And off they ran! I know it's hard to believe, but it really did happen.

• • •

One day after breakfast, I was walking toward my daughter's room thinking about what else I could do instead of giving her a long lecture about not leaving milk out on the counter. But I was preceded by my son, eight, who was already outside her door saying, "Milk turns sour when it's left out of the refrigerator."

To my surprise the door opened, and out came my six-year-old, who immediately went to the kitchen and put the milk away.

• • •

I was in the living room and overheard this conversation between my ten-year-old daughter, Liz, and her friend Sharon, who was searching through a kitchen cabinet.

SHARON: (*in a whiny voice*) I'm hungry. Why does your mother keep all the snacks up so high? She never puts things where you can reach them.

LIZ: Sharon, in our house we don't blame. Just tell me what you want and I'll get it for you.

I stood there thinking, you try and you try and never know if you're getting through. And then one day it happens!

• • •

The big thing I got from your book is that it's okay to be angry—as long as you don't say anything that hurts anybody. I used to try to keep calm and keep it all in and would always end up yelling stuff I'd regret. As a matter of fact, lately I've been letting the kids know early on when I'm even beginning to feel uptight or out of patience, or when I just need to take some time for myself.

Yesterday I got my reward.

I was shopping with Ryan, my thirteen-year-old, who had shot up during the summer and needed a new winter jacket. We went to two stores and found nothing he liked. We were on our way to a third when he said, "Let's go home."

ME: Ryan, when that first cold snap hits, you won't have anything to wear.

RYAN: Mom, please. I want to go home.

ME: But, Ryan . . .

RYAN: Mom, I'm trying to tell you! I feel myself getting into a bad mood and I don't want to let it out on you.

As we headed home, I felt so proud and so cared about. Thank you for giving my kids and me ways to protect each other when we're about to "lose it."

• • •

I've been attending your *How to Talk* . . . classes for the last month. Recently I had a conversation with my eight-year-old son that I had to share with you.

ERIC: (*as he was getting off the school bus*) Guess what happened at recess today?

ME: I'm all ears.

ERIC: Michael got into trouble 'cause he hit someone and Mrs. M. yelled at him. He started to cry and she told him to stop and called him a crybaby.

ME: That must have made you feel bad to see that happen to Michael.

ERIC: Yeah! I put my arm around him like this. (*He curves his arm around an invisible boy and pats an invisible shoulder.*)

ME: I bet that made Michael feel better.

ERIC: Uh-huh. Mrs. M. should go to those classes you go to, Mom.

I believe that the new way I'm talking and listening to my son has helped him become a more sensitive person who doesn't just stand by when he sees injustice.

• • •

So far, we've been looking at children using skills. In this final letter, a woman describes her own journey to internalize this "new language."

As I sit here feeling the tears of joy, revelation, and pride, I just have to write and say thank you. A thousand thank-you's. Today I realize how much I have changed, how much I am putting into practice naturally. It was a small incident. My three-year-old's cousin (age nine) was visiting. He was showing my son how to pile boards so that he could reach the top of the fence. I looked out and said, in a calm and friendly tone, "Hey, I see a pile of boards that is tippy and unsafe. And fences are not for climbing. Feet on the ground, please."

Then I went away. I looked out the window a couple of minutes later and *they had dismantled the pile and were playing at something else—safely!* It struck me suddenly that I had gotten more than the desired result (just to get them away from the pile) without:

1. Having to first think about which of your skills to apply. The words just flowed, naturally.
2. Screaming like a banshee—the usual result of my gripping fear at the image of the harm that could come to my child.

3. Physically being part of the correction. Even after I said my piece, it was not a conscious decision to leave the scene. It just happened. I just walked away and let them decide what to do. So unconscious was leaving the scene that it didn't even occur to me until I'd done it, until I sat down to write this letter! I'm really learning! I'm really learning! Hurrah!

Afterward, I reflected on, and will not print, how I would have handled that situation as little as a year ago. And I cringe. Then I cry to think of what my child's life would have been like without your books. You have given the likes of me—a perfectionist, workaholic, adult child of an alcoholic—the incredible gift of communicating with my precious children in a loving, uncritical way.

My mother and I recently shed tears when she reflected on how she had talked to us as children: "When I hear how you speak to your son, I am ashamed of how I spoke to you kids." I was quick to forgive. She is quick to learn. She's also spurred on by the warm feelings that a parent or grandparent can bask in after a success.

My sister—having recently fled from an abusive husband—spoke to her children in such a demeaning tone that I reached the point where I could not be in her company. I felt so much hurt for her children that I just couldn't listen anymore. I bought her *How to Talk* . . . and *Siblings Without Rivalry* and suggested that she just skim the cartoons for the gist, hoping she would be drawn in. My mother reports seeing a change in the way my sister communicates with her kids. The self-esteem of another two children is being saved by your books.

I truly cannot convey the depth of my gratitude to you for sharing your skills.

Jane

P.S. Alcoholism is ugly and my family can't yet own up to it. I, therefore, can't release my surname.

Thank you, Jane. Thank all of you who have taken the time to put your thoughts and experiences in writing. It is when we read letters such as these, from home and abroad, that we permit ourselves, once again, our fondest fantasy: The one where all of us together—parents, teachers, mental-health professionals, and workshop leaders—spread the principles of caring communication so far and so wide that the time comes when the children of the world grow up to be strong, compassionate human beings, confident in themselves and committed to living in peace with one another.

# 30th Anniversary

Another decade has flown by. An updated edition of *How to Talk* . . . is being readied to go to press. Our editor asks if there's anything we'd like to add for today's parents.

Elaine has an idea. "Let's ask Joanna."

"My Joanna? . . . Why?"

"Because, Adele, she's grown up in your home. Everything that took us so long to learn is as natural to her as breathing."

"So?"

"So she's the next generation. She's been putting her skills into action as a teacher, as a parent, as a speaker, and as a workshop leader who's been running our group workshop programs for years now. She's right there on the front lines of the parent-child battles. I think our readers would love to hear about her experiences and discoveries."

"Are you saying we should ask her if she'd be willing to add her perspective to this new edition?"

"It would be a loss if we didn't."

When I broached the idea to Joanna, she barely hesitated. "How soon do you need it?" she asked.

The following pages are hers.

# The Next Generation

It feels a little strange to be writing about being the daughter of parenting guru Adele Faber. As a young mother I was not eager to discuss my illustrious background. I was trying to survive each day on that crazy roller coaster of life with toddlers. At home, one moment would be pure joy as my little boy mastered the leap from sofa to beanbag chair; the next was narrowly averted tragedy as he attempted to make the game more interesting by leaping over his helpless infant brother. At the playground, we moms would beam fondly as our children happily zipped down the slide together, and then rush to separate them as one landed with a foot in the other one's face and the offended party retaliated with a bite that elicited shrieks of pain and outrage.

I remember one miserable outing to the mall when my son was about two. He was going through a period where he hated to have his hand held. He needed to be free! The mall was crowded that day. As Dan eagerly darted off to see some shiny thing that caught his eye, I grabbed his arm. I was terrified that I would lose him. As soon as he felt my grip he started to struggle. I held on tighter. I was hurting him! He began to yell and twist.

I scooped my now hysterical child up in my arms. As I walked rapidly toward the exit with my kicking, screaming prisoner, my eyes darted anxiously around, anticipating an encounter with a mall security guard, accusing me of kidnapping a child. I actually thought about giving a false name.

What if I said my name is Joanna Faber, and then somehow it got around that I was the daughter of a child-rearing expert? I would be humiliated and my mother discredited!

I had a group of friends, moms of toddlers and babies, who would get together on a regular basis for group "playdates." It was really more of a playdate for the adults. The kids would mostly play on their own, when they weren't battling over toy possession. Even though I had a close relationship with these friends, I stayed undercover. I was afraid that if I admitted that my own mother had written a book about child-rearing, I'd be looked upon with suspicion. They'd think I was judging them as they struggled with their uncooperative toddlers. And worse yet, they would judge *me* as they watched me struggle. "Her mother wrote a book about parent-child communication? Humph!" I imagined them thinking.

My anonymity was not fated to last. During one gathering, my friend Cathy said to me, "Joanna, you have to read this book I have. I'm sure you'd love it. It's just your style. Everything in it reminds me of how you talk to your kids. It's called *How to Talk So Kids Will Listen & Listen So Kids Will Talk.*"

I was startled. I had no plan for this! I mumbled, "Yeah, my mom and her friend Elaine wrote that book." Cathy was astonished. Her face lit up. "Oh, one of the authors is Adele *Faber*! I can't believe I never noticed that. Hey, everybody, listen up. Joanna's mother wrote this great book about child-rearing and she never told us!"

And so I was outed.

A little while later Cathy told me she was organizing a series of lectures at her church. She asked me if I would give a talk about growing up as the daughter of Adele Faber. The date she mentioned was several months in the future, so I happily agreed. Surely I would think of something to say by then! As the date drew nearer with frightening rapidity, I began to think that maybe the church group would disband or the pipes would burst and flood the building, or I would get sick—something disastrous enough to cancel the speech but not really hurt anybody. What was I thinking? How can I present myself to this group of people as the product of ideal parenting? It's just plain weird! Am I supposed to have come out perfectly? And to be able to effortlessly parent my own children?

Finally, I realized that I could do this. I didn't have to be perfect. All I had to do was share the skills I used every day with my family. There is no such thing as a calm, conflict-free life with young children. I was expecting too much. What I had was pretty darn useful—the skills to deal with all those conflicts and survive with good feelings and good relationships intact.

I started out by admitting to my audience that I had in fact been raised by a mom who respected her children's feelings, encouraged our autonomy, and used creative problem-solving rather than punishment for our conflicts. I grew up listening to and discussing all kinds of stories of human interaction with her, and immersed myself from a very young age in her library of books: Carl Rogers, *On Becoming a Person*; Haim Ginott, *Between Parent and Child*; Virginia Axline, *Dibs: In Search of Self*; Herbert Kohl, *36 Children*; John Holt, *How Children Learn,* and many others were all devoured by me as a preteen. From a very early age I had decided I was going to teach, to work with children and heal any wounds the world had inflicted on them. I was also inspired by my father, who was a guidance counselor in an inner-city school and ran a college-bound program for disadvantaged young people.

As a young child I remember saving up the frustrations of my school day to tell my mother. I knew that I could bear it when the teacher was mean, or some terrible injustice occurred on the playground, because when I got home I could tell my mom. She'd listen to my outrage, and I would be soothed and strengthened for the next assault. Even as a little girl I noticed that other parents were different, and I remember wondering how other kids got by without having anyone to listen to their sorrows.

# The Next Generation

I entered the working world as a teacher in an elementary school in West Harlem. I was determined that my skills and my understanding of human nature would lead to great things. Of course, I met challenges there that humbled me, but I still maintained my basic belief that my abilities were sound. It was just that some of these kids were so damaged by their parents that it was hard to get through to them.

I was sure that when I had my own kids, and raised them the right way from the start, it would be smooth sailing. There would be no damage to undo. I remember sitting with a fellow teacher who had her four-year-old daughter at work that day. The little girl was sobbing because her mother had just slapped her for picking up a lollipop that had dropped on the dirty floor. My colleague said to me, "You think it's so easy. Just wait till you have a kid of your own and that sweet little thing just outright defies your authority. Then you'll see what you can do with all your theories."

I thought to myself, "How wrong you are! When I have a daughter of my own, I'll never treat her like that. I'll respect and celebrate her independent little spirit. I am not like you, with your authoritarian approach to motherhood!"

Then at one point I jumped off that cliff of no return and created little humans of my own who would live with me all day and keep me up all night. And, finally, I was brought to my knees. Parenthood was just so *relentless*. You never get to go home at the end of a good day's work. I found my voice reaching that high, desperate pitch as I formulated classic, non-self-esteem-enhancing statements such as:

"What is the *matter* with you?"
"I've told you a *million* times!"
"How could you do that to your brother?"

And the reprehensible:

"Okay, that's it. I'm going to leave without you." (And wishing I really could do it).

Also, the ever-helpful philosophical question:

"Why did you do that when I *just* told you not to?"

Somehow I had imagined that when my children got over being babies and were able to walk and talk and grab things they would be a little bit more reasonable. They certainly wouldn't kick or bite or shove their little brother when they had been raised in such a gentle and accepting environment.

Even though most of the skills my mother had to learn as a whole new language were second nature to me, when it came to being on the front line of parenthood day and night, I still needed to review my material. Sure, many times all the right words flowed effortlessly from my lips, as my friend Cathy pointed out when she noticed my "style" of parenting. But at other times, worn out and frustrated by the constant barrage of the needs of three small children, the right words did not flow. I would lash out with supremely unhelpful outbursts that touched off emotional eruptions and meltdowns in my children. And that is when I *really* appreciated those skills. Because with children you always get another chance. You can be confident that the latest battle over who gets the red cup, or who knocked over the blocks, will not be the last. And knowing what to do with that second chance is what saves me every time!

After the speech at the church, there was a lot of excitement among the audience. A group of parents wanted me to lead a workshop series. And so I was launched into the whole business of helping parents communicate with their children while still finding my own way through that challenging maze. Here are some of the memorable moments from each of our meetings.

### Session 1—Acknowledging Feelings

I was afraid that the parents would be disappointed with our first meeting. My message was a cliché. Acknowledge feelings.

Who hasn't heard of that? I imagined them rolling their eyes at one another. Is this what we got a babysitter for? To my great relief, they found it challenging. There is a wide gap between knowing something intellectually and applying it on the battlefield under fire.

One of the objections parents had to accepting feelings was that often the feelings their children expressed were so downright unacceptable! And yet they were willing to suspend disbelief and give it a try. This first story is from Max's mom. She was often at her wits' end. Her four-year-old son had been diagnosed with "oppositional defiant disorder." He was constantly challenging her and had many tantrums every day. A therapist had helped them to set up a chart with points and rewards for good behavior, but so far it hadn't made a difference.

After our first session Max's mom came back with this report to the group:

### Max at the Mall

Last Saturday was cold and rainy. I made plans with a friend to meet her and her children at an indoor play area at the mall. When we got to the place, Max stopped at the entrance and refused to budge. He declared, "I'm not going in there. It's boring and stupid and dumb!"

I thought, "Uh-oh, here we go again with another tantrum." I almost said, "What do you mean? You wanted to come! Look at all the great things there are to play with. All the kids in there are having so much fun."

Instead, I took a deep breath and said, "So, you don't like anything about this place. All these slides and trampolines and cars and ride-on trucks look boring and stupid and dumb to you!"

He said, "YEAH!" and then he went in to play. I was stunned. Later, when he came out, he looked up at me and said, "You understand me." He's never said anything like that before.

**Picture This**

A few days later I received this e-mail from Max's mother:

Max has a lot of very strong feelings. I've always tried to calm him down, but now I realize it really helps when I am dramatic with him. Yesterday he was looking forward to a playdate. At the very last minute the mom called to postpone, saying that her daughter was too tired to handle coming here.

Max was so upset! He let out a huge wail. I went over to the chalkboard and said, "You sound so disappointed! You were really looking forward to your playdate." I drew a stick figure of a boy with enormous tears (the tears were bigger than his face) flowing into a gigantic puddle. Max wanted me to draw the puddle bigger and bigger. Then he put the whole picture inside a giant teardrop and wrote the words SAD and BOO HOO!! There wasn't an empty spot on that chalkboard.

Finally, we talked about what to do to feel better. He said he could call another friend, and he did. While he was waiting for the other friend, he told me how lucky he was, because now he had two playdates—one today and one another day with the first friend.

Maybe this seems like a lot of trouble to go through to acknowledge a feeling. But in the past I would have tried to stop him from making such a big deal over nothing and he would have been impossible for the rest of the day.

**Calm Down?**

One parent told the group that this "feeling stuff" wasn't working in her home. Sometimes her daughter became even more enraged when she accepted her feelings. I asked the mom for an example. "Well," she said, "like just this morning. Megan was pitching a fit because her pink sneakers were wet and I told her she couldn't wear them to school. I kept my cool and said, "Megan, I can see that you're disappointed. You wanted to wear those shoes, but they're too wet." She screamed even louder and started kicking at me!

I listened to Megan's mother's soothing, singsong voice and said, "Your words are telling me you understand, but your tone of voice is saying, 'Shhhh . . . Calm down. It can't be that bad. There's nothing to be so upset about.'"

One of the other mothers piped up, "Calm down? Those two words are not allowed in my house. When I'm angry, telling me to calm down makes me even angrier. If my husband says that to me, I will rip his head off, and he knows it!"

"Well," said the first mom, "I *was* trying to use a calm voice to calm her down. I didn't want to add fuel to the fire."

If you want to calm a child down, it helps to try to match her strong feelings rather than minimize them: "Oh no! You were planning to wear your pink shoes and now they're all *wet*! What a disappointment! Those are your favorites! Darn it! I wish we had time to dry them. Do you think if we put them over the heater now they might be ready when you get home?"

And sometimes a choice helps a child move on. "What should we do for now? Do you want to wear your purple sneakers or your sandals?"

### Starving

A few weeks later Megan's mom reported this conversation:

Megan was starting to melt down because she was hungry. I told her (calmly!) that she needed to be patient and that dinner would be ready in just five minutes. The whining got louder.

Then I remembered about matching the emotion, so

I threw myself on the floor next to her and said, "Five minutes is a LONG time to wait when you're starving! It feels like you could almost *die* of hunger in that time!" I pounded on the floor with my fist. "We need food now!" Megan giggled and said, "You're silly, Mommy." She really enjoyed the drama. It completely changed her mood.

## Two (or Three) at a Time

A nursery school teacher in my group wondered about accepting feelings when there's more than one child involved. It seems like such a one-on-one activity. Here's what she had to say after giving it a try:

"I used to put myself in charge of settling the kids' conflicts. That often ended up with one unhappy child sulking in a corner and the other gloating over having won. Now I just listen and reflect back what each child is saying. I'm like the narrator. Here's an example from last week:

Jared, you didn't like it when Jose grabbed that block from you!

And, Jose, you *needed* that block to support your racetrack.

Ah, so, Jared, you were going to use that block on your tower . . . I see.

And, Jose, you feel it isn't fair, because Jared has a *lot* of blocks and you just need that one."

(Then, to my surprise, the coat-closet door pops open a crack and I hear a little voice say, "And Lily is in the closet because Jose stepped on my finger!")

When I do this, most of the time the children finish saying their piece and then they just calm down and go off to play. I don't even have to do anything. It's really quite amazing. Sometimes I help them find a solution (Can you help Jose find another block for his bridge?), but often just being heard is enough.

**Granola Grief**

One of the parents declared:

"Giving in fantasy is my favorite skill. Listen to what happened at my house when I tried it. Kristen, my four-year-old, only likes peanut butter–flavored granola bars. Her older sister, Jenna, was busy polishing off the last peanut butter bar from the variety pack. As Kristen started to cry, Jenna quickly shoved the whole bar into her mouth.

I gave Jenna a disapproving look. She scooped a damp wad from her cheek and offered it to her sister. No good. Too late! Kristen was screaming and sobbing. I assured her that we'd buy more as soon as possible, but she was not impressed. She continued to scream. I told her she had to use her indoor voice. She screamed louder. My eardrums were breaking, so I took her outside into the backyard. Now the whole neighborhood got to share in the grief! On and on it went until I finally remembered . . . "Oh yeah, give in fantasy."

In my most dramatic voice I said, "Kristen, do you know what I wish?" She stopped crying to say, "What?" I looked around the yard for inspiration. Aha, got it. "I wish we had a granola bar as big as that picnic table." Kristen's eyes grew wide. She said, "No, Mom. That would be *too* big."

"Well, then . . . I wish we had a granola bar as big as that rock over there." Kristen sighed happily, "That would be good!"

Crisis over. I guess having someone know just how much you want something can be almost as good as getting the real thing.

**Take Me to Oz**

One mother wondered if acknowledging feelings could possibly work with her nine-year-old son, who had been diagnosed with autism. Robbie had serious cognitive delays and most of his service providers were sure that a behavioral system with simple, concrete rewards and punishments was the only way to help such a child get himself under control. "I don't know," I hated to admit. "I don't have any experience with this."

Here's what she reported the following week:

> Robbie got it into his head that he wanted to see *The Wizard of Oz* on Broadway. He's watched the movie dozens of times and has memorized all the songs. I explained to him over and over that it wasn't playing in theaters right now, but that didn't help. One of the issues we have is that when Robbie wants something he just can't let it go. The anger and the crying can last for hours. He was starting to get really wound up when I figured, I'll try the fantasy thing."
>
> I patted the bed and said, "Robbie, do you want to come on my magic carpet with me and go visit Oz?"
>
> Robbie ran to the bed and snuggled in beside me. We "flew" over Oz. I looked down over the edge of the bed and started pointing out the characters. "I think I see the Scarecrow down there. What is he doing? And is that the Cowardly Lion?"
>
> "I see the Tin Man!" Robbie yelled.
>
> "Oh no, he's not moving," I said. "I think he's rusted."
>
> We visited all the characters and had a lovely time together. I felt good that I was able to meet his needs instead of just trying to suppress his endless frustration. It's so much better than offering him a star on a chart for controlling his temper, especially when he really can't control himself, and then he has to be doubly upset because he didn't get the star!

### I Hate School

This next example came from the mother of a child with Asperger's syndrome:

Justin has been giving me a hard time about going to school for over a year now. Transitions are difficult for him. We were having terrible mornings. He would cry and scream and have to be dragged to the car. I've been making changes—working with his teachers and reducing his school hours—but I've also started acknowledging his feelings. At the same time, I've stopped trying to reassure him and push away his anxiety. I used to say things like "You know I'll pick you up at twelve thirty," or "You know you *have* to go to school," or "You'll feel better once you're there," or "You'll see your friends," or "You love doing math at school"—all of which just enraged him.

Here's how it goes now (every day still):

Me: "Justin, time to put your jacket on for school, we're going to the car." (*horrified pause*)

Justin: "But I HATE SCHOOL!"

Me: "I KNOW! School is not your favorite place to be. You like being at home, playing with your cars . . . sigh . . . Well, here's your jacket."

Justin (*coming to the front door*) repeats: "It's *not* my favorite place!" and puts on his jacket.

It's funny. I think I used to do this a bit sarcastically ("Yeah, I know you hate it. I heard they torture kindergartners every afternoon"). Now that I know I don't have to fix all his worries, I can completely and honestly accept his feelings. And I think he knows it.

### More Questions

The parents continued to challenge me: Surely there are some feelings that are too insignificant to merit sympathy. "What about the kid who falls apart over the littlest thing? Someone brushed against his elbow? 'OWOWOW! It hurts!' Are we supposed to acknowledge the feelings of a kid who is just seeking attention? Won't that encourage him to complain about ever more insignificant slights?"

A child's day can be filled with all kinds of frustrations and emotionally intense experiences. (As four-year-old Max said after a long, tough morning of being cooperative and well-behaved at preschool, "Mom, I am freaking out!") Maybe that little brush of the elbow was the proverbial last straw. Maybe it was an excuse to weep a little.

If a child *just* wants attention and comfort, we can *just* give it to him. If we don't, he may well seek other, more annoying strategies for getting our attention!

You can scoop him up and say, "Where does it hurt? This needs a kiss." You can keep a special supply of Band-Aids dedicated to invisible injuries. A child who feels low can have two raisin "pills" or a teaspoon of grape juice "medicine." It is enormously cheering to have a few moments with an adult who ladles out a little emotional first aid in times of need.

And one last issue: "Often I will see that my daughter is upset, but when I ask her what's wrong she says, 'Nothing.' The more I question her, the less she will tell me."

It makes an enormous difference to a child when we accept her feelings from the get-go, without any questions. Instead of *asking* what's wrong, we can simply say, "You look sad," or "Something upset you," or "Seems like you had a rough day."

Statements like these help a child relax and feel free to share. She doesn't have to defend her feelings as she would if we had said, "Why do you feel sad?" She can talk to us if she wants to or just take comfort from our understanding.

I remember feeling the power of this skill of accepting the feelings without questions when I was teaching at PS 161 in Manhattan. One morning, as I checked in at the main office, I saw a tangle of teachers and secretaries surrounding a weeping sixth grader. The adults were desperate to find out what was wrong. They took turns firing questions at the child: "Why are you crying? What's wrong? Did something happen to you? Are you okay?" With every question, the girl sobbed harder, until she was almost breathless.

I took her arm and steered her out of the circle of attentive adults. "I'll sit with her," I said. We sat in a corner and I waited a bit, then I said, "Something really upset you." The girl started to talk, telling me that she had heard a car backfire on the street, and she thought it was a gunshot. Someone on her block had been shot that weekend, and now she thought they were shooting at her. "That must have been really scary," I offered. "Yeah" she agreed, as her breathing slowed and became less spasmodic.

If I had any doubt as to the power of my simple acceptance, it was quickly erased. Two adults in the office, seeing that the girl had calmed down, approached and started questioning us. "Did you find out what happened?" . . . "Is she okay now?" . . . "What was wrong?" The girl immediately went back into her panicked sobbing. I said, "She got scared, she's going to be okay," and the well-meaning adults backed away.

I felt very grateful at that moment that I had this little key to help a stressed and panicked child. The urge to question is so strong. If we find out what the problem is, we feel we have a chance to fix it. But often the fix is simple acceptance. Even if this girl hadn't told me what was wrong, I feel sure that having an adult just sit with her and acknowledge her distress without question would have been the most healing remedy.

### Session 2—Engaging Cooperation

One issue that jumped out at me when I started conducting workshops was that parents aren't just worried about getting through the day. Sure that's a top priority, but there's always the underlying anxiety: What kind of child am I raising? How did I create this little monster who has no sense of responsibility, hits his sister, tells lies, won't clean up his messes, whines, and is generally about as cooperative as an angry hornet? He was such a sweet little baby! Where did I go wrong?

I remember how I felt when my own son Danny, at two

years of age, figured out a new game to play with our small, elderly terrier mix. He would approach the sleeping dog, swing back his chubby little foot, and kick. The poor dog would jump up in alarm, and Danny would laugh delightedly at the excitement he had created. What kind of a human being kicks a dog for fun? What kind of a mother raised such a horror?

It helps to keep in mind that a two-year-old doesn't yet fully understand that other people (and creatures) have feelings. He understands that *his* leg hurts when *he* is kicked, but he doesn't really get it that *your* leg hurts when he kicks *you*. He isn't feeling any pain! Sure he'll cry if you yell at him, but that's because it's scary and unpleasant to be yelled at.

That knowledge freed me from feeling bad about myself as a mom, or angry at my son, and allowed me to focus on helping my child figure out a better way to interact with the dog. I stuck to the simple formula—acknowledge the feeling, limit the action. And throw in a choice to make it easier to move on.

"I see you're in a kicking mood, Danny. Dogs are *not* for kicking. Dogs like to be touched very gently! Let's see . . . what can you kick? Would you like to kick a balloon, or your foam ball?"

And of course it helps to remember that no matter what approach you take with a two-year-old you are sure to have to repeat yourself endlessly (and so I did!). I am pleased to report that Dan grew up to be a person who is exceedingly gentle with animals as well as people. He is the guy who will catch a wasp in a cup and put it outside rather than swat it with a flyswatter. And by three years of age he did learn to stroke the dog gently, to the great relief of his mother!

The parents in my group came up with lots of creative solutions with their own children once they abandoned the notion that their kids should behave out of a sense of moral obligation.

One of the favorite methods for engaging the cooperation of their young children was to be playful rather than stern. Kids love play. The day can get pretty grim with all the things they have to do. It is a nice relief to be goofy. For a preschooler it's a safe bet that making an inanimate object talk will be irresistible. They're eager to help socks that plead, "Won't somebody please put a foot in me. I feel so flat and empty"; toys that whine, "I'm lonely here on the floor. I want to be in the closet with my friends"; soap that sobs, "Poor me, I need some dirty hands to wash!"

## The Hungry Bag

In the land of toddlers you can beg, you can threaten, and you can punish, but there is no way you can compel your child to pick up those blocks. One mom tried. She was so annoyed with her son for refusing to clean up his mess that in a fit of rage she found herself stuffing blocks into his hand and clamping down hard on his fingers so he couldn't fling them away, as she forced him to drop each block into a bag. Not exactly the most efficient way of cleaning up! After our session here's what she told us:

> Yesterday another battle was brewing over the damn blocks. This time I had a brain wave. I held out the bag and said in a deep, scratchy voice, "I am so hungry . . . I want to eat blocks!" and we were off. The bag really liked purple ones . . . He had been waiting all day to eat that green one over there . . . "Hmm, they taste like broccoli . . . Not baaad . . . Oh no, I'm getting full now . . . *No,* don't make me eat the pink ones, they make me sick, please no, I'll vomit!" My eight-year-old daughter came over to "play" and made the cleanup even faster. Today they were both dying to do it again, and now the bag has a name—Boris, the hungry bag. Long may he last!

My personal favorite skill in this session is the one where we parents get to express our own feelings. The parents in my group seem to expect themselves to be endlessly patient and feel terribly guilty when, time after time, they fail.

A mother says to me, "*You* would have known just what to say. You would have been calm. You wouldn't have lost it like I did!" I am taken aback. Have I given the impression that I'm a calm person? Nothing could be further from the truth, I protest. "When I get frustrated my volume goes straight up. If you had been in my house last night (or even outside my house!), you would have heard me pounding on the bathroom door where my teenage son was taking an endless shower. You would have heard me yelling, "I don't like being late! Five people are waiting for us! I hate leaving people hanging! We have to leave NOW!"

We don't need to stay calm. We can express ourselves with all the heat we're feeling, as long as we remember to describe our own feelings and give information, instead of attacking our children.

When your kids get a little older you'll be grateful you've taught them the skill of simply giving information, because you'll often find yourself on the receiving end.

Recently, I asked my son Dan if I could borrow his new GPS. He was showing me how to program it, and I kept tapping the screen sharply with my finger. Dan said to me, "All it needs is a touch." I kept on tapping. Dan, seeing his prized new $100 purchase continue to be abused, repeated more forcefully, "Mom, the screen is sensitive! Watch. It responds to a very light touch." This time I got it.

Imagine if he had said to me, "MOM, what is the matter with you? You're going to break my GPS! You are being way too rough. Let me do it for you." Clearly, that would be a disrespectful way to talk to a parent! But where do kids learn how to talk to their parents? At least partly from how their parents talk to them.

## Close the Bar!

Some of the parents particularly loved the idea of writing notes.

The mother of a sixteen-year-old reported:

David will not go to bed without doing his workout, which includes several sets of pull-ups. Unfortunately, the only place in the house that has a doorway with a tall enough ceiling to mount the pull-up bar is right outside our bedroom. I've pleaded with him, again and again, to do the pull-ups earlier so he doesn't wake us just as we've fallen asleep. He promises to make an effort, but nothing changes. The next night there he is, doing his late-night workout again.

Finally, I wrote a note and hung it on the pull-up bar.

### BAR CLOSES AT TEN.
### THIS MEANS YOU! NO EXCEPTIONS!
### The Management.

It's been a week, and so far he's finished his exercises before ten every night. I asked him how he managed that, and he just gave me a funny look and said, "Well, I have to get it done before the bar closes, Mom."

I don't quite understand why the written word seems to have so much more power than the spoken one, but it is working for us!

And another parent found that note-writing helped when her son was too upset to talk.

## I'm Not Going to School!

Last night Kevin got really mad because his team lost the Super Bowl *and* he didn't win any of the quarters on the football pool we did. So he yelled, "I'm not going to school tomorrow!" and went up to his room and wrote a note:

Hi I'm not going to Shcool
oh and Tak everything I Have away

From Kevin

ps. I **hate you**

Needless to say, I was not looking forward to the morning and getting him ready for school. So I wrote a note back and left it on his bed:

*Dear Kevin,*
*There is no need to take everything you have away. You didn't do anything wrong. You are just really sad because the Cardinals lost and you didn't win the football pool. It is okay to be mad. Especially since your team lost last year, too. You probably don't want to go to school because you don't want to be embarrassed.*

*Write back,*
*Love, Mom*

Then this morning I went in to make sure he was awake, and saw he had written back:

Yeh I Gess So Thats What Happened last year But I Still Don't like Football.

So I pretended I thought he was still sleeping and wrote back to him and left his room:

*Dear Kevin,*

*I wouldn't like football either—why can't your team win? Maybe someday you can play and help your team win.*

*Love, Mom*

*PS We need to get ready for school*

After about five minutes he was dressed and ready to go to school. Not in a great mood, but decent.

## *Session 3—Alternatives to Punishment*

The idea that we need to punish in order to teach is deeply ingrained in most of us. We feel it is part of our duty as parents. I'm always a little bit nervous about making a case against such a powerful social norm. So I begin the session by asking parents if any of them can recall being punished as children. Here are some of the responses I've gotten:

"I was grounded but it didn't stick. We got away with a lot."

"When my parents grounded me it was pathetic. There was no way they could control me. I just lost more respect for them."

"My mom hit me with a spoon. It didn't stop me."

"My dad hit me with a belt. It didn't stop me."

"When I was hit, I just got sneakier."

"My mom used to make me put soap in my mouth. It just made me mad."

"I was put in a corner. I felt ashamed. It was scary."

Then one father threw me a curveball:

"My mother always spanked us when we were bad. We respected her and followed her rules. I spanked my son whenever he was bad. It works. But now I have a daughter, and when I spank her it makes her so angry that she gets worse. So I'd like to learn your alternatives. Also, we now have a foster child, and we're not allowed to spank him, so this is very important to me!"

After I hear from the parents, I pull out a newspaper clipping I'd saved and read excerpts to the group. I found this article striking because a teenager died when his friends were so focused on avoiding punishment that they neglected to take him to the hospital when he was severely injured.

### A Nightmare for Real

**Teen athlete's death, actions of others shake entire region.**

A 17-year-old popular high school student athlete died Tuesday night, his devastated family by his side, after being taken off life support five hours earlier. Rob Viscome had been in a coma at the Westchester medical center since hitting his head at an impromptu after-school beer party at a friend's home. . . .

The teens lied about where the party took place and cleaned up evidence. . . . Many of the witnesses gave conflicting stories. It is still not clear why they didn't call police or how long the teen lay bleeding before friends finally drove him to the hospital. . . .

We pray that young persons, despite possible short-term *consequences* with their parents, will be more apt to dial 911 if one of them becomes injured or sick. Precious moments and precious lives may be at stake.[*]

Why would we be surprised that in a moment of crisis our children's first thoughts turn to self-protection, rather than how to fix the problem? We have trained them to expect that our response to their misdeeds is to punish them.

An incident of much smaller import occurred to my son when he was in fifth-grade English class. A girl seated near the teacher's desk put her foot up and accidentally knocked a snow globe to the floor, where it shattered. Everyone froze, except Dan. He jumped up and began to pick up the broken glass. Of course, no good deed goes unpunished! The teacher erupted in a rage at him, thinking that he was the culprit. She screamed at him so furiously that he wasn't even able to get out that he hadn't done it. In the face of this onslaught, no one else confessed.

What I came away with from this experience was that when faced with a problem, *my* kid was the one who reacted instantly to fix it, because that's how he was raised. Everyone else drew back in fear (as well they should have!).

The challenge for us is to find some response to misbehavior

---

[*] An editorial from the *Journal News*, Westchester edition, May 3, 2002.

that actually inspires change, instead of hanging on to the old ways that cause resentment and, more important, distract from the real problem.

But parents continue to wonder, "Shouldn't there be consequences for children who continue to misbehave? How will they learn if they don't suffer for their crimes?"

My objection to the word "consequences" is that it is so often used as a new label to stick on an old, self-defeating idea. In the mind of the parent, "No TV for a week" becomes a "consequence" rather than a punishment. It doesn't change the dynamic. The child does something wrong, and the parent thinks of some way to make the child feel bad in the hope that he will learn to behave better. Whether we call it a consequence or a punishment, it doesn't get us the result we're looking for. We need to decide what we want our children to think and feel when they do something wrong. Do we want them to focus on which TV shows they will miss, how resentful they are at being grounded, what hopelessly bad people they are . . . or do we want them to think about how to fix the mistake, make it better, what to do next time?

Parents were still skeptical. "So are you saying that even *consequences* aren't allowed? How about when a child deliberately disobeys? Then what are we left with? That's too permissive for me! Don't we need some kind of bottom line?"

I'm not suggesting that we give up our authority as parents. We can assert our authority by taking action. We can take action to protect a child from harm, to protect him from hurting others, to protect property from being damaged, to protect ourselves or our relationship. We can state our values and give choices. We can give our children a way to fix the problem or to make amends. And we can do it all without punishing.

Here are some examples of parents taking action to protect, rather than imposing "consequences."

# The Next Generation

Protecting your property:
- Throwing blocks can break windows. I'm putting the wooden blocks away for now.
- I'm not willing to lend any more tools. I'll feel better about sharing my tools again when the drill you brought to your friend's house last week is returned or replaced.
- I'm very upset that the car was taken without permission. I'm holding on to the keys until we can come up with a system that we're both comfortable with. Let's take awhile to think about it.

Protecting others:
- No hitting! I can see how angry you are with your brother. I'm taking you (or him) into the kitchen with me right now so that nobody gets hurt.
- Throwing sand can injure people's eyes. Let's go play on the grass for now.
- I'm holding on to your paintball gun until you can come up with a way to assure me that it will be used safely. Pointing it at people's ears is too dangerous.

Protecting yourself:
- I'm too tired to read bedtime stories after nine o'clock. We can try again tomorrow night as long as you're ready for bed on time.
- We're going home now. I don't want to do any more shopping today. I know you need clothes for your camping trip, but right now I'm too upset at being spoken to so sarcastically, especially in front of the salesperson.
- Last time we went to the lake, I was really angry that I had to yell and beg for fifteen minutes to get you all out of the water when it was closing time. I'm not willing to go back until we come up with a better plan for leaving.

Protecting your child:
- I'm putting the bike away for now. I can see you're in no

mood to wear a helmet, and I'm too worried about injury to let you ride without one. What can we find to play with that doesn't require headgear?
- I can't give you permission to go to another unsupervised party. I'm sure you know why. If you'd like, you can invite some friends over to our house.

Protecting your relationship with your child:
- I need the house to be clean before the guests come tonight. I'll take you to your friend's house as soon as this clutter is put away. Yes, I hear you saying that I could do it myself because they're *my* friends. The problem is that I'd feel very resentful if I had to clean up your stuff while you were out playing, and I don't want to feel that way about my daughter!
- I'm very upset right now! I don't like the way you're talking to me, and I don't like the way I'm talking to you! I'm going into my bedroom now and closing the door. I need some time to cool down.

These kinds of statements let your children know, without attacking them, that you respect your own feelings as well as theirs, and that you have your limits. Not only does it motivate them to cooperate and make amends, it helps teach them how to stand their ground respectfully with their own friends. In most of our relationships we don't have the power to punish people, but we often do have the power to protect ourselves and others.

As I drove home from the meeting, I thought about the time Dan spent the afternoon with his friends exploring the woods behind our house. He was twelve then. That evening he said to me, "Mom, it's really weird. Steve and Henry wanted to climb those rocks by the ice cave, and I told them I didn't think we should do it.

"Steve said, 'Don't worry, it'll be okay.' And I said to him, 'I know if my mom were here I'd be saying the exact same thing that you're saying. But I just don't feel comfortable with you guys climbing up there. Because if you got hurt I'd feel responsible.' And they stopped! I think I'm getting to be like a grown-up. I could never imagine myself saying something like that."

I was dumbfounded. I couldn't imagine it either. My reckless little boy was telling someone else to be careful? But he had the language for it. He couldn't have given orders to his friends. ("Don't you dare do that!") Or threatened them. ("I'll ground you!") But he knew how to respectfully describe his feelings and state his limits (who knew he even had limits!). A useful tool in any relationship.

The next week, parents were eager to share the results of their experiments with alternatives to punishment.

## Young Vandal

One of the workshop moms had a home that was a real showcase. It was filled with elegant furniture, plush white carpeting, and beautiful rugs. She also had Ivan, a destructive little three-year-old. He would use black marker on the couch cushions, the walls, the floor, and he'd poke at the pillows with scissors. Ivan was a menace. Whenever she wasn't looking, he was redecorating. She would scold him and give him time-outs, but the behavior continued. Here's what she reported:

> The week after we had our alternative-to-punishment session, I caught Ivan cutting the fringes on one of my rugs. I grabbed the scissors from him and said, "I am very upset! This was the Oriental rug my grandmother gave me! Now the fringes are all messed up. I expect you to fix it." I handed the scissors back to him, found a ruler, and placed it along the line of fringes. "This has to be cut very carefully to even it out."
>
> Ivan said, "I'm sorry, Mommy," and carefully evened out the fringes while I held the ruler. The next day he spilled a drop of water on a tablecloth. He ran to me and

said, "Mom, there's water on the tablecloth. What can we do to fix it?"

I was astonished. My son has done a complete turn-about, from the destroyer to the fixer. I also took him on a special shopping trip to buy him art materials—all kinds of things for him to draw on, paint on, and cut. I keep the supplies in a special box for him, and there have been no art attacks on my house since.

## A Big Mess

I have to admit, Andy is a pretty wild little four-year-old. I do understand that "boys will be boys." I gave my parents a hard time in my day. Still, I want Andy to learn to face up to his bad behavior instead of running away. The day after our meeting on alternatives to punishment, I walked into the living room and saw white powder all over the floor. Apparently, Andy needed something to carry in his dump truck, and decided that his little sister's baby powder would be a good cargo. I yelled, "Who made this big mess?"

Andy said, "Trouble!" and ran to hide behind the couch.

Then I remembered, and I changed tactics. I said, "Oh no, we have a problem. What should we do?"

Andy poked his head out from behind the couch. He yelled "Water!" and ran to the bathroom and came back with a wet paper towel.

## The Little Green Man

I shared my own first attempt to introduce problem-solving to my toddler. (My mom told me he was probably much too young for this, but I was desperate.)

When Dan was two years and nine months old (I know this, because he was toilet trained at two years and eight months, and, yes, I *was* counting), we had our first formal problem-solving session. I was the frustrated parent of a boy who, having shown his ability to deposit bodily fluids in the pot, had now lost interest in this activity. He would play, clutching himself until it was absolutely too late, and then let loose and pee freely on the carpet. He'd then happily climb up on the stool to reach the foam-action carpet cleaner and scrub brush to clean up the mess. If I tried to urge him to use the bathroom during the clutching period, he would vehemently protest that he did not need to go. This had gone on for a week. My long-awaited toilet-training triumph was crumbling before my eyes. I got out my pad and pencil and read aloud as I wrote:

The problem—Dan does not like to stop playing to go to the bathroom. Mom does not like peepee on the floor.

Dan asks, "What are you writing?"

"I'm writing down ideas to solve this problem . . . one, two, three, four."

1. (I go first) Mom will remind Dan in a friendly way to go to the bathroom.
2. (Dan offers the next idea) Dan will clean the floor with carpet cleaner.
3. (My turn) Dan can wear diapers if he doesn't want to pee in the potty (I'm hoping he won't take this option).
4. (Dan is looking around the room. His gaze falls on a small plastic Statue of Liberty souvenir.) The little green man will tell me. He will say, "Peepee in the pot."

I am thinking that this is not working, but I forge ahead. "Okay, let's look at our ideas to see which ones we want to use and which we don't like."

1. Dan violently objects to a friendly reminder. I cross it out.
2. Mom objects. Carpet is getting too smelly.
3. Dan says okay to diapers, but Mom objects to her own idea.
4. The little green man. Dan thinks this is a good one, although Mom lacks conviction.

I post the list on the fridge and lie in wait for the next crotch-clutching incident. Finally, it happens. It's dinnertime and Dan has no thought of leaving the table. He is content to squeeze and wiggle. I take Miss Liberty, put it to his ear, and whisper, "Peepee in the pot." He takes the statue and whispers something back to it (I never found out what), and he went to the bathroom. Hallelujah!

For the next month or so I carry the little green man everywhere with me. He is my emissary to my son's bladder. It caused me only one awkward social moment. Once, when I was rummaging through my pack, I found my Swedish friend giving me an odd look. She had spied the statue. "My, aren't we getting patriotic lately. Should I be carrying the Swedish flag?"

## Inappropriate Attire

Eight-year-old Carly has always been a tomboy. She absolutely hates getting dressed up. Usually I let her pick her own clothes. But last Sunday was my mother-in-law's funeral. My husband was distraught, and so were the other children. His mom had been very close with them all. She was no long-distance grandmother. Carly chooses to stage a clothing revolt right before we get in the car. Instead of the outfit I had laid out for her, she came to the car in a stained T-shirt, jeans, and her Yankees cap. My husband was ready to give her a good, hard spanking.

I grabbed Carly and went inside. I told her that I knew she hated dress-up clothes. The problem, I said, is that Daddy is very sad about his mom dying. And to him and a lot of other people dressing up is a sign of respect. I can't let you go to the funeral like this because it would make other people feel bad.

Carly didn't say anything, but her bottom lip was pushed out and she wasn't about to cave in. I said I'd bring her nice black pants (I wasn't even making her wear a dress, mind you!) and two blouses to choose from. When we got there, she could change in the car. If she didn't want to change, we would not be going into the funeral. I would wait outside in the car with her.

When we got there, Carly squirmed into the nice clothes and came in with us. Later on at the reception, I told her she could change back into her jeans, but she insisted that she liked her fancy outfit.

I was very relieved to be able to save the day when my husband was under so much stress! Describing our feelings and giving Carly a choice let her cooperate without losing face. She can be really tough. A direct confrontation would have been a disaster!

Finally, one parent who complained of being a short-order chef shared this experience:

## Mealtime Misery

Mealtimes at my house are miserable. Josh, my five-year-old, will start to complain that he doesn't want to eat the chicken. He says it's disgusting, and I yell at him for being rude. Then the seven-year-old twins act up. If he isn't eating it, why do we have to? We end up in a big fight every night.

I decided to give problem-solving a try. I told the kids I worked hard at making dinner and it hurt my feelings when they said it was disgusting. Josh said he didn't want to be *forced* to eat something he didn't like. I realized that one of the reasons he was being so rude was that I was giving him no choice. He would be willing to be polite if I would back off a little.

I told them we needed to write down all our ideas for making dinnertime more pleasant for everyone. They were excited about that. Here are the ideas we all finally agreed on:

Josh would be allowed to make himself a sandwich for dinner if it was something he felt he really couldn't eat. But he had to do it ahead of time. No complaining about food and jumping up to visit the refrigerator during the meal.

The twins didn't want to make their own sandwiches. They didn't really mind the food. But they decided to make a rule of "no singing at the dinner table." That would make mealtimes more pleasant, because the singing made the kids annoyed with one another and usually led to fighting.

We also decided to put a suggestion sheet on the refrigerator where they could write their dinner ideas, and at least once a week I would make something from the sheet.

So far, it's been working beautifully. The kids don't complain anymore, and my son makes his own sandwich two or three times a week. I no longer dread mealtimes!

With only a few minutes of our session left, a parent waved her hand. "Wait, how about homework?" Others immediately chimed in: "Yeah, that's the worst!" . . . "Torture every night!" It was time to go home, but we all decided to schedule one extra meeting before moving on.

**Homework**

I was glad we'd be devoting an evening to this topic. It's hard to think of a single issue that has caused more children to melt down and more parents to tear out their hair in frustration than homework.

I told the group that when I was a kid homework didn't exist in kindergarten. It was barely introduced in first and second grade. We had an occasional assignment along the lines of "If you would like, you can bring in something to talk about for show-and-tell." Decades later when I sent my own children to school, I encountered a whole new world. They came home from kindergarten with nightly assignments, such as "Write the letter *B* ten times. Then draw four objects that begin with *B*." Sounds simple, doesn't it?

I remember watching my Dan tearing through the paper with his eraser as he struggled to draw the bicycle that existed in his head. There was no way I could convince my sobbing son to "Please, just draw a *ball*," instead of an infernally complicated two-wheeler. That was just the second day of kindergarten! In grade school it got worse. Pages of long division problems, five-paragraph persuasive essays, science webquests, all designed to bring a parent with a tired child to the edge of insanity.

Eventually, I discovered that every parent imagines that his or her child is the only one having such trouble. Surely the other children are happily scribbling cute little drawings of bubbles, balls, and bottles, while your own is becoming mentally unhinged. Some children may handle homework with relatively little stress, but I haven't met many. There's no simple solution. We need to tackle the problem from all angles.

"I'm ready to try anything," said the mom who had introduced the topic. "Please, can we use my son as an example?" Without hesitation, she launched into her tale of woe:

Tommy started sixth grade this year. He did okay for the first quarter, but then things started falling apart. There is so much homework, and it takes him so long to do it, that he has just given up. He has difficulty with his handwriting and it is very slow and tedious for him to write out assignments. We have massive fights about it every night.

He has had to give up playdates because he won't finish his homework first, and I know he won't do it afterward. I've taken away his Xbox and his TV-watching privileges. I've yelled at him until I'm blue in the face. I don't know what else to do. Last night I followed him upstairs, saying, "Tommy, you *have* to do this penmanship homework. It's very important!" Tommy snatched the sheet from my hand and said, "No . . . I . . . don't!" as he ripped it into little pieces and threw them down the stairs.

The school called me in to a conference with his teachers and the guidance counselor. They told me that Tommy was in danger of repeating the grade. Every time he misses a homework, he gets a zero. Even if he passes all his tests, he may still fail. I was too upset to say much. I just told them I'd talk to my son and get back to them.

Everyone in the group had something to say. Could you use problem-solving? What about acknowledging feelings? Would choices help? This situation seemed too complicated for a simple fix. We explored all possibilities. Tommy's mother took lots of notes. The following week she could hardly wait to tell us how it went:

The first thing I decided was that I had to change my whole attitude. Instead of being on the school's side, I had to be on my child's side. I'd stop trying to convince Tommy that homework is "good for him" or "not really such a big deal if he'd only get down to it." I kept the thought in my mind that for an active kid like Tommy, sitting down to homework after a long day at school really did feel like torture, especially with his learning disabilities.

I told him I needed his help in solving the homework problem. I said, "I hate having this battle every night. I find myself screaming at you and getting all angry and frustrated, and I don't want to do that anymore."

Then I spent a long time acknowledging his feelings, the way we practiced in the group. I said things like "It's a really difficult problem. Here you are coming home each day after six and a half long hours at school, and then you're supposed to sit down and do even more schoolwork. That stinks! You'd rather watch TV and relax, or run around, or play video games, or eat—*anything* but more schoolwork. It's not as if you don't work hard when you have an interesting assignment. Like with that egg-drop lab. You spent all afternoon working on your contraption."

Tommy looked suspicious at first, but then he got more enthusiastic, nodding as I went on. Then I said, "The problem is, the school can really give you a hard time if you don't do any homework, and I don't want that to happen. So we have to find the *least* painful way to get through this. We need ideas! What could we try that might work?" I got a piece of paper and I wrote "Horrible Homework Ideas" on top.

I started out the list with some outrageous ideas, because Tommy loves humor. It is really the way to his heart. So I wrote, "Tell them the dog peed on it." Tommy said, "Yeah!" Then he suggested, "Say Emily [his little sister] peed on it!" I wrote it down. Then he offered, "Use a mind-wipe laser like in *Men in Black,* so they'll forget they assigned it." I added, "Pray for a snowstorm on heavy homework nights." Tommy said, "Pray for a blackout if it's too warm for snow."

I decided the mood was right for a few more realistic ideas.

Me: Start homework after you have a snack.

Me: Do it in the kitchen while I'm making dinner.

Tommy: Eat ice cream while doing homework. (He knows he's not allowed to have ice cream before dinner!)

Tommy: Eat three raisins after each spelling word.

Me: Do five jumping jacks after five math problems.

Tommy: Do HW while watching TV.

Me: Do it while listening to music.

Me: Set the timer and stop when it rings.

Me: Maybe you can write the longer assignments on the computer. (Tommy said that wasn't allowed, but I said we had to put down *all* the ideas, so we left it in with a question mark.)

We looked over our list. Tommy laughed heartily at the

first few ideas, and said, "I think we need something a little bit more *practical,* Mom." So I crossed them out. I also crossed out the TV idea, because I thought that would be too distracting. Tommy really liked the idea of the timer. I'm sure that one of the reasons he refuses to start homework is that he finds so many ways to distract himself that it goes on forever, and that is all he does until bedtime. The school says the standard is sixty minutes a night for a sixth grader, so we decided that we would set the timer for twenty minutes of math, then twenty minutes of English, and twenty minutes of reading, which we would do together. If the timer went off before he was finished, I'd write a note to the teacher *if* he had worked steadily. Tommy was really excited about this idea. He also liked the idea of working to music.

Here are the results. I no longer ask him about homework as soon as he gets off the bus.

I wait until after his snack. Then I say something like "Twenty vocabulary words to look up? That's a lot! Three pages of math? Ugh! Twenty sentences? Well, how many do you think you could bear to do? Five or seven?"

When I start dinner I call him inside for homework. He spends some time choosing certain songs to listen to on his iPod during homework, and setting out his snacks. Then we start the timer. It helps him to know that there's an end to the ordeal. He often surprises me by going beyond the time to finish up his work. "Just two more sentences, Ma. I can do it!" Sometimes he quits when the timer rings, but then will finish up in the morning before the bus comes. I never would have thought of leaving homework until the last minute as a good idea, but I am amazed at how much more efficiently he can work after a night's sleep.

But that's not all. I wrote a letter to his teachers saying, "I appreciate your support and my husband and I are very grateful that you took the time to discuss Tommy's issues with us. After the conference with you, we all had a long talk about how to improve the homework situation. One of the things we concluded is that Tommy gets overwhelmed and resists doing homework partly because it takes him so long to do it. Part of our new plan is to put a time limit on the homework, so that it isn't as overwhelming to him. We feel this is the way to get him back on the right track. I hope you will support us in this endeavor!

"In addition, we plan to have Tommy use the computer when he has more than one written assignment in a given night. He can practice his handwriting with shorter assignments like spelling words and definitions. This way, we will get the best of both worlds: more motivation from Tommy, and regular handwriting practice without tears."

The teacher actually agreed! He has never been flexible with Tommy in the past. But I guess the way I put it was hard to resist. This has made our lives so much more *livable*!

The group beamed and applauded. It was a lot to absorb. I thought I'd better summarize. "So when it comes to homework," I said, "here are your new strategies."

1. Be on your child's side. Acknowledge his feelings!
2. Problem-solve. Consider everything.
3. Be your child's advocate. Communicate with the teacher when homework gets overwhelming. Don't worry about what other people's kids are doing.

### *Session 4—Encouraging Autonomy*

Probably the hands-down favorite of parents in this session is the simple substitution of a choice for a command. Kids usually respond with enthusiasm to choices. Not only can we feel good about encouraging our children to become independent individuals; we get a little cooperation on the side. Not a bad collateral benefit!

## Don't Fence Me In

With some kids (mine, for example) the choice needs to be open-ended.

Me: Dan, I can't let you cut the carpet with your scissors. Do you want to cut paper or cardboard?

Dan: No!

Me: Well, I don't want my carpet cut. What else *can* you cut with the scissors?

Dan gets a gleam in his eye. He looks around. "I can cut string, I can cut tissues, I can't cut the laundry . . . I KNOW, I can cut weeds!" He runs outside.

Another one:

Me: Dan, don't throw that ball in the house. (He throws it again, predictably I might add.)

Me: I can see you're in a throwing mood. You can throw a balloon in the house or you can throw the ball outside.

Dan: I'll throw my paper plane in the house.

Me: Oh, I didn't think of that.

## Up a Tree

A father shared this encounter:

My son's eleven-year-old friend Aiden was visiting. When his older brother came to take him home, Aiden was up in the top of our maple tree. His brother ordered him to come down . . . now! Aiden refused. I tried to help. I explained to Aiden that it really was time to go, and he shouldn't make his brother wait. Aiden said, "I'm staying in my tree!"

Then I thought, this kid loves to joke around, so I called up, "Aiden you have a choice. You can come down very, very slowly like a three-toed sloth or . . . you can jump down fast like a monkey. Aiden yelled, "Monkey!" and jumped out of the tree.

The cartoon that caused parents to protest was the one about not asking too many questions. "But if I don't ask," they complained, "I don't find out anything!" Even though we've all experienced for ourselves just how unwelcome those questions can be (for example, Tell me all about your vacation. How many places did you visit? Did you have fun? Make any new friends? How much money did you spend? Are you going back next year?), it's still hard to just sit there and say nothing, especially when we're dying to know! Besides, not asking could seem uncaring.

Here's one alternative to interrogation that I use when I want to encourage communication. Everyone who tried it liked it.

**An Invitation to Talk**

Instead of asking "How was your class trip? Did you have fun?" Or "How did your PowerPoint presentation go? Did the class like it? What did the teacher say?" substitute an invitation to talk:

"I'd love to hear about your class trip when you're ready to tell about it." Or "I'm interested to know how your presentation went. Come tell me about it when you're in the mood."

Parents found that often their child would approach them a few minutes, or even hours, later saying, "I'm ready to tell now. Do you want to hear?"

### Session 5—Praise

One of the challenges that came up in this session was how to summon the genie of praise when the first thing that leaps to our lips is criticism. I admitted to the group that when my son lost his cell phone at the mall I really wanted to rip into him: "How can you be so casual about such an expensive thing? You knew that it slips out of those gym pants pockets when you sit down, because it's happened before. Why would you not either get a clip for it or wear different pants? Do you realize how much it will cost to replace?"

But when I looked at the woeful expression on his face, I was unable to muster up a scolding. I thought about all the things I have lost, and how upset I felt when I lost something valuable. How awful it would be to have someone kicking me when I was down. So I praised him instead. (With description instead of evaluation, of course.)

"Gee, Dan, you've kept track of that phone for two years and never lost it. And it's not as if it stays in your room. It's been to school and on trips and to soccer games. It's pretty amazing if you think of it."

Dan said, "I'll check the bench I was sitting on when I texted Sam." There was a teenager at the bench holding Dan's phone. "Did you lose this?" he asked, seeing Dan dive under the bench, obviously in search of something.

Phew! The phone was back. Dan turned to me and proclaimed, "I'm never going to wear these shorts again when I'm carrying my cell phone!"

Criticism would have torn him down and defeated him in his lowest moment. Descriptive praise gave him the strength to carry on the search and to plan to fix the problem in the future. What's more, it demonstrates that in times of need we support rather than attack each other.

## The Bad Grade

One of the parents remembered that story when she received her son's report card:

I'm so glad you told us about your son's cell phone. When I read Eric's report card I was really mad at him. He was failing math, and he hadn't given me a clue that he was struggling with it. I said, "Eric, I noticed that in the past you've always done pretty well in math. And you're so good at explaining it to Joey [his younger brother] when he has trouble with his homework. Something must be happening here with this D."

Eric started telling me he really didn't like his teacher this year. She was always putting a lot of notes on the board, and he couldn't write fast enough to copy the formulas before she erased them. Last year the kids had worked in groups and discussed their answers, but this year it was all lecture. We had a friendly discussion, and Eric agreed to go for after-school help if he missed the notes in class. In the past I have scolded him for a low grade and he has gotten really sullen and angry with me. He never talked with me before about what kind of problems he was having.

One temptation that parents have to watch out for is the urge to praise by comparison. Parents with more than one child found it particularly hard to resist statements like:

"You got your shoes tied without any help. The baby can't do that."

"Look at what a big girl you are, reading your book all by yourself. Your little sister can't read a single word."

"You cleaned your room without being asked. That's more than I can say for your older brother!"

The danger here is that this kind of praise puts relationships on thin ice. Might the big brother feel threatened when his little brother learns to tie his shoes? Will his accomplishment be diminished? And how will big sister feel when the "baby" starts learning to read? And will the brothers be likely to work together and help each other out with cleanups when one's achievement depends on the other's failure?

Consider these alternatives:

"You got your shoes tied all by yourself. I know who will be teaching little Joey when he is ready for his big-boy shoes."

"You are reading! I think your little sister is going to be excited when she finds out that her big sister can read to her."

"The two of you make quite a cleanup team. Jason put the Legos away and Joel picked up all the books."

One dad brought this story to the group:

**This Is Music!**

When my son was in fourth grade he learned a solo jazz piece on his saxophone to play at the school concert. He worked hard on it. He had to learn to play notes that hadn't been taught yet by the band teacher. At the concert we were treated to a program that only a parent could love. The children squeaked and squawked through a C scale, and then "Hot Cross Buns." Finally, my son came to the front of the stage and started to play. People were bobbing their heads and tapping their fingers. This was music! My heart swelled with pride. When I saw my son afterward I had a powerful urge to say, "You were the best one! Everybody else up there could hardly play, but you, you were great!" But I knew we weren't supposed to do that anymore.

What I finally came up with was "You sounded so smooth and confident up there, like you were really into the music. And the audience got into it, too. I could see people swaying and tapping their toes. It was like being at a real jazz club." How's that for a masterpiece of descriptive praise?

The next day my son came home from school very excited. He told me that he was teaching a bunch of kids how to play his piece, because they all liked it so much. I felt pretty good about my restraint. What if I had told him that I was proud of him because he was better than all the other kids? Would he have allowed himself the experience of sharing his music with his friends?

### *Session 6—Freeing Children from Roles*

Parents often find themselves putting their children in roles just to explain their behavior to the outside world. When you are at a relative's house for dinner and your son rejects the entrée, you say in self-defense, "Ah, well, he's a picky eater."

When a visiting relative talks to your daughter and she turns her face away, you feel compelled to explain, "She's just shy." When your five-year-old doesn't join the others in the pool, you tell the other parents, "He is afraid of the water. He takes a long time to warm up to new things." Of course, our kids are hearing all this and taking it to heart. "My parent sees me as a shy, picky eater who is fearful and takes a long time to warm up. Ah, so that's who I am. I guess I'd better stay away from that pool!"

But what *can* we say? We can't just sit there silently while Aunt Rose nags at Johnny about not eating the roast beef. How can we support our kids, while not making them feel stuck in a role, and simultaneously politely fend off well-meaning friends and relatives?

A very useful phrase that seems to do it all is "when he is ready."

"Johnny will try a new food when he's ready."

"Don't worry, I'm sure Maria will talk to you when she's ready."

"Sammy, I know you'll try out the swimming pool when you're ready."

Now your child is getting the message that you're not pushing him to do something he's not comfortable with, but you don't expect him to be stuck at that stage forever. He can decide to make a change when he feels right about it.

## The Olden Days

Max's mom thought she could use this idea. She often found herself in the position of having to explain his difficult behavior to others within his earshot. She was eager to try something different. She told us:

> I think this new language is having an effect. For the first time, Max stayed to play at the next-door neighbor's house all by himself. In the past I've always had to stay

with him. If I tried to convince him to let me do an errand, he'd cry, "No, Mommy, don't leave me!" I used to urge him to be a big boy, but that didn't help. Lately, I've just been telling him that he will do it when he is ready. It seems to have made a difference. The next day he wanted to go next door by himself again. He said to me, "Mom, remember in the olden days when I was afraid to stay at Ryan's house?"

Isn't that cute? We all laughed.

## Who Will Carry the Hammers?

One parent reported on her experience helping out in her son's third-grade classroom:

We were doing a book-making project. It involved hammering nails into a stack of papers to make holes for the binding, and then sewing the papers together with embroidery thread. I came to the classroom with a bag of hammers, among other supplies. We needed to transport the materials down to the gym, where we would work.

I remember that when I was in elementary school only the boys were asked to help out with physical tasks, and I always resented it. So I looked around the room and caught the eye of a thin, pale girl, and asked, "Bridget, would you like to carry the bag of hammers?" Sure enough, several boys jumped up, yelling, "I will! I will!" But Bridget shouldered the bag. As we walked down to the gym, she started to complain. The bag was too heavy. It was hurting her shoulder. She shifted her grip. Now it was hurting her hand. How much did these hammers weigh, anyway? I felt guilty. In my political zeal to be fair and feminist, I had picked this poor kid who was too frail for the task.

We spent a happy hour working on the books, and when it was time to move the supplies back to the classroom I asked who wanted to carry the hammers. Again, several boys vociferously volunteered, but Bridget grabbed the bag and said fiercely, *"That's my job!"*

"But I thought it hurt your shoulder," I said.

"I figured out a better way to carry it," she snapped back.

Score a point for skinny girls!

The cartoon that caused the most consternation in this session was the one about not being a sore loser. Turns out that *all* of our children are sore losers, and that everyone thinks that they have done something terribly wrong for their kids to be so deficient in this area.

When my firstborn child was almost four years old, I bought him his first board game. I was excited. We were about to start a whole new level of interaction. I remembered my childhood game-playing days with great fondness. So we opened up Hi Ho Cherry-O with great anticipation. Dan was happy to put together the spinner and baskets, and to poke the little plastic cherries into the holes in the cardboard trees. Then we started to play.

My goodness, where was the sportsmanship? What was wrong with my child? He insisted on taking endless turns, spinning over and over until he got the number he wanted. He refused to put cherries back when the spinner landed on "spilled basket." I soldiered on, trying to explain the concept of taking turns, winning and losing, being a good sport. Dan ignored me and got annoyed when I tried to stop him from playing his way. Fortunately, my sluggish brain caught up to reality before meltdown occurred. I gave up my quest, and Cherry-O became a favorite activity involving flicking a spinner and rearranging plastic cherries.

What I've come to realize, after raising three children to teenagerhood, and hearing from many parents in my groups, is that formal game playing, from sports to cards, is not a terrific activity for preschoolers. Those fond memories I had were of a much later stage in my development as a child. Three- and four-year-olds cannot comprehend why they should be made to lose, wait for someone else to have a turn, follow the unpleasant demands of a roll of the dice or the flick of a spinner. Parents worry that their children are behaving like spoiled brats. That they won't have the proper social skills they need to have friendships if they can't learn to be gracious losers. Give it time! A preschooler isn't ready for that, and she doesn't need to be.

For school-age children, games become social coin of the realm. But it still can be difficult for them to accept the idea of losing without feeling angry and discouraged. Heck, it's difficult for many adults! One of the ways we can teach our kids the fun and satisfaction of game playing without the emotional drama is to alter the games a bit, so that the competition factor is lessened. Here are just two of the successful variations that we have come up with:

Kids love to play racing games. But there are often tears and accusations of cheating. The best purchase I made was a big stopwatch. The kids come up with some kind of challenge or obstacle course, then one of them will run while the other keeps the time. On the next round, each child tries to beat his own time. I am amazed at how well this works! You would think they'd insist on comparing, but they don't.

When we play board games like Candyland, the one who gets around the board first is the official "first-place winner." But the rest of the family keeps on playing. I started this tradition because it was too frustrating for the other kids not to be allowed to get to the end. I said, "I'm going to keep playing until I finish. I don't care how many turns it takes!" Now everyone gets the satisfaction of finishing the game.

This may sound overly indulgent. But I have seen my three boys grow into teens who enjoy competitive sports, card games, computer games, and all manner of board games (at least during blackouts and "family game nights"). They are gracious winners and good losers. They modify their intensity for younger children. They laugh a lot while they play. I believe that the work I did when they were younger, racking my brain to figure out ways for them to enjoy playing without feeling like losers, helped that happen.

## Our Last Session

When we meet for the last time, I ask the parents which skill they found most useful. Without fail, most say that the language of accepting feelings is what has profoundly changed their relationship with their children. It's interesting to me that this is what they choose. Way back in session one, when we first talk about this skill, I can tell that the parents are impatient. They want to get past the touchy-feely stuff and move on to the real tricks of the trade. They accept the idea of acknowledging feelings, but what they really want to know is "Then what?" After I do all that, how do I make my child get ready for school, stop having temper tantrums, stop poking his baby sister in the eye, eat his vegetables, brush his teeth, go to bed? It really takes the whole six-week series for it to sink in. Acknowledging feelings is not the prologue; it's the main event. All the other skills build on that foundation. Many problems evaporate without anything more. And the whole nature of the relationship is so transformed that many problems never even get started.

It is an ongoing challenge to live life without constantly contradicting the experience of those around us. Often, when we're talking to an adult friend, we can empathize easily, without even thinking about it. We don't try to scold or instruct or advise. We have a natural sense that this would be insulting. But sometimes, even with other adults, our instincts fail us. Empathy seems counterintuitive.

Recently, I was talking to a friend who was having some medical tests done. She told me that she was worried that she might have cancer. Every instinct told me to dismiss her fears. "Don't even *think* that! Of course you don't have cancer. You're going to be fine!" I sat in silence for a moment before I was able say, "That's a huge worry to be carrying around."

My friend gave a sigh of relief and said, "YES! *Everyone* is telling me not to worry about it. But how can you *not* worry?"

"Yeah," I said, "it's like telling someone not to look at the pink elephant in the living room." She laughed, and the mood lightened. I was so glad I had been able to help, even just for the moment.

That knowledge is not always at the tip of my fingers, but I'm grateful it's there when I reach for it. It gives me the starting point to connect with the people in my life—even when I'm scared or frustrated or downright enraged. It is a powerful gift my mom passed on to me.

# Some Books
# You May Find Interesting

Axline, Virginia M. *Dibs: In Search of Self.* New York: Ballantine Books, 1986.

Bradley, Michael. *When Things Get Crazy with Your Teen.* New York: McGraw-Hill, 2008.

Cohen, Lawrence. *Playful Parenting.* New York: Ballantine Books, 2002.

Faber, Adele, and Elaine Mazlish. *Siblings Without Rivalry.* New York: W. W. Norton & Company, 2004.

> *How to Talk So Kids Can Learn.* New York: Scribner, 1996.

> *How to Talk So Teens Will Listen & Listen So Teens Will Talk.* New York: Harper Paperbacks, 2006.

> *Liberated Parents/Liberated Children.* New York: HarperCollins (Perennial Currents), 2004.

Fraiberg, Selma. *The Magic Years.* New York: Scribner, 1959.

Ginott, Haim. *Between Parent and Child.* New York: Three Rivers Press, 2003.

> *Between Parent and Teenager.* New York: The Macmillan Company, 1969.

> *Teacher and Child.* New York: Avon, 1975.

Gordon, Thomas. *PET in Action.* New York: Bantam Books, 1979.

Kohn, Alfie. *Punished by Rewards.* Boston: Houghton Mifflin, 1999.

# Some Books You May Find Interesting

Kurcinka, Mary Sheedy. *Raising Your Spirited Child.* New York: Harper Perennial, 1992.

Leach, Penelope. *Your Baby and Child: From Birth to Age Five.* New York: Alfred A. Knopf, 1997.

Rogers, Carl. *On Becoming a Person.* Boston: Houghton Mifflin Co., 1961.

# For Further Study . . .

If you are interested in a chance to discuss and practice the communication skills in this book with others, you can request information about the "How to Talk So Kids Will Listen Kit" created by Adele Faber and Elaine Mazlish. The kit consists of a leader's guide, parents' workbooks, and CDs or a DVD of the authors conducting each workshop session. For further details, please visit our website: www.fabermazlish.com or contact us directly:

info@fabermazlish.com
1-800-944-8454
Faber Mazlish Workshops, LLC
P.O. Box 1072
Carmel, NY 10512

# Index

Page numbers in *italics* refer to illustrations.

# Index

# Index

# Index

# Index

# Index

Moralizing to gain cooperation, 53, 56

Motivating child to take ownership of problem, 257

Nagging, 79

Name-calling:
  to gain cooperation, 52, 55
  parents' stories, 249

Naming a child's feelings, 9, *15*, 26
  misidentification, 29–30

*Newsday,* 119

*New York Times,* 243

Next Generation, 287–332

"Nos":
  alternatives to, 163–64
  watching out for too many, 163

Note, writing a, 170–71, 217, 225
  engaging cooperation and, 57, *66–68*, 70, 75, 85–88, 304–5
  as problem-solving method, 127

Ochberg, Dr. Frank M., 118

*On Becoming a Person* (Rogers), 289

One-word statement, engaging cooperation and, 57, *62–63*, 69, 75, 83

Outside sources, encouraging children to use, 142, *147*, 150, 152, 156, 160, 166, 169

Parents' feelings. *See* Feelings of parents

Parents' stories, 249–56, 258–64

responsible behavior, encouraging, 255

Permissiveness, 33

Philosophical response to a problem, 6

Physical activity as outlet for anger, 30–32

Physical privacy, child's, 161

Pity as response to a problem, 7

Playfulness, power of, 79, 274–77, 301–2

Playing roles, freeing children from, 205–31, 232, 326–31
  exercise, 217–19
  labeling children, 205–10, 222, 229–30, 326–27
    effects on self-esteem, 209
  parents' stories, 224–31, 250, 327–29
  skills for, 210, 218–19, 221–22, 223
    be storehouse for child's special moments, 210, *215*, 221, 223
    let children overhear positive statements about them, 210, *213*, 221, 223
    model the behavior you'd like to see, 210, *214*, 221, 223
    put children in different situations, 210, *212*, 221, 223
    show child new picture of himself, 210, *211*, 221, 223
    when child acts according to old label, 210, *216*, 222, 223

# Index

Protecting, taking action for, 308–10

*Psychology of Self-Esteem, The* (Branden), 177

Punishment, alternatives to, 90–138, 232, 306–21

allow child to experience consequences, 95, *98,* 113–15, 308

assignment, 110–11

coming up with, 94–95, 122–23

exercise, 101–3

experts' opinions on punishment, 117–19

express strong disapproval, 95, *96,* 112, 116–17, 123, 309–10

feelings of children and, 92, 93–94, 290–91, 306, 307–8, 321

give a choice, 95, *97, 100,* 112

with little children, 113

motivations for punishment, 92, 93

parents' questions, 113–17

parents' stories, 119–23, 251, 311–21

point out way to be helpful, 95, *96*

preventive measures, 95

problem-solving. *See* Problem-solving

show child how to make amends, 95, *99,* 112, 116–17, 119–22, 229, 311–12

state expectations, 95, *99,* 112, 309–10

taking action, 95, *100,* 112, 308–10

Putting it all together, 232–38

Questions:

to ask yourself when not getting through, 77–78

not rushing to answer, 142, *146,* 150, 152, 156, 168–69

parents':

about children's feelings, 27–34

about engaging cooperation, 76–80

about praise, 191–95

about punishment, 113–17

refraining from asking too many, 142, *145,* 149, 152, 156, 159, 299–300, 323

as response to a problem, 6–7, *12,* 270, 290–91

restating problem as, 165–66

"Readiness," showing respect for child's eventual, 162–63, 327, 328

Repeating yourself, 79, 113, 301

Report card, 171–73, 324–25

Respect, 124, 253, 259

to encourage autonomy, 142, *144, 145,* 151, 156, 158–59

Responsibility. *See* Autonomy, encouraging

Rogers, Carl, 289

Role-playing, 23–25

child's situation, 23

parent's situation, 24–25

parents' stories, 262–63

# Index

Adele Faber                                    Elaine Mazlish

Internationally acclaimed experts on communication between adults and children, Adele Faber and Elaine Mazlish have won the gratitude of parents and the enthusiastic endorsement of the professional community.

Their first book, *Liberated Parents/Liberated Children*, received the Christopher Award for "literary achievement affirming the highest values of the human spirit." Their subsequent books, *How to Talk So Kids Will Listen & Listen So Kids Will Talk* and the #1 *New York Times* bestseller *Siblings Without Rivalry,* have sold more than four million copies and have been translated into over thirty languages. *How to Talk So Kids Can Learn: At Home and in School* was cited by *Child* magazine as the "best book of the year for excellence in family issues in education." The authors' group workshop programs and videos produced by PBS are currently being used by thousands of parent and teacher groups worldwide to improve relationships with children. Their most recent book, *How to Talk So Teens Will Listen & Listen So Teens Will Talk*, tackles the tough problems of the teenage years.

Both authors studied with the late child psychologist Dr. Haim Ginott and are former members of the faculty of the New School for Social Research in New York and the Family Life Institute of Long Island University. In addition to their frequent lectures throughout the United States, Canada, and abroad, they have appeared on every major television talk show from *Oprah* to *Good Morning America*. They currently reside in Long Island, New York, and each is the parent of three children.

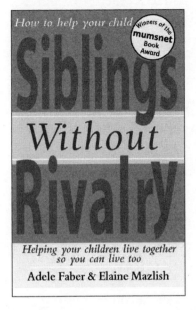

'Full of insights and techniques that can help restore harmony in warring households.'
*Time Out*

'No peace-loving parent should be without a copy.'
*Good Housekeeping*

One of the ten best parenting books chosen by *The Independent*.

'He hit me!'
'She hit me first!'

Having children is wonderful,
but they can seriously endanger your sanity!

Discover Faber and Mazlish's practical guidelines and
examples for how to cope with – and deflect – sibling rivalry.

Written with humour, understanding and compassion,
*Siblings Without Rivalry* challenges the idea that constant,
unpleasant conflict is natural and unavoidable.
Complete with anecdotes and stories, this book shows
the many ways you teach your children how to get along.

What Every Parent and Teacher Needs to Know

**"HOW TO TALK SO KIDS CAN LEARN"**

**AT HOME AND IN SCHOOL**

Adele Faber & Elaine Mazlish

Bestselling Authors of
How to Talk So Kids Will Listen & Listen So Kids Will Talk
with Lisa Nyberg & Rosalyn Anstine Templeton

'If you're a teacher or parent, you simply can't get along without this book.'
*The Washington Post*

'Will encourage teachers to reflect on their strategies to motivate, interest and increase their pupils' self-esteem.'
*The School Librarian*

The leading experts on parent-child communication show parents and teachers how to motivate kids to learn and succeed in school.

Using the unique communication strategies, down-to-earth dialogues and cartoons that are the hallmark of their bestselling *How To Talk So Kids Will Listen*, Adele Faber and Elaine Mazlish show parents and teachers how to help children handle the everyday problems that interfere with learning.

This breakthrough book demonstrates how adults can join forces to inspire kids to be self-directed, self-disciplined, and responsive to the wonders of learning.

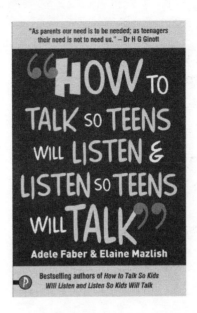

"As parents our need is to be needed; as teenagers their need is not to need us." – Dr H G Ginott

# HOW TO TALK SO TEENS WILL LISTEN & LISTEN SO TEENS WILL TALK

**Adele Faber & Elaine Mazlish**

Bestselling authors of *How to Talk So Kids Will Listen and Listen So Kids Will Talk*

'Just read this brilliant
exposé on the
teenage psyche.'
*Lovereading*

'Could save your sanity
and help your child
get through puberty.'
*Best*

'Recommended.'
*Woman's Weekly*

In this revolutionary, must-have book for parents,
bestselling authors Adele Faber and Elaine Mazlish
turn their down-to-earth, respectful approach to parenting
to the specific troubles of the teenage years.

Written in their trademark practical, sensible and accessible
style, and reinforced with cartoons and reminder pages,
*How to Talk So Teens Will Listen & Listen So Teens Will Talk*
offers innovative suggestions that can be put into
immediate action and practical ways to build
the foundation for lasting relationships.

Covering topics ranging from curfews and cliques to sex
and drugs, the authors give parents and teens the tools
they need to safely navigate the often stormy years
of adolescence.